THE TRANSFORMATION OF
AMERICAN ABOLITIONISM

THE TRANSFORMATION OF AMERICAN ABOLITIONISM

FIGHTING SLAVERY IN THE EARLY REPUBLIC

RICHARD S. NEWMAN

The University of North Carolina Press

Chapel Hill and London

© 2002 The University of North Carolina Press
All rights reserved
Manufactured in the United States of America

Designed by April Leidig-Higgins
Set in Carter & Cone Galliard by Keystone Typesetting, Inc.

The paper in this book meets the guidelines for
permanence and durability of the Committee on
Production Guidelines for Book Longevity
of the Council on Library Resources.

Library of Congress Cataloging-in-Publication Data
Newman, Richard S.   The transformation of American abolitionism:
fighting slavery in the early Republic / by Richard S. Newman.
p. cm.   Based upon the author's dissertation.
Includes bibliographical references (p.   ) and index.
ISBN 0-8078-2671-5 (cloth: alk. paper)
ISBN 0-8078-4998-7 (pbk.: alk. paper)
1. Antislavery movements — United States — History — 18th century.
2. Antislavery movements — United States — History — 19th century.
3. Abolitionists — United States — History. 4. African Americans —
Politics and government — 18th century. 5. African Americans — Politics
and government — 19th century. 6. United States — Race relations.
7. Pennsylvania Society for Promoting the Abolition of Slavery.
8. Massachusetts Anti-Slavery Society. 9. Social change — United
States — History — 18th century. 10. Social change — United States —
History — 19th century. I. Title.
E446 .N58 2002   326.8'0973 — dc21   2001027913

06 05 04 03 02   5 4 3 2 1

For my mother and father

CONTENTS

Preface   ix

HISTORY IS THE study of change over time. While my undergraduate and graduate mentors constantly drummed this historian's axiom into my head, I began this project to study the continuity of the American abolitionist movement between the American Revolution and the 1830s. Although abolitionism is a well-studied topic, I wanted to examine the less-well-known pre-Garrisonian phase as a prelude to movements of the 1830s. An abolitionist was always an abolitionist, I thought.

Yet as I researched the tactics and strategies of the Pennsylvania Abolition Society, the world's first and now oldest such group, I discovered that early abolitionism differed almost completely from later movements to end slavery — in terms of racial and gender composition, day-to-day tactics, and overall strategies. In the middle of the project, then, and with some critical mentoring, I realized that I had to talk about change: the transformation of abolitionism during the early republic. The task thus became one of explaining how the abolition movement started in one place, ended in another, and completely altered its public face to become the well-known movement we still remember today.

I AM ONE OF THOSE people who turns first to the acknowledgments section of any book I pick up. Did the author go it alone or surf on a wave of help — and did he or she thank properly those renderers of aid? I could not imagine finishing this book without the incredible support of dozens of generous people. It is a pleasure to thank them now in print. I will start with those institutions that provided funding at various stages of the dissertation on which this work is based. At the State University of New York at Buffalo, I received support from The Mark Diamond Foundation (in the form of extended travel grants), the Department of History (in the form of a critical Plesur fifth-year dissertation fellowship), and both the Graduate Student Association and the Graduate History Association (for supporting shorter research trips). The Library Company of Philadelphia and the Massachusetts Historical Society provided invaluable support in the form of Andrew W. Mellon Fellowships. Rummaging through stacks of Americana in Philadelphia and Boston, exchanging views with other scholars in residence or passing through, and generally benefiting from the enormous wisdom of the staffs of these two wonderful institutions, I felt lucky indeed. At the Library Company, I wish to express my particular gratitude to John C. Van Horne, Phil Lapsansky, and James Green, each of whom made me feel at home during an early research summer. At the Massachusetts Historical Society, I similarly would like to thank Conrad Wright, Donald Yacovone, and Virginia Smith for always being wise and helpful. I also must thank the staffs of the Historical Society of Pennsylvania, the Boston Public Library, and the Boston Athenaeum for their courtesy and help.

At conferences, numerous scholars have molded my thought, challenged my claims, and illustrated how much I still have to learn. Both the dissertation and the revised manuscript benefited from informative and sometimes lively exchanges with James and Lois Horton, Robert Forbes, Donald Yacovone, Julie Winch, Ron Walters, Robert McColley, David Waldstreicher, J. Morgan Kousser, Michael Morrison, Jim Green, Richard Dunn, Chris Densmore, Susan Wyly-Jones, Eva Sheppard, George Price, Roy Finkenbine, and Patrick Rael. They are not responsible for any errors that remain, but they must assume responsibility for making this a better book than it otherwise would have been. James Brewer Stewart deserves special mention for his advice and friendship — two invaluable commodities to a young scholar. Jim has been a tireless advocate of my work and a model in more ways than I can recount here. I can only hope to repay him more properly someday. At Brown University, Gordon Wood and Abbott Gleason provided critical support for which I remain eternally in their debt. At SUNY Buffalo, where I received a terrific undergraduate and graduate education, numerous professors, colleagues, and friends helped me along the way: Richard Fly, Ken Dauber, Neil Schmitz, John Milligan, Susan Cahn, John Naylor, Orville Murphy, Georg Iggers, William Allen, Chris Forth, among many others. I also thank Scott Henderson for his eternal good cheer and support and Derrick Krisoff for many spirited conversations. Legendary teacher Robert Pope taught me to always be a teacher, and rarely a day goes by when I fail to think of his words and example. I have been the richer for his advice, but the profession lost much when he retired early.

I was lucky to have the support of some great friends during the early stages of the work. David and Jennifer Blaustein welcomed me to their home in Philadelphia when I was first researching the Pennsylvania Abolition Society and then miraculously moved to Boston when I announced that I needed to research Massachusetts abolitionists. I cannot imagine having done the same work without them. At Clarion University, the crew of Paul Hart, Tim Collins, Catherine Petrassans, Dwayne and Pam Mulder, and Carol Englehart offered constant diversion. Beverly Smaby and Frank Towers provided a temporary but critical home for me to begin thinking about the revised manuscript. At the Rochester Institute of Technology, my thanks go to Rebecca Edwards, Glenn Kist, Ken Nelson, and my colleagues in both the History Department and the Liberal Arts College for their continued support. Andrew Moore generously provided monetary support from the Dean's Office for the manuscript's timely completion. Frank Annuziata called me one night and asked, "Are you a cool guy?" Little did I know that I would be in Rochester soon and loving it; I still owe Frank much.

Everyone at the University of North Carolina Press has helped make this a better book through their constant encouragement and friendly assistance. My thanks to Ruth Homrighaus, Ron Maner, and Mark Simpson-Vos for their aid and support. Stevie Champion did heroic work copyediting the manuscript, for which I want to thank her deeply. Charles Grench seamlessly assumed the project after arriving at the UNC Press and assured its success. Although no longer at the Press, Alison Waldenberg also deserves special mention for expressing early and continued interest in the project. Finally, thank you to the anonymous reviewers and to Waldo Martin for their supportive, generous comments.

My dissertation committee members remain the most important group of all. They moved me with their concern, intimidated me with their critiques, and humbled me with their wisdom. Richard Ellis virtually compelled me to become a historian by virtue of his dynamic classroom presence and scholarly example. Tamara P. Thornton taught me much about cultural history and professionalism — she never let me off the hook at any stage of the project. Michael Frisch influenced nearly every aspect of my teaching and research. The questions he asked me and all of his students about the processes of historical change will always remain vividly in my mind. In addition, he provided career counsel and opportunities — and some memorable quips about Buffalo Bills' wins and losses. I owe most to my adviser William Freehling, who has taught me so much about the teaching and writing of history that I must quote Otis Redding: I owe him "more than words can ever say." But I will try: When I sent him a chapter, he returned it virtually the next day awash in red or black. When I thought I had all the answers, he always asked another vexing but necessary question. When I felt like I had had enough of the dissertation, he called out of the blue and offered the most reassuring words. Even now, when I publish a book or an essay and send him a copy, he reads it fully, contacts me immediately, chats about it for what seems like hours, and leaves me dazzled all over again. He has remained a wonderful adviser and friend, a continuing inspiration.

My family has been a constant source of love and encouragement at every twist and turn. Thanks Eric, Ruth, Mom, and Dad.

THE TRANSFORMATION OF

AMERICAN ABOLITIONISM

Abolitionist Transformations

There are no second acts in American Lives.
— F. Scott Fitzgerald

IN JANUARY 1831 William Lloyd Garrison began publishing the *Liberator*, a radical abolitionist newspaper dedicated to immediate abolition and full equality for African Americans. "I will not equivocate," Garrison thundered, "AND I WILL BE HEARD."

In both the popular imagination and in many scholarly accounts, Garrison's debut remains *the* benchmark of abolitionism. Against the backdrop of religious revivals, a broader reform sensibility, and an emerging market system of free labor, a radical abolition movement appeared almost overnight. The early struggle against slavery (described variously as "gradualist" and "Quaker-oriented") had long since died out; a brand-new age was born. Indeed, despite the impressive growth in abolitionist literature over the previous two decades (described by one well-known scholar as an "avalanche"), abolitionism as an organized movement is still understood in this post–1830 context. Many prominent historians (including Robert Abzug, Richard Blackett, Aileen Kraditor, Lewis Perry, Ron Walters, and most recently Paul Goodman and Julie Jeffery) slight the work of early abolitionists, placing meaningful debates over strategy, tactics, and personnel only in later years. Conversely, scholars detailing the push for slavery's eradication after the American Revolution (such as Gary Nash and Jean Soderlund, Merton Dillon, Arthur Zilversmit, and Shane White) have neglected abolition's continuity through the 1800s. Even David Brion Davis's magisterial work on slavery in the post-Revolutionary world, which focuses on antislavery philosophies rather than tactics, stops at the Missouri Compromise. Only a few historians of abolitionism, most prominently James Brewer Stewart, transcend these timelines.[1]

Abolitionism was born with the American republic. It did not fade until the nation's near-death experience of the Civil War. Yet while abolitionists worked consistently to destroy slavery and racial injustice in these years, their strategy and tactics constantly evolved. The era between the American Revolution and the 1830s was the first great period of transformation. What began as an elite abolitionist movement in Pennsylvania during the post-Revolutionary period yielded to an egalitarian movement based in Massachusetts during the early 1830s. With this shift in location, abolitionist strategy, tactics, and, perhaps most significantly, personnel shifted too. Whereas Pennsylvanians sought politicians' support for gradual abolition, "modern" abolitionists roused the masses — including blacks and women — to end slavery immediately. Instead of Pennsylvanians' specialized legal tactics designed to persuade jurists to end bondage, Bay Staters dispatched traveling agents to organize local antislavery societies; instead of learned legal briefs, they crafted emotional appeals emphasizing the horrors of slavery. Profound changes in American political culture and social life influenced abolition's transformation in the 1820s and early 1830s, from the advent of revivalism and egalitarian political theories to the rising prominence of free black and female activists. Massachusetts agitators seized these cultural developments to turn the abolitionist movement itself into a revolutionary force over and against Pennsylvanians' conservative tradition of reform.

This study probes more deeply abolition's transformation during the early republic. It revolves around several questions: Just who were Pennsylvania abolitionists, and how did they function tactically? Why did abolitionism change *when* it did in the 1830s? What roles did African Americans and women (long ignored by first-generation reformers as public activists) play in forming more radical abolitionist activities, and how did the Pennsylvania Abolition Society (PAS) react? Finally, how exactly did abolition's strategy and tactics change so that Americans would ever remember the aggressive post–1830s movement as the essence of organized antislavery?

It is important to make two caveats at the outset of this study. First, this work does not delve deeply into the religious inspirations of abolitionists. Historians have long known that religion was the primary motivator for generations of abolitionists. However, this focus on motivation has often pulled scholars' attention away from what abolitionists did and how their activities shifted over time. Yet whatever their reasons, reformers' tactics often made more of an impression on slaveholders and skeptical northern politicians. In the 1830s Governor Edward Everett worried less about the inducements of new abolitionists and more about their aggressive speaking campaigns in the Massachusetts hinterland, which he sought to ban. Similarly, just before the Civil War some southern slaveholders referred to the earliest petition campaigns of Pennsylvania abolitionists as the beginning of an abolitionist offensive — and a just reason to secede finally from a Union soon to be overrun by abolitionist policies.

The second caveat is that although the transformation of abolitionism is considered here largely from the perspective of Pennsylvania and Massachusetts activists, it would be an oversimplification to reduce the antislavery movement to these two states. In the early national era, for example, the New York Manumission Society and the American Convention of Abolition Societies joined the Pennsylvania Abolition Society as leaders in the fight against slavery. Similarly, the Massachusetts Antislavery Society was but one of a whole new generation of immediatist organizations that formed in the early 1830s, particularly in New York City, where black and white activists formed crucial ties. Nevertheless, the Pennsylvania and Massachusetts campaigns became virtual personifications of the abolitionist struggle during the early republic. Following the American Revolution, a variety of American and European reformers recognized the PAS as the preeminent organization to end slavery. The flow of information relating to abolitionist tactics went through the group's headquarters in Philadelphia more so than any other locale. Fifty years later, however, Massachusetts served as abolitionism's tactical center. "I like the spirit of Massachusetts abolitionism," one Maine reformer wrote at the end of the 1830s, for "it is energetic." Pennsylvania reformers realized that a transition had occurred, and that abolitionists in Massachusetts (whom they labeled "Garrisonian" or "modern" reformers) now occupied a leadership position. "To Pennsylvania belongs the honor of first organizing a society" for abolishing slavery, one Quaker State activist somberly wrote in the late 1830s. "Its members were amongst the most excellent and virtuous of the day. They were animated by clear and lofty benevolence . . . and thus constituted and recognized, they wielded moral power, the effect of which is now felt among their descendants." But, he made clear, the present belonged to the younger generation of Massachusetts radicals. "Has abolition gone defunct in Pennsylvania?" one Bucks County, Pennsylvania, reformer wanted to know. "For a long time it has seemed as though the spirit of freedom had fled from our citizens' bosoms," a new local abolitionist society in Pennsylvania answered in 1837. The new group was Garrisonian.[2]

The transformation of abolitionism strained relations between first- and second-wave reformers in Pennsylvania and Massachusetts. For a time the PAS even refused to admit "modern" abolitionists, and during the transition of the early 1830s its members often did not support public speeches by Garrisonians in the Quaker State. "Modern" abolitionists labeled the old guard as "halfway" abolitionists at best. "The cause must come out of their hands," one Philadelphia woman aligned with Massachusetts reformers wrote in 1838. As perhaps the ultimate snub, second-wave abolitionists' histories of the movement paid little attention to their predecessors. "The cradle of abolition," Boston's James Freeman Clark summarily declared after the Civil War, "was Massachusetts."[3] Hence the belief, still very much alive, that abolition really began in the 1830s.

THE TRANSFORMATION OF abolitionism is best told in the tale of two organizations: the Pennsylvania Abolition Society and the Massachusetts Antislavery Society (which became the model for the American Antislavery Society). Together, they dominated the first fifty years of organized abolitionism, spanning not just many years and numerous activists but two completely different tactical styles and political/social worlds. The PAS created the world's first abolitionist organization and set the tone for the American abolitionist movement before 1830. Though initially composed of Quaker antislavery theorists who sought private conversions of slaveholders, the PAS quickly established itself as a prestigious organization of politically oriented strategists. Based on an examination of the tactical leadership and strategy of the society, abolitionism appears to have been part and parcel of a post-Revolutionary world marked by deferential governing styles and Enlightenment sensibilities. Dominated by societal elites — wealthy philanthropists, political representatives, businessmen, and, above all, well-known lawyers — the PAS advocated gradual abolitionism by means of painstaking legal work and legislative action. As William Rawle, the organization's longtime president and a noted lawyer, soberly put it, the Pennsylvania Abolition Society engaged in a particular mode of "dispassionate" reform. Emotional appeals to the public and religious zeal had no place in its procedure.[4]

Despite this careful approach, the PAS became a controversial participant in post-Revolutionary debates over American slavery. In an era when most political leaders avoided the divisive issue, PAS strategy emphasized that government and its representative legal and political institutions should gradually attack the institution of slavery. By pressuring state and federal officials to craft abolitionist statutes, and by challenging courts to hand down pro-abolitionist decisions, Pennsylvania activists tried to delegitimize slavery's legal standing in the nation. Government interference, the PAS argued again and again, was the key to broad emancipation in American society.

This strategy of striking at bondage via government power stood out in two PAS tactics: petitioning and providing legal aid to African Americans. Abolitionist petitions routinely pushed state and federal governments to prohibit the domestic and overseas slave trade, to stop slavery's westward expansion, and to eradicate the institution itself in federally controlled areas, such as the District of Columbia. Before 1830, the group drafted over twenty petitions to Congress on such issues and over twice as many to the Pennsylvania legislature. And well before the gag rule debates of the 1830s, southern congressmen sought to ban antislavery memorials from the federal legislature.

The PAS viewed litigation against masters as another important way to strike at bondage gradually. By representing kidnapped free blacks in court, by bargaining with slaveholders for a fugitive slave's freedom, and by requiring northern courts to protect the constitutional rights of blacks, the PAS hampered slavery's legal protections nationally—turning bondage into a distinctly sectional institution with different legal sanctions in northern and southern courts. Pennsylvania abolitionists spent most of their time and money planning legal tactics and achieved a national reputation as blacks' legal representatives.

The group did not do it alone. In fact, PAS litigation illuminated the remarkable struggles of African Americans (both free and enslaved, in Pennsylvania as well as in southern states where bondage remained entrenched following the Revolution) to fight slavery throughout the early republic. On a consistent basis, Pennsylvania blacks ran away from masters who tried either to circumvent the Quaker State's gradual abolition law or more boldly attempted to kidnap free blacks into servitude. African Americans fought back not just by fleeing but by trying to secure abolitionist representation in Pennsylvania courts. On several occasions, African Methodist Episcopal leader Richard Allen was contacted in Philadelphia by endangered blacks. He, in turn, engaged white lawyers to assist them. Eventually, slaves from neighboring states sought refuge in Pennsylvania, and they too gained PAS legal aid—under the right legal circumstances. All the same, black activists were not officially invited to join the Pennsylvania Abolition Society until decades later.

The PAS's tactical and strategic arsenal reflected a late-eighteenth-century republican worldview. The group operated in a rational, enlightened, and highly dispassionate manner. It worked conscientiously within the American political and legal system. And it believed that only certain individuals could serve the abolitionist cause: elite white males who could bolster the group's legislative strategy and tactics, lawyers who could manipulate legal codes, and wealthy benefactors who could fund legal work. In the hands of the PAS elite, abolitionism operated like a sober business.

Massachusetts abolitionists diverged strikingly from their Pennsylvania competitors. Operating from within the "modern" abolitionist organizations that emerged in Massachusetts during the early 1830s, they demanded immediate — not gradual — emancipation of southern slaves. Equally important, these second-wave agitators revolutionized abolitionist strategy and tactics. Arguing that the PAS's republican style of reform was outdated in an increasingly egalitarian and romantic age, modern abolitionists emphasized the power of nonelites to halt slavery. Indeed, mobilizing the masses (including blacks and women), not careful legal and political planning, became the central abolitionist strategy after 1830. Only by opening up the movement to democratic activists and egalitarian sensibilities could reformers eradicate bondage. If enough people joined the abolitionist cause, Bay Staters argued, then the people themselves could compel governments to act — for instance, to amend the federal constitution to outlaw slavery, drop fugitive slave laws, and curtail racist laws. As one Massachusetts activist proclaimed in 1835, the new reformers would turn the "entire American continent into one big Anti-slavery society."[5]

Although an important part of early abolitionist legal maneuvering, African Americans had long been denied membership in the PAS. Black leaders created their own parallel antislavery movement. In the abolitionist world of the 1830s, African American reformers quickly became coworkers and allies, bringing with them a protest tradition that emphasized national action, public and often emotional attacks on bondage, and immediate emancipation. Similarly, female abolitionists who came to prominence in Massachusetts during the late 1820s focused intensively on people's reform potential as well as slavery's moral evil. For both groups of activists, mass mobilization and emotional outrage formed the core of new abolitionist activities.

A mass action strategy necessitated tactical innovations. To funnel masses of citizens into the abolitionist movement, Bay State activists spent most of their time and money lecturing, pamphleteering, and organizing in every town and community possible. Their relentless work in the countryside paid big dividends in the 1830s: local abolition societies proliferated, petition signatures exploded, and abolitionists gained favorable coverage of their strategy and tactics in many small newspapers. Agents also connected to an ever-widening circle of nonelite activists, particularly women. When elite citizens refused to support abolitionism, these grassroots participants filled the void. To cite one critical trend, women purchased twice as many *Liberator* subscriptions as professional men and other prominent figures.

Finally, Massachusetts abolitionists provoked citizens' outrage by publishing gripping accounts of bondage and emotional slave narratives. Pennsylvania abolitionists vetoed such "literary" tactics, favoring instead erudite legal briefs. Bay Staters argued that the PAS's dispassionate works elided slavery's immorality and restricted abolitionist activity to the educated few. To properly understand the plight of slaves, these reformers announced in the 1830s, citizens should now consult black authors and "modern" abolitionist narratives of black suffering. Befitting a romantic age, Massachusetts activists sought to pierce the American heart as a critical first step to obliterating slavery nationally. "I shall never forget his first speech," William Lloyd Garrison recalled of Frederick Douglass's debut in the Bay State, "the powerful impression it created upon a crowded auditorium . . . I never hated slavery so intensely as at that moment." Though this event occurred after the transformation of abolitionism, it merely continued interracial efforts begun in the early 1830s. Garrison's 1832 anticolonization pamphlet was so firmly grounded in the black public protest tradition that one colonizationist wrote that he paid little attention to the bombastic white printer. Black anticolonizationist voices, he said, made more of an impression than anything else in the document.[6]

The PAS deplored these new abolitionist approaches. Some members of the old guard referred derisively to second-wave activists as young upstarts who knew nothing of moderation or the skills of backroom politicking. From black and female membership and grassroots organizing campaigns to immediatist ideology and emotive appeals to the citizenry at large, the PAS worried that Massachusetts radicals would ruin the American republic before they destroyed slavery. The venerable PAS impeded the new abolition's growth in its own state, closing meetinghouses to traveling lecturers and limiting the distribution of "modern" abolitionist publications. Yet for a whole new generation of American abolitionists after 1830, Massachusetts activists, not the PAS, became the defining force of abolitionist strategy and tactics. Indeed, despite PAS opposition, "modern" abolition societies eventually assumed supremacy in the Quaker State. Moreover, some of the PAS's most notable activists transferred their allegiance to Massachusetts abolitionist societies in the 1830s.

WHAT PROMPTED THE shift from first- to second-wave abolitionism during the early republic?[7] And why did it occur precisely in the early 1830s? Several background factors help answer these vexing questions. American abolition changed as American society and culture evolved. During the early republic political and economic life intensified, both with the advent of democratic politics and with the formation of an integrated national market economy. A great wave of revivalism swept across the nation, lasting for decades and touching many aspects of political and social life. Finally, the early national period saw the rising prominence of African Americans and women in the public sphere at a time when newspapers and the print media were becoming a parallel universe for political and social debate. Abolitionism mirrored many of these changes in politics, economy, religion, and culture, with reformers themselves contributing to America's dynamic political and social character between the 1790s and 1830s.

Religion was a cornerstone of abolitionism throughout the Revolutionary and early national periods. As David Brion Davis has argued in *Slavery and Human Progress* (1984), liberal religious thinkers continually broadened the antislavery struggle in Anglo-American culture. "In the 1760s, black slavery was sanctioned by Catholic, Anglican, Lutheran, Presbyterian, and reformed churchmen and theologians," he writes. Quakers unleashed the first sustained abolitionist initiative during the Revolutionary era. With the Second Great Awakening, evangelicals advanced the antislavery cause in the early 1800s.[8]

Revivalism also created a new intellectual framework for nineteenth-century Americans, democratizing both religion and society. Revival preachers such as Charles Finney and Theodore Weld promulgated doctrines of universal salvation based not on clerical authority or Calvinist predestination but on an individual's ecstatic conversion experience and good works. As Robert Abzug has put it, "old structures" of church life were "blown apart" by the new mode of lay conversions. In celebrating emotion as the key to salvation, nineteenth-century revivalists challenged the rationalistic worldviews of the founding generation. Sentiment and feeling arose alongside what Timothy Smith long ago called a "revivalist movement of massive proportions." Were Thomas Paine, the free-thinking pamphleteer of the American and French Revolutions, to have visited America in the mid-1800s, he would have been amazed to find that the nation conceived in rational liberty was now fulfilling its democratic promise through the power of evangelical faith. For Paine, man was the ultimate scientific instrument: Rational thinking could solve even the most vexing problems, from governance to social problems such as slavery. Religion seemed to be part of a premodern world to Paine, and his book *The Age of Reason* (1793) relegated it to the dustbin of history. The evangelical upsurge, Timothy Smith concluded, proved Paine wrong, for "common grace, not common wisdom, was the keynote of the age!"[9]

Although it would operate with particular intensity in several locations, by the 1820s and 1830s the Second Great Awakening became identified with many Bay State reform causes, from transcendentalism to communalism. At this cultural moment, Boston regained national prominence as a reform capital. As far as abolitionism was concerned, revivalism profoundly affected the way reformers in Massachusetts viewed their world and crafted their tactics. Ideologically, of course, evangelical thinking now embraced a new antislavery ideology based on the concept of immediately stamping out the sin of slavery. Strategically, the missionary impulse that accompanied the evangelical uprising helped new generations of abolitionists mobilize partisans in the countryside, far beyond the statehouses and courtrooms favored by first-wave abolitionists. In short, revivalism decisively shaped American reform culture during the early republic.

Political changes influenced abolition's transformation, too. Reformers of the 1820s and 1830s sat on the cusp of an age where ordinary people began to shape the nation's political direction. Whereas formerly democracy in its crudest, purest form had been feared as a precursor to mob rule or even anarchy, by the 1820s many Americans saw mass democracy as the defining characteristic of the nation. "Democratized public opinion became the 'vital principle' underlying American government, society and culture," Gordon Wood notes, "a new standard for everything."[10] The Jacksonian era, as Harry Watson observes, "liberated ordinary white men from many of the deferential restraints of 18th century politics," thus according them a "new respect in the public sphere."[11] Although Massachusetts had strong Federalist roots, even Bay Staters believed in what one Concord paper called "the sovereignty of the people." "Whiggism," the founding generation's belief in elite rule and deference to the better sort, had finally "died."[12]

To shape popular majorities nationally, new party politicians led by New York Democratic leader Martin Van Buren utilized new political tactics.

Nominating conventions, massive press coverage, and grassroots organizing strategy became the watchwords of politicians at every level of government. And more than ever, campaigning was a matter of public relations, as mass rallies, sloganeering, and parades advertised candidates' credentials to the people at large. According to Robert Remini, these activities "recast the style and tone of American politics." Gone were the political clubs and elite congressional caucuses of the Revolutionary era. As Andrew Jackson himself declared, the new political tactics would rally the masses and allow the people to exert their "full influence on government."[13]

This new age of people power also embraced a radical new individualism.[14] Philosophers began extolling the individual soul. "All barriers to growth and achievement seemed to crumble," Lewis Perry writes, and a commoner could now "dream of expressing one's deepest genius, of gaining fame, of furnishing leadership to the new age." Moreover, Perry continues, a new sense of "inborn intuition made ALL MEN AND WOMEN immediately equal." In Massachusetts, transcendentalists emphasized the importance of the "individual conscience," personal "feeling," and "private experience." "The individual is the world," Emerson declared. Like other idealists of the new age, Emerson believed that radical individualism would emancipate Americans from society's restraining conventions — conventions that the PAS had upheld for years.[15]

William Lloyd Garrison was part of this political age before he became a professional abolitionist. As a young man, Garrison threw himself into electioneering for John Quincy Adams, particularly as editor of the *New-buryport Herald* in 1828. Although possessing neither a college education nor social connections ("a plain, unlettered man," as he referred to himself), Garrison sought to become a player in American political debates. Indeed, even though he had begun his journalistic career as an ardent Federalist, he bristled at deferential codes of political behavior. Each "man is his own master," he wrote of the dawning age of mass politics. Though he might respect their abilities, Garrison no longer viewed men like John Quincy Adams and Daniel Webster as "idols." Nor did he have to "soothe the delicate nerves and republican sensibility" of any gentleman. Garrison, like thousands of other common men, could now shape and define his political and social worlds. Attending political rallies in Boston, skirmishing with established political hands and "respectable" editors in state politics, and jousting with national figures such as Andrew Jackson and "Governor Troup" of Georgia, Garrison placed himself squarely in the coming democratic tide of popular movers and shakers. As he made clear, the "great body of the people" reigned supreme in American culture. How different from the previous age's conception—and the PAS's governing principle— that a small body of gentlemen must rule. According to Garrison's most recent biographer, in fact, the young printer's genius lay in his melding of politics and reform. Garrison's *Liberator* brought his ardent and hectoring electioneering style to the sensitive slavery issue.[16]

Mass democracy cut many ways, often hindering as well as helping the struggle for racial justice. As scholars such as Alexander Saxton, David Roediger, and Noel Ignatiev have shown, white democratic advances often came at the expense of black liberty.[17] In New York and Pennsylvania, for example, black suffrage was taken away as white suffrage expanded. "Is this the light of the 19th century?" exasperated Pennsylvania black activists asked in the 1840s, a few years after the Quaker State revoked black voting rights.[18] Yet at the same time, as scholars studying women's and African Americans' response to antebellum political changes have pointed out, gender and racial conventions came under more intense attacks than ever before as new generations of reformers challenged the social status quo. Long advocates of universal freedom, black activists in many northern (and some southern) locales inaugurated new tactics to reinvigorate the cause of racial justice. Organizing local, state, and national protest organizations, founding autonomous newspapers, and creating new educational institutions, African American reformers vowed to bring the twin evils of American slavery and racism to a halt. Black Philadelphians alone established thirty-five reform or benevolent institutions between 1820 and 1830 (twenty-two of them female groups)—four times the number formed between the 1780s and 1810s.[19] Even more impressive, perhaps, in 1826 Boston's black community created the General Colored Association, calling on blacks everywhere to combine their protest efforts into a coordinated national movement. "The civil rights of a people being of the greatest value," the editors of the first black-owned newspaper *Freedom's Journal* called out, "it shall be ever our duty to vindicate our oppressed brethren" in the eyes of white society. Thus, they continued, "this paper shall lay our cause before [the entire American] public . . . urge our brethren to use the elective franchise [where possible], [and] bring together . . . from the different states" black activists to shatter "the iron fetters of bondage."[20]

Female reformers forged newly prominent roles for themselves in the public sphere by pushing for temperance, educational, and religious reform in cities and towns throughout the North. As Nancy Hewitt has written, "women stepped beyond the prescribed boundaries" of motherhood and home in unprecedented numbers beginning in the 1820s. The Pennsylvania Abolition Society noticed this surge of female activism at the close of the decade, when a group of Philadelphia women began renting a PAS building for meetings of female educators and abolitionists. In North Carolina, female reformers stunned members of the state abolition society in 1826 by asking how they might attack southern slavery. According to these women, "the assistance of our sisters in the work of benevolence" signaled a possible integrated future of organized abolitionism. In fact, many northern women would move from local reform activities into the national movement against slavery — taking over petition drives to Congress, raising money for state and national abolitionist organizations, and becoming a forceful abolitionist constituency in their own right.[21]

For both women and African Americans, the political and cultural strands of the Jacksonian era would meld in second-wave abolitionists' mass action strategy that defined abolitionism itself as a movement of all Americans. Some of these "new" public reformers pushed this approach before the 1830s even began. In 1829, for instance, David Walker urged the black masses in Boston to become the vanguard of a new national movement against racial injustice. If only a fraction of "two million and a half of colored people in these United States" organized, he challenged, "what mighty deeds could [not] be done by them for the good of our cause?" At virtually the same time, a young Philadelphia woman called out from the pages of the *Genius of Universal Emancipation* for women everywhere to step outside the home and agitate for political solutions to slavery. "You can give it *your* active exertions," Elizabeth Chandler proclaimed, "and you must."[22]

Massachusetts abolitionists exploited these political and cultural developments to revolutionize the movement to end slavery in America. Combining transcendentalism's belief in the innate power of *every* individual to change society with the new mass politics' emphasis on a collective "people power," Bay State abolitionists formulated a strategy of grassroots activism. As Charles Follen announced at an 1836 meeting, "every human being, whether colored or white, foreigner or citizen, man or woman, is a rightful and responsible defender of the natural rights of all." Massachusetts abolitionists, Follen concluded, must "make this whole nation one great antislavery society."[23]

As the written appeals of second-wave activists such as Margaret Chandler, David Walker, and William Lloyd Garrison would indicate, print culture became a valuable and viable weapon for attacking the nation's racial ills. Black activists' literary tactics provided a firm foundation of the new abolitionists' crusade. Americans' broader emphasis on literacy and print technology also had an impact on the evolving abolitionist movement. Between the 1790s and 1830 American literary production steadily increased. After 1830, however, it exploded. The number of newspapers grew fourfold between that decade and the 1850s. American printers increased their activities in virtually every corner of the nation. Much of the impetus for printed matter came from the market revolution. In many Americans' minds economic progress became linked with the diffusion of knowledge and information. As John Quist has shown, even slave-holding regions of the Deep South (such as Alabama) witnessed an expansion of printed materials after 1830. Similarly, scholars of African American life in the North have pointed out that literacy rates increased among black as well as white Americans. Across lines of class, color, and gender, Americans increasingly viewed the printed word as a vital means of both self-expression and diffusion of knowledge.[24]

It was through print, moreover, that women and African Americans exerted a profound tactical influence on American reform, working as editors and writers for journals emerging in Philadelphia, Baltimore, Boston, and New York.[25] The classic example was the inauguration of *Freedom's Journal* in New York City in 1827. The famous opening line of the editors called attention to blacks' redoubled efforts to make their voices heard: "for too long others have spoken for us." Of course, the editors, John Russwurm and Samuel Cornish, often demonstrated their indebtedness to black pamphleteers and petitioners dating back to the Revolutionary era. In one prominent case, they republished an 1813 pamphlet by James Forten (*Series of Letters by a Man of Color*) for the edification of younger black activists. Yet *Freedom's Journal* publicized African American protest as never before. As the editors and correspondents noted during its brief two-year run, the paper could be found on ships, in private homes, in barbershops, and in all manner of public places. Furthermore, it promulgated a different strategy from that favored by the first generation of white abolitionists. The American people at large must be stirred to fight slavery, not merely statesmen and judges. To do this, black writers had to create new public images of African American society (ones that would convince the white citizenry at-large to accept black equality) and to focus as much on the emotional impact of slavery and racism as on its philosophical evil. At a time in the 1820s when the colonization movement was gaining increasing converts and slavery itself was continuing to expand, black writers sought to make anger and moral outrage a central part of abolitionist discourse.[26]

Although the inaugural African American newspaper folded in 1829, black viewpoints pervaded abolitionism during the 1830s and beyond. In the most impressive example, nearly one-fifth of the *Liberator*'s writers during its first year of operation were African American. African Americans continued to publish more pamphlets, more narratives, and more newspapers during each of the three decades leading to the Civil War. It did not take that long for the nation's oldest abolitionist group to recognize that this new trend was taking shape. At an 1827 PAS meeting it was noted that African Americans were publishing a new paper entitled *Freedom's Journal*. The venerable abolitionist group subscribed to it and watched a new abolitionist future appear.

THE YEAR 1830 marked a transitional moment for both American culture and American abolitionism. Religious revivals heralded a new age of perfectionism in which sin would not be tolerated. Egalitarian rhetoric celebrated commoners as the essence of the republic, challenging the deferential political styles that had dominated American statecraft for decades. Cultural politics intensified as northern black communities matured and asserted themselves anew in public demonstrations for racial justice. Moreover, female reformers joined a variety of causes, from colonization to religious revivals, and they increasingly viewed themselves as legitimate actors within the broader spectrum of American political culture. Despite the impact of these extensive societal changes, second-wave abolitionists were not merely "reactors" (suddenly set in motion by a change in economic philosophy or political ideology) but agents of history who changed with the times and changed their times. When Elizabeth Chandler told would-be abolitionist women that they "*must* give it their active exertions" to finally end slavery, she spoke the keynote for a whole new generation of activists — black as well as white, women as well as men, nonelites as well as the so-called better sort.

Movements for social change in American history have often followed abolition's path. After establishing an exclusive movement of activists with a relatively narrow strategic vision, and after achieving initial successes in government and law, social movements evolve into more populist phases. As new people with new ideas about now to attack social problems become involved, they challenge both old reformers and society at large to come to terms with new strategies. The civil rights struggle, women's rights movement, even gay and lesbian movements — all have evolved from relatively conservative strategies to much more radical ones.

Abolitionism became the first social movement to so completely transform itself. This strategic overhaul explains not simply how and why new abolitionists helped make slavery the most divisive antebellum issue, but how abolitionism itself became an increasingly radical outlook on American democracy.[27]

Republican Strategists

The Pennsylvania Abolition Society

The sentiment of Thomas Jefferson was very fine in theory, but it would
have been enhanced a thousand fold if Jefferson had practiced what he
preached. Precept without example is like faith without works — it is dead.
— *Genius of Universal Emancipation*, July 1834

ALTHOUGH THE YEAR 1775 is remembered for the shot at Lexington,
Massachusetts, that started the American Revolution, it also marked the
beginning of another auspicious battle. With Revolutionary events swirling
around them, a handful of reformers met at Philadelphia's Sun Tavern to
form the Pennsylvania Society for the Abolition of Slavery, the world's first
organization dedicated to securing slavery's end. Dominated by the state's
legal and political elites, this exclusive group set the standard for abolitionist activity during the early republic. But more than merely the inaugural
abolitionist group, the Pennsylvania Abolition Society (PAS) became famous for its distinctly conservative style of activism. Elite patronage, re-
fined legal and political strategy, and careful tactics guided the group's work
for over fifty years.[1] In a republican world dominated by the "exertions of
great and good men," the PAS believed that only its exclusive strategy and
tactics would halt slavery.[2]

THE PAS GREW from Quaker roots. Quaker antislavery theory dated to
1688, when a Philadelphia-area group issued the Germantown Protest criticizing the institution of bondage. With its high concentration of Quakers,
who adopted George Fox's belief that all human beings were equal before
God, Pennsylvania became the epicenter of American antislavery thought.
By the 1750s, the Philadelphia Yearly Meeting formulated its own abolition-

ist policy: Quaker slaveholders must relinquish either their chattels or their ties to the religious society. Over the next several decades, Friends in New York and New England adopted similar schemes, and Quakers became a critical base of abolitionist organizations from Rhode Island to Virginia.[3]

A host of Pennsylvania Quakers gained national and international fame for their early tactics as well, among them John Woolman, Anthony Benezet, Benjamin Lay, Warner Mifflin, and John Parrish. These celebrated activists preached or published their antislavery beliefs in the years leading up to the American Revolution. Most early Quaker reformers favored a "privatist" strategy: individual emancipation by masters. One privatist tactic was group coercion: members of the society would pressure recalcitrant Friends until they either manumitted their bondsmen or were banished from monthly meetings. The New Jersey Quaker Meeting provides one of the best examples of Pennsylvania-style privatism in action. The group spent what one member recalled as a "considerable deal of labor" trying to convince John Corlis of Monmouth County to stop "keeping Negroes." Because Corlis "continues to decline complying with the yearly meeting's [slave-holding] ban," the New Jersey group expelled him. Corlis kept his four slaves but lost his place among Friends.[4]

John Woolman and Warner Mifflin tried to expand privatist tactics among other religious sects. By undertaking extensive travels through Pennsylvania, Maryland, Delaware, and Virginia, they hoped to persuade other groups to weed out slaveholders. Less-well-known Quakers emulated this itinerant activity. In 1789 one Maryland Friend began a preaching mission to free "200–300 slaves," according to his hopeful estimate.[5] Philadelphia schoolteacher Anthony Benezet preferred a pen to preaching missions. Before his death in the 1780s, Benezet published nine influential antislavery treatises. The PAS held these forebears in the highest esteem, frequently punctuating its messages and reports with allusions to the "spirit of Benezet" or a similar motto. Benjamin Lundy, a PAS member, editor of the influential abolitionist newspaper the *Genius of Universal Emancipation* during the 1820s, and a Quaker himself, ran a series of biographical sketches on these noble men in the early 1830s to invigorate a new generation of activists. To him, as to countless others, they had been the first antislavery activists in American culture.[6]

DESPITE THEIR theoretical work, Quaker activists lacked a coherent plan to systematically attack slavery throughout American society. Some Pennsylvania Friends abhorred broader political attacks on bondage. Quakers, they asserted, should focus only on their own transgressions, not on trans-Quaker political debates over slavery.[7] A group of Philadelphians disagreed: reformers needed to expand their political tactics to end the evil institution. This faction founded the world's inaugural "abolition society" in 1775. The first Pennsylvania Abolition Society was a loosely formed group of twelve men who met sporadically at the beginning of the Revolution, disbanded while the War of Independence raged, and then reorganized in 1784. The latter year also saw the establishment of the New York Manumission Society (NYMS), and soon other groups organized in New Jersey, Connecticut, and Rhode Island and abortively in Maryland, Virginia, and Kentucky. Abroad, groups with varying commitments (from abolishing the slave trade to slavery itself) formed in Great Britain and France.

The New York society joined its Pennsylvania counterpart as one of the most visible first-generation abolitionist organizations. Inaugurated in New York City in January 1784, the NYMS advocated the gradual abolition of slavery, established schools for free blacks, aided African Americans in courts of law, and fought to end the overseas and domestic slave trades. Like the PAS, the New York group received official incorporation from the state government and welcomed prominent statesmen into its ranks, including John Jay and Alexander Hamilton. Quaker and Anglican members stood out as well; in fact, during its first three decades of operation the Society of Friends contributed over 50 percent of its membership. In many ways, the New York Manumission Society faced a more daunting task than reformers in Pennsylvania. New York remained the largest slave-holding polity north of Maryland and Virginia, with 21,000 enslaved people during the 1790s. The NYMS petitioned the New York legislature to pass gradual abolitionist statutes but was rebuffed several times. Even John Jay's gubernatorial administration in the mid-1790s failed to win passage of such legislation. Just before the century ended, however, New York adopted a statute similar to that of Pennsylvania. According to the new law, all slaves born after July 4, 1799, must be registered at a state office; men were to be liberated at age twenty-five and women at age twenty-eight.[8] In 1827 the legislature would issue a final emancipation decree.

The New York society earned a reputation for assisting distressed blacks in both New York City and New Jersey. It confronted sea captains who brought slaves into port in violation of federal statutes and established a legal aid system to help kidnapped blacks secure their freedom. New York City masters often evaded the state's gradual abolition act by selling slaves

South before they were to be freed. This domestic slave trade also ensnared free blacks, as slave traders unscrupulously captured black men and women who could not prove their freedom. Perhaps as important, the New Yorkers helped abolish a local law that allowed masters to bring unruly slaves to city prisons for punishment as well as the slave catchers' practice of using local jails to hold fugitives captured in surrounding states.

The Manumission Society's sponsorship of free African schools proved to be one of its most enduring legacies. Between 1787, when the NYMS established its first school in New York City, and the 1820s, when it administered nearly a half-dozen schools, over two thousand black pupils received an education at NYMS-sponsored schools. Graduates included such future luminaries in black protest as Henry Highland Garnet, Alexander Crummel, and Samuel Ringgold Ward. Although New York abolitionists utilized black teachers, some of the city's leading African American figures began criticizing the paternalistic attitudes of the society. This development revealed tensions inherent in early abolitionism, in both New York and Pennsylvania. The New York Manumission Society did not encourage black members to join, and black activists were often treated as less-than-equal participants in the broader struggle against slavery. When *Freedom's Journal* began publication in New York City in 1827, it highlighted the protests of activists such as William Hamilton, who sought more autonomy in black education. By the early 1830s black reformers had gained more control of the schools.[9]

The American Convention of Abolition Societies was the third main abolitionist organization during the early national era. Formed in 1794 to give the movement national scope, the convention became a clearinghouse for abolitionist tactics. Although it met biennially between the 1790s and early 1830s (when it disbanded), and although it attracted abolitionists from the South and West, the group never became a potent national protest organization. In fact, it was dominated by the Pennsylvania and New York groups. Nevertheless, the American Convention did have prominent moments, such as spearheading a petition drive in the early 1790s to urge Congress to ban the slave trade. This effort produced petitions from several abolitionist groups. Congress responded in 1794 by passing a measure that somewhat limited American participation in the Middle Passage. According to the new law, ship captains could not use foreign ports for their human cargo. (The PAS prosecuted several captains who violated the statute.) The American Convention was interesting for one final reason: it did not prohibit any state abolitionist society from admitting slaveholders. Al-

though the Pennsylvania Abolition Society in particular encouraged southern abolitionist groups to expel slaveholders, even it realized that northern
abolitionists could not dictate terms to their would-be brethren. Abolitionist groups in Kentucky, Maryland, and Virginia appreciated the PAS's understanding position. Still, it quickly became clear to Pennsylvania and New
York abolitionists that the American Convention would never build a
united front against bondage.

At the same time, first-generation abolitionists believed that their movement would slowly but surely destroy American slavery. The backdrop of
Revolutionary events had much to do with this optimism. The American
Revolution spawned the first consistent secular challenge to slavery in the
Western world, reversing, in essence, the institution's centuries-long nor-
mative standing among philosophers and statesmen. By focusing attention
on natural rights theory and self-determination, the Revolution unleashed
a utopian vision of human freedom and possibility. Utilizing the works
of European philosophers, from Jean-Jacques Rousseau to Adam Smith,
American colonists battling Britain began rigorously defining the meaning
of freedom, liberty, and equality in human society. These libertarian trends
soon affected slavery, as guilt-ridden American masters manumitted thousands of slaves following the Revolution. A transatlantic spirit had clearly
taken shape by the 1770s, making slavery anathema to emerging republican
governmental systems. Indeed, slavery became one of the dirtiest words in
the English language.[10]

The Pennsylvania Abolition Society hoped to make these antislavery
trends the basis for firm abolitionist policies in government and law. "The
sentiment of Thomas Jefferson was very fine in theory," one Pennsylvania
abolitionist subsequently remarked about the difference between mere anti-
slavery philosophies and abolitionist action, "but it would have been enhanced a thousand fold if Jefferson had practiced what he preached. Precept
without example is like faith without works — it is dead."[11] Calling for less
antislavery talk and more abolitionist laws and court decisions, the PAS
dedicated itself to crafting concrete solutions for governments and statesmen now conscious of slavery's evil.

Founding an abolitionist society to formulate abolitionist action had
several virtues, PAS members asserted. First, it allowed abolitionists to coordinate specific activities aimed at eradicating slavery. The PAS devised a
Quarterly Meeting schedule to plan various tactics, such as representing
blacks in court and drafting legislative petitions. Four times a year, the
society convened a general meeting to hear reports from a host of spe-

cialized committees. For instance, the aptly named Acting Committee summarized recent PAS work (particularly the group's ever-expanding docket of court cases) and set the agenda for future political action. The Corresponding Committee communicated PAS plans to members and allies in America and Europe. Other committees dealt with concerns ranging from membership to black educational institutions.

The PAS worked rigidly within the committee model to achieve its goals. If it was no longer just a religious trend or secular spirit, the group argued, then abolition itself needed to be a highly structured and efficient movement. The PAS committee system, like its Quarterly Meeting schedule, bylaws, and official constitution, established firm guidelines for abolitionist procedures. Pennsylvania reformers never improvised tactics or transcended the society's rules. For instance, to attack the domestic slave trade during the 1810s, the PAS formed several committees with specialized tasks. A preliminary committee interviewed black kidnapping victims, white eyewitnesses, and legal officials to obtain statistics and depositions on the domestic slave trade. Another committee drafted petitions asking state and federal governments to take appropriate steps to curtail the domestic trade in blacks. A third committee corresponded with various statesmen (and haunted legislative chambers) until an anti-slave-trading bill had been crafted. On any number of other issues — the overseas slave trade, slavery's constitutional existence in the District of Columbia, legal action of all kinds — Pennsylvania abolitionists carefully proceeded through their maze of committees.

Forming an abolitionist society offered more than mere structure: it brought together elite activists who could better promote abolitionist action among political and legal officials. A lone antislavery preacher might be easily ignored or discounted, but an organized group of "weighty and influential" abolitionists would have an impact in legislative halls, courtrooms, and the private chambers of statesmen. Although the PAS attracted nearly four hundred dues-paying members in its first twenty-five years, it prized the elite above all. Potential activists had to be nominated by PAS members and, if elected to the society, pay annual dues. The support of figures such as Benjamin Franklin (the group's first president) or Nicholas Waln (a prominent Pennsylvania lawyer and congressman) provided access to other statesmen and civic leaders, thereby magnifying abolition's impact on governing elites.[12] The PAS bragged when personages like Benjamin Rush, Tench Coxe, and Albert Gallatin joined the group. In addition, some of America's most distinguished statesmen and philanthropists counted themselves corresponding members — among them, Noah Webster, Theodore Sedgewick, and Elbridge Gerry. General Lafayette became a corresponding member from France, as did William Wilberforce, Grenville Sharpe, and other celebrities from Britain.[13]

To further enhance its credentials in the government sector, the PAS gained official incorporation from the Pennsylvania General Assembly in 1789. This formal sanction provided "force and stability," as one PAS correspondent put it, to organized abolition, for it put political representatives, judges, and even slaveholders on notice that the legally recognized body of activists could sue individuals in court, bargain with slaveholders for blacks' freedom, and request civil authorities (sheriffs, jailers, justices of the peace) to support abolitionist activities.[14] Far from a band of ad hoc preachers or well-intentioned philanthropists, the PAS now claimed the same official standing as a chartered bank or business enterprise.

Members emphasized this fact. James Pemberton, who succeeded Benjamin Franklin as PAS president in 1790, took every opportunity to tell statesmen around the country about the Pennsylvania Abolition Society. "You have heard that an association has been formed in this city to advocate the cause of the oppressed blacks," Pemberton wrote to New Jersey governor William Livingston in the late 1780s, "under the name of the Society for the abolition of slavery." To buttress its systematic legal and political "exertions," he explained, the PAS was writing to governors throughout the United States for information on slave laws and to inform them about this exclusive abolitionist organization. Pemberton asked Livingston to help him, as one prominent official to another, to "obtain authenticated copies of . . . those laws lately enacted by the Legislature of New Jersey" relating to blacks and slavery. Pemberton found a fast friend in Livingston, who became a correspondent with, and advocate for, the PAS before his death in 1790.[15] Pemberton remained convinced that his success with Livingston and other luminaries stemmed directly from the PAS's incorporation by the state legislature.

Again and again, the PAS used its official standing to penetrate legislative bodies and gain special hearings from statesmen. The society continually used its legislative contacts to defend Pennsylvania's gradual abolition plan from attempts to repeal it before 1800. Antiabolitionists constantly tried to impede, obstruct, and even halt the abolitionist law, which had been implemented in 1780 to gradually emancipate slaves in the Quaker State. Yet legislators heeded PAS pleas to rebuff repeal bills. This was no small feat even in Pennsylvania, which had contained nearly seven thousand chattels and several thousand slaveholders through the 1790s. As letters from legislative contacts indicate, the PAS's official standing and reputation among elites provided clout to the abolitionist cause. Even antiabolitionist assemblymen had to respect the group's petitions and viewpoints.

The society's official standing also preceded it in courts of law, often with ironic consequences. In a violent 1795 kidnapping case, for instance, the southern slaveholder's attorney tried to weed out PAS members from the jury pool precisely because of their potential influence over other members. The case involved Toby, who claimed to have been emancipated on entering "free" Pennsylvania with the Sevier family of "the Southwestern Territory," which claimed him as an escaped slave. Abolitionists brought suit against the family for kidnapping the black man. The case eventually made it to the state supreme court, Chief Justice Thomas McKean presiding. The judge, well aware of the PAS, agreed with defense motions to prohibit its members from becoming jurors. "The society for the abolition of slavery," McKean observed, was "incorporated 8th December 1789, by law" and essentially assumed the position of an influential corporate body. Toby's freedom claim did not hold up in court, and the Sevier family was acquitted of the kidnapping charges.[16]

Although it clearly worked against the PAS on this occasion, legal incorporation would pay dividends in the group's subsequent legal work, as local magistrates, sheriffs, and slaveholders were compelled to deal with official actions of the Pennsylvania abolitionists.

THE PAS'S RAPID development during the Revolutionary era (its efficient organizational culture, official incorporation, and elite membership) marked a distinctly new phase in the struggle to abolish slavery in America. Abolitionism was no longer simply a religious or philosophical trend; a formal society had emerged to systematically agitate for abolitionist policies in government and law. Indeed, the PAS's use of government institutions to achieve its mission often engendered fractious debate over slavery and abolitionism in American culture. These gradualist reformers pushed for laws that worked slowly but surely to drain slavery from American society; they believed that state and federal governments must be the central means of abolishing the institution of slavery. American abolitionists, PAS strategists argued over and over again, had to pressure government leaders to act on behalf of the abolitionist cause.

The American Revolution's intense focus on the meaning and uses of representative government decisively shaped PAS strategy. As Americans established new governments and constitutions following the War of Independence, republican governance attained the spotlight as never before. Broad debates raged over such issues as the scope of federal power in relation to state governments, protection of citizen's liberties, and the meaning of judicial and executive branches in republican society. A small but significant debate also developed over slavery's relationship to representative government. Could representative government destroy slavery through laws and judicial action? statesmen and reformers began to ask. Did any government have even the coercive power to emancipate blacks?

Northern states used sovereign power to end slavery through a series of gradual abolition acts. Pennsylvania's abolitionist law of 1780, the world's first such statute, freed slaves over a period of time. Masters had to register their slaves with local magistrates. Those born *after* 1780 would be freed at a specific time in their life: men at age twenty-one, women at eighteen. Scholars have only recently detailed how halting and often disappointing was this road of gradual emancipation for many northern blacks. As Shane White's book on New York's gradualist scheme indicates, for instance, northern masters often sold their slaves South before state emancipation decrees took effect.[17]

Yet by invoking government power over slavery, these schemes were abolitionist milestones. Where previously private manumission had been the only route to black freedom, now abolitionists (in concert with various statesmen and legislative bodies) focused on government emancipation decrees. As Pennsylvania's abolition act stated, "we intend to extend that freedom which we enjoy . . . to others." By the early 1800s Connecticut, New Jersey, and New York instituted similar schemes, often after fractious debates. Slaveholders in many of these northern states lashed out at gradualist laws, continually challenging their legitimacy in courts and assemblies. In Pennsylvania, slaveholders howled at the prospect of legislating slavery out of existence — that was not a legitimate power of *their* representative government![18]

Pennsylvania abolitionists never doubted government's power to gradually destroy bondage, nor abolition's relevance to the Revolutionary era's main constitutional and political dialogues. They viewed government as a critical ally, for government alone had the legal tools and civil authority — the coercive power — to quash slavery and stand up to slaveholder opposition. As the PAS wrote to Kentucky abolitionists in 1809, abolitionists must ever view representative government as the vehicle for killing slavery, not individual citizens or religious groups. Without government action, abolitionists worried, slavery would prosper.

The focus on government's abolitionist potential excited a whole generation of reformers, not just Pennsylvania activists. Britain's Grenville Sharpe applauded the PAS's legislative strategy, urging Americans to pressure their government leaders to pass abolitionist laws. A Rhode Island activist agreed: putting slavery on the legislative agenda and pressuring prominent representatives to oppose it offered the surest route to national emancipation. The PAS predicted a time "not too distant" when abolitionism would be "universally and firmly established" as government policy, not simply "debated" in speeches and books.[19]

Attacking slavery via government required a specialized tactical arsenal. Two PAS activities stood out: petitioning and legal work. Abolitionist petitions continually pushed state and federal officials to use their power to attack slavery. Though often warning against "overzealous" tactics, the PAS argued that slavery was legally and constitutionally actionable.[20] Petitions pointed not only to specific problems stemming from the institution of slavery (such as increases in the domestic slave trade and slavery's southern and westward expansion in places like Missouri and Florida) but also the legitimacy of governmental solutions to these problems. The federal government, as the PAS's first national petition put it, had "many and important powers" for banning the overseas slave trade outright or taking other abolitionist action. Petition after petition made this same point, beginning with the foreign slave trade and culminating in efforts to outlaw slavery in the District of Columbia during the 1820s.[21] By the 1830s the PAS had drafted over twenty separate petitions and addresses to the national government on a variety of issues and twice as many to the Pennsylvania legislature.

Benjamin Rush bragged to prominent friends in New York and Boston about his society's legislative tactics. "Our Society for Abolishing Negro Slavery [is] about to address the legislature" on the overseas slave trade, he excitedly wrote of one early petition to the Pennsylvania General Assembly.[22] Even when friends decried such action, Rush lauded it. For, he asserted, without government-sanctioned abolitionist plans, emancipation would remain a distant vision.[23] As a Rhode Island abolitionist wrote to the PAS in 1789, simply pushing abolitionism in the legislative realm "requires [making] a much stronger impression upon the mind" of public officials than any other topic, for there was no natural "abolitionist" constituency to support it, "no private interest" behind abolitionism.[24] PAS petitions put abolition squarely in front of the nation's politicians and implored them to adopt an abolitionist strategy.

The group's legal work also emphasized the possibility of government intervention. Slavery, in the PAS's eyes, had a legal standing in American culture; by manipulating various laws, the society hoped to undercut the institution's legal stability.[25] Thus slavery's demise, as PAS president William Rawle would argue throughout his career, depended on careful but crafty legal tactics. These included litigation in cases involving kidnapped free blacks and, in some important cases, runaway slaves; juridical opinions questioning slavery's constitutionality in northern states; and the recasting of legal codes to protect black freedom. The Pennsylvania society expended tremendous amounts of money on legal tactics, from traveling to other states to deliver a kidnapped person's "free papers," to taking depositions, to bargaining with southern masters for a fugitive slave's freedom. Like petitions, PAS legal work tried to put the slavery issue before the nation's judicial leaders for learned and favorable decisions.

The PAS viewed America's institutional machinery as a rigid guide to ending slavery.[26] The nation's legal and political institutions defined the very possibilities of the group's activism. Like all early abolitionist organizations, the PAS opposed anything outside the narrowly focused framework of the law and civil government, particularly the use of violence.[27] This is important, for several of America's most prominent slave rebellions occurred during the society's heyday: the Haitian Rebellion of the 1790s, Gabriel's Rebellion in Virginia during the early 1800s, and Denmark Vesey's South Carolina Revolt in 1822. Revolutionary plots such as these, the organization believed, undercut the slow but steady progress of government-backed abolitionism. Rarely, in fact, does one encounter sympathy with revolutionary doctrines of any kind. An 1828 proposal to forward PAS money directly to "slaves in the southern states" fell on deaf ears. As early as 1791, when a sister organization in southern Pennsylvania broached the subject of vigilantelike means to recover a kidnapped free black man, the PAS strongly counseled against such action. Mobs had no place in proper abolitionist procedure.[28]

In contrast to black revolutionary action, the PAS steered people's attention back to government-sanctioned abolition plans. In 1792, for instance, the group reprinted five hundred copies of a pamphlet entitled *An Inquiry into the Causes of the Insurrection of the Negroes in the Island of St. Domingo*. Originally issued for the British Parliament, the pamphlet quickly attracted the attention of Pennsylvania abolitionists, for its main point meshed with their own: blacks would revolt against masters unless Western governments developed a strategy for gradual abolition. "Those dreadful disorders" in St. Domingo, the publication began, "are chargeable to" the French government alone, because "IT DID NOT INTERFERE" in the slavery problem at an early and decisive moment. Indeed, government apathy left "black laborers" at the "mercy of their masters," thereby contradicting "the first principles of their Constitution" that "all mankind were born equal."[29]

Moreover, the pamphlet urged governments in the Western world to attack, not safeguard, slavery. White reformers and governments had to curtail the slave trade and then gradually abolish slavery itself to quell further black violence. Lack of such government "interference" had caused black rebellions in the first place. Thus, the document emphasized, legislators should ignore masters' calls to further safeguard slavery. The British Parliament should continue "daily considering and fully deciding" on a slave trade ban. And it should enact emancipation statutes in all of its colonial possessions.[30]

The PAS found the pamphlet to be a sensible guide. American reformers needed to publicize a similar call to government action. Statesmen must heed this call. Slavery had to be removed from the realms of private interest and long-standing custom and put on the scales of justice. The result, Pennsylvania abolitionists hoped, would be a safe and equitable draining of slavery through government action. Anything less would lead to more ominous, and violent, results. PAS members adopted this sentiment in the wake of nearly every major slave rebellion.

Similarly, the PAS condemned "overzealous" abolitionist activity, including emotionalism, enthusiasm, or anything that smacked of fervent behavior. Fever-pitched tactics, many of the group's legal counselors and official representatives warned, threatened the reasoned, sure-handed approach of PAS elites. The Pennsylvania society regarded its members as diligent reformers and respectable men who pursued specific legal and political objectives with vigor but never fervency. Exertions on behalf of blacks were good; zealotry was bad. Prodding statesmen to support anti-slave-trade petitions was likewise acceptable procedure, but disobeying seemingly unjust laws to free a fugitive slave was not. To the PAS, slaveholders and antiabolitionists were society's zealots. Their "warm" and "heated" conduct, like their passionate defense of slavery's inherent good, provoked acrimonious legislative debate and sectional discord.[31] For Pennsylvania activists, abolitionism was too deadly serious to turn into a crusade.

SUCH SOBER VIEWS about abolitionist strategy and tactics derived from the PAS's elite cadre of civic leaders, businessmen, and political officials. The group contained a virtual who's who of prominent citizens: the Pemberton brothers, descendants of a wealthy Philadelphia merchant family; William Rawle, an eminent lawyer and constitutional commentator; Caspar Wistar, a long-standing political figure in Philadelphia; Roberts Vaux, philanthropist and member of the business elite; as well as legislators and jurists such as Charles Miner, William B. Reed, and Samuel McKean. As men who knew politics and the law, they preferred to wage their abolitionist battles within the privileged realm of legislative chambers and courtrooms. These "weighty" leaders imparted an unmistakably genteel manner to the PAS strategy and tactics. The Pennsylvania society never demanded action or lectured statesmen, it never supported revolutionary action, and it never transcended the limits of the law.[32]

Of the PAS's influential figures, none stood out more than the lawyers. They dominated committees, policy decisions, and the very definition of the PAS strategy. The roster of top-notch legal men included prominent barristers beyond Pennsylvania as well as stars in the state bar. Theodore Sedgewick, the well-known Massachusetts Federalist who defended black freedom claimants in the 1780s, joined the group during the 1790s, as did Timothy Pickering, another Bay State lawyer. New York's John Jay and Alexander Hamilton (both members of the New York Manumission Society) held corresponding status in the PAS. William B. Reed, Enoch Lewis, Peter Du Ponceau, and several of Pennsylvania's most respected attorneys represented the PAS at some point in their careers.[33]

Both the law and the legal process became increasingly important components of American society after the Revolution. Perhaps as significant, the legal professions ascended as never before. One scholar has estimated that after 1780 the number of lawyers nationally grew at a rate four times that of the general population. Of the Constitutional Convention's fifty-five delegates, perhaps three-fourths were lawyers. And many of the founding generation's leading citizens — from Thomas Jefferson, James Madison, and Alexander Hamilton to Albert Gallatin and Timothy Pickering — were trained in the law. After 1776 law impinged on slavery as never before. New slavery-related statutes proliferated throughout the United States. Northern gradual abolition schemes, southern slave laws and anti-emancipation statutes, federal fugitive slave provisions, black challenges to slavery in court — these developments required a core of competent lawyers. Black freedom suits multiplied so rapidly in Pennsylvania that the PAS had to appoint several new legal counselors and hold special strategy sessions just to keep pace.[34]

Its expanding legal team kept the group abreast of these legal developments. PAS lawyers had the task of finding abolitionist loopholes in certain laws, crafting abstracts of new laws and legislative proposals relating to slavery and free blacks, and determining legal action in certain cases. Southern masters, when wishing to manumit slaves, began writing the PAS for advice on their state's tricky emancipation procedures. The group turned to its lawyers for answers. Similarly, PAS lawyers continually analyzed Pennsylvania's gradual abolition act after 1780, looking for loopholes that masters as well as slaves might try to exploit in court. If the society's own lawyers could not provide answers to tricky legal questions, they were responsible for contacting attorneys who could.

In this manner, the PAS created a specialized niche for itself in the brandnew area of abolitionist law. Perhaps no single law firm or organization in antebellum America could boast such an impressive group of legal minds: William Rawle, Evan Lewis, David Paul Brown, John Sergeant, Charles Minor, Jonathan Roberts, and a cast of other legal elites. They all trained their eyes on slavery. William Rawle alone provided the PAS a towering legal reputation, as he literally wrote the book on constitutional law in Pennsylvania. Once nominated as U.S. attorney general by George Washington, Rawle also served as president of the Pennsylvania bar in the 1810s and 1820s. For over forty years (from the 1790s throughout the 1830s), he offered legal advice to the PAS on everything from fugitive slave laws to the types of writs required to gain blacks' freedom.

Rawle counseled legal preparedness to fellow abolitionists. But like his colleagues, he could also be crafty with the law. In the 1790s, for example, he argued that Pennsylvania courts could declare slavery unconstitutional. The state's bill of rights — protecting every person's "right to life and liberty" — supported such judicial activism; in Rawle's eyes, there was nothing radical about it. He therefore urged the PAS to bring a "test case" to the state supreme court that would declare bondage null and void within the state's geographic limits.[35]

David Paul Brown, Rawle's protégé in law and at the PAS, became perhaps the most celebrated of early abolitionist lawyers. Also one of Philadelphia's leading orators by the 1830s, Brown represented myriad blacks in court cases between the 1820s and 1840s, most of them pro bono. He lived lavishly, frequently to his own detriment. Colleagues often scoffed at his appalling lack of monetary sense (he was repeatedly threatened with eviction from his law office for nonpayment of rent), though no one laughed at his record in court, least of all African Americans. In 1841 Philadelphia's black community saluted Brown in a moving ceremony at the Second Presbyterian Church. Robert Purvis, one of "Philadelphia's Black Elite," gave the keynote address and presented a gift to Brown on behalf of his brethren: a silver bowl inscribed with appreciation for the man who never failed to defend a black person in court.[36]

Showmanship, not legal precision, marked Brown's court manner. "He excels in extravagance, not in the law," one PAS member who knew Philadelphia's foremost attorneys later wrote. But Brown, like Rawle, always worked within the law. Slaveholders had legal rights, Brown admitted, which no court, or lawyer, could abrogate. Yet he insisted that blacks had essential constitutional rights too, and that solidified his reputation as a tireless legal advocate for blacks.[37]

Jonathan Roberts, John Sergeant, Nicholas Waln, Charles Miner, William B. Reed, and Thomas Earle, among others, anchored the PAS's lawyerly contingent, each offering legal counsel at some time in their careers. All of these men enjoyed excellent reputations in the Philadelphia bar. Roberts was considered one of the nation's undervalued lawyers. He argued before the U.S. Supreme Court in several high-profile cases (including *Worcester v. Georgia* and *Ogden v. United States Bank*), becoming one of only a few men to defeat Daniel Webster in court. He even turned down a seat on the Supreme Court. Sergeant served in the PAS for a number of years between 1800 and the 1830s. A student of the celebrated Philadelphia lawyer Jared Ingersoll, he quickly established himself as a leader of the city's legal elite, becoming deputy attorney general for Philadelphia County in his early twenties. Waln, Miner, Reed, and Earle were mainstays on the PAS legal staff, as well as leading lights in Pennsylvania politics between the 1790s and 1830s. Reed, for example, served as attorney general of Pennsylvania. Earle remained a stalwart abolitionist from the 1820s through the 1840s, when he was a vice presidential candidate for the Liberty Party.

The PAS staffed a second tier of legal workers who were not formally trained in the law. These men bolstered the group's legal activism by securing and delivering writs to slaveholders and justices of the peace, apprising detained blacks of their rights, and questioning judges and legal officials about the meaning of a particular law. This contingent included less prominent names: Thomas Shipley, Isaac T. Hopper, Thomas Harrison, and Arnold Buffum. But by learning legal tricks of the trade at the PAS, they served vital roles as utility men. They traveled to prisons and courthouses in Pennsylvania, New Jersey, Maryland, and Virginia to check on tips about fugitive slaves or to identify kidnapped free blacks in need of legal aid, researched case histories and interviewed deponents for pending court cases, counseled black families and friends as "agents" in such matters as indentures, and chased down crucial legal papers for blacks that often turned a big case around. One example of the legal footwork done by this group was provided in 1836, when Thomas Shipley traveled to New Jersey and Maryland to get a copy of a black man's free papers before returning to Philadelphia for a formal legal hearing. Without the documentation, which eventually led to freedom, the freeman would have remained in bondage or even been sold South.

Thomas Harrison, a tailor, represented numerous African Americans in binding proceedings with slaveholders. Hopper, also trained as a tailor, took depositions from blacks for court cases. Shipley, brought up in the hardware trade, traveled throughout the mid-Atlantic region to obtain critical legal documents for kidnapped free blacks. One counselor, underlining the demands of PAS legal work, lamented that he had spent "14 days without monetary reimbursement" working on a single case for black freedom. In another example, Shipley himself spent eighteen days on a single case. Finding deponents (black as well as white), seeking legal advice, building a compelling legal argument with facts and case histories — this was taxing work for the utility men. But it made a significant difference to the PAS's specialized legal work, not to mention the lives of many black Americans.[38]

THE STRATEGY AND tactics of the Pennsylvania Abolition Society reflected a late-eighteenth-century, republican worldview. In terms of sensibility, the group favored reason above all else. In terms of attack, it condoned state-backed legal and political action while eschewing violence and extralegal, extrapolitical, or extraconstitutional means. Moreover, the group cherished elite activists, particularly lawyers. In short, the PAS believed that abolitionism would succeed only by utilizing the governmental and legal institutions of men (certain men), not the universe of God, to end slavery.

In both membership and tactical style, the PAS fit the profile of benevolent reformers in the post-Revolutionary world. As recent scholarship has demonstrated, early national America witnessed an explosion of benevolent organizations, particularly in the New England states and Pennsylvania. Many of these reform groups revolved around men of status and power. From Philadelphia, Benjamin Rush proclaimed that the philanthropic work of "great men" would usher in an American golden age of liberty, sobriety, and moral worth. Prominent friends in New York City, Providence, and Boston picked up Rush's call to benevolent action, establishing moral reform societies, early temperance groups, and charities.[39]

Despite its own weighty leadership and conservative tactics, the PAS often provoked intense opposition during the early republic. Many statesmen outside of Pennsylvania viewed abolitionists, in general, and the PAS, more particularly, as a bunch of government "meddlers." An early petition to Congress moved one Georgian to decry the PAS's entire legislative strategy: if the "general government" heeded the group's words and abolished the overseas slave trade, then congressional power over bondage would be unquestioned — and "total emancipation" decrees would quickly follow in southern states. If American leaders did not want to bring on "a civil war," the Georgian declared, they would "take no notice" of abolitionist petitions.[40]

Even sympathetic figures remained wary of the PAS approach. For instance, Massachusetts minister Jeremy Belknap, informed that he had been elected to the PAS's sister organization — the Providence Abolition Society — and that the society would petition Congress to curtail the slave trade, expressed considerable dismay at such abolitionist tactics. "The proposition [of petitioning Congress] does not strike me agreeably," he wrote to Ebenezer Hazard, a conservative New York City Quaker and member of the New York Manumission Society. Belknap doubted the legitimacy of abolitionist strategy, too. Preaching or publishing one's antislavery scruples was fine, he observed, but not organizing an elite band of activists to agitate government and legal bodies for slavery's demise, especially at the federal level. The Constitution itself "precluded" any congressional prohibition of the overseas slave trade until "1808" and any abolitionist action in the southern states forever. Thus, Belknap asserted, with the abolitionist strategy preemptively foiled, their legislative and legal tactics could only threaten the brand-new American Union. Even a congressional petition urging (not demanding) government "interference" in the overseas slave trade would provoke sectional discord. "I apprehend that stirring up controversy on this subject may endanger the Union," he concluded. For that reason Belknap was "not pleased" to learn of abolitionist petition efforts or even of his "honorary" inclusion in an abolitionist society.[41]

A number of the Revolutionary era's most influential thinkers and states-men (John Adams, Thomas Jefferson, Edmund Randolph, James Madison, George Washington, among others) echoed Belknap's concerns. In their eyes, Pennsylvania abolitionists' vision of using the government to destroy slavery threatened America's grand experiment in republican nationhood. Indeed, as prominent citizens of the republic, they viewed abolitionist strat-egy as a political and social threat. PAS petitions to Congress in 1790 ex-hausted Washington's patience, for, as he observed, they brought sectional discord to the new nation at a time when it needed national harmony. John Adams questioned the very justice of government-sponsored abolitionist plans. As he explained, "Justice to the negroes would require that they not be generally abandoned . . . and turned loose on a world which they had no capacity to procure a subsistence . . . [And] Justice to the world . . . would forbid that such numbers should be turned out *by decree* to live by violence, theft or fraud." Americans, Adams concluded, should slowly curb slave imports and then gradually press for better treatment of those already en-slaved, until whites became so numerous that small, private liberations could begin to take place, provided, of course, that masters as well as slaves agreed. As vice president and leader of the Senate, Adams derided PAS congressional memorials that sought government solutions to the private problem of slavery.[42]

Virginians Thomas Jefferson and Edmund Randolph agreed with Adams's logic: abolitionist strategy augured ill for the American republic. In the face of heated opposition from Virginia planters, Jefferson retreated from his own legislative plans to abolish slavery. His *Notes on the State of Virginia* (1787) expressed antislavery sympathies but argued that abolition-ism should remain a master's prerogative. Jefferson's well-known lament about slavery's evil — "I tremble for my country when I think that God is just" — remained just that, for he also argued that abolition must remain largely a personal, not a governmental, concern. Randolph, who followed Jefferson as governor of Virginia, wrote the PAS (which had approached him about sponsoring abolitionist memorials) that he could never embrace abolitionist strategy or tactics. Though he supported private manumission, he opposed an abolitionist government strategy.[43]

This elite opposition hampered the PAS. The group hoped to befriend political and judicial figures nationally whose "worthy" sponsorship of state abolition societies everywhere would help activists build legislative, judicial, and political walls around slavery. The American Convention of Abolition Societies did, of course, bring together abolitionist groups from

Connecticut, New Jersey, Delaware, and, on occasion, Virginia and North Carolina. Yet to their chagrin and even shock, PAS members encountered stony receptions from many elite figures, North as well as South.

When Virginia abolitionists tried to implement the PAS's strategy, they found precious little room to operate within the Old Dominion's legal or political bodies. Laws prevented them from representing blacks in court, statesmen refused to support abolitionist petitions, and abolitionist meetings were often disrupted by angry slaveholders without any legal recourse. For a state whose leaders had talked so much about the evils of slavery during the Revolution, Virginia abolitionists complained to the Pennsylvanian society, the Old Dominion seemed intolerant of "those associations" that planned its demise. The PAS encouraged their abolitionist associates to persevere. It realized, of course, that Virginians would be wary of abolitionist strategy and that abolitionists needed to cultivate elite contacts in Virginia before they could succeed. Yet the Old Dominion's worthies never warmed to abolitionism, and the speed with which Virginia abolitionists were routed by the early 1800s shocked the usually optimistic Pennsylvanians.[44]

Virginia abolitionists established societies in both Richmond and Alexandria at the end of the 1780s. But as early as 1794, the Virginia General Assembly railed against their "menacing" activities at the bar and in the legislature. One member of the state assembly warned both Virginia and Pennsylvania abolitionists about the "impropriety" of their legislative tactics in the Old Dominion.[45] In 1796 a wealthy slaveholder further denounced abolitionists' legislative agitation and legal work with blacks. "This Society," he shouted at one abolitionist meeting, would produce "dangerous consequences . . . by infusing into the slaves a spirit of insurrection and rebellion which might eventually destroy the tranquility of the state." As a letter to the PAS recounted, "the alarm soon spread" until "a remonstrance against the society was drawn up, signed by a number of state magistrates," and brought to the General Assembly. The state's worthy men sought "legislative action against the Society," as one Virginia reformer explained, "ABOLISHING the ABOLITION of slavery throughout . . . Virginia." Abolition societies, according to a new law, could no longer represent black claimants at the bar. More broadly, the legislature instructed those "voluntary associations instituted for the purpose of abolishing slavery" to cease and desist their political activities.[46]

This dark warning had unfortunate consequences, for blacks often relied on white legal aid in Virginia. The state's abolitionists, like their Pennsylvania colleagues, faced an ever-increasing number of black freedom claims. During one year, over one hundred such cases came to their attention. But, Virginia abolitionists reported, "the friends of the society are too small to operate properly . . . for the purposes of the institution." Legislative warnings about *any* abolitionist action in courts or legislatures further threatened what little legal aid Virginia abolitionists could offer.[47]

Virginia activists held on until 1804, when two recent slave rebellions finally forced them to shut down. As the Virginians stressed to the PAS, however, Gabriel's Rebellion only provided the state's leaders with a convenient excuse to pressure abolitionist societies out of existence. In actuality, Virginia's leading men had never supported abolitionism. "The predominance of interest combined with power," wrote Archibald McLean, founding member of Alexandria's short-lived abolitionist society, neutralized "the principles of reason, justice, humanity and every benevolent and sympathetic" action undertaken by Virginia abolitionists. In other words, prominent political figures rigidly opposed abolitionists' government strategy; without their support, McLean argued, abolitionists could never defeat slavery in Virginia.[48]

To the PAS's dismay, many of the Bay State's distinguished citizens also were against abolitionism. Massachusetts had banned slavery in the early 1780s, when, in the wake of several successful black freedom suits, its highest court declared bondage null and void. For that reason, the PAS believed, a Massachusetts Abolition Society would bring great respect to any national abolitionist movement. The state's well-known political figures could expound on the virtues of broad emancipation decrees and abolitionist adjudication. Moreover, prominent Bay Staters could help abolitionists gain influence in Congress.[49] Finally, Massachusetts reformers could help the PAS track and prosecute New England's slave traders, who, according to PAS reports, brought the bulk of Africans to American shores between 1790 and 1800. Thus throughout the 1790s, the Pennsylvanians urged Boston's political and religious leaders "to form . . . an [abolitionist] society in that place."[50]

Despite the PAS's outreach efforts, leading citizens of Massachusetts remained wary of planning slavery's end nationally. With so much else of national economic and political importance, some officials argued, national abolitionism remained a low priority. Baptist minister Isaac Backus, though a self-professed antislavery man, objected to treating abolitionism (or even the overseas slave trade) as a national political concern. Other officials claimed that nonslaveholding states such as Massachusetts had no business "interfering" in what was becoming a distinctly southern institution. Massachusetts representative Harrison Gray Otis routinely attacked abolitionists' congressional petitions for "meddling" in "business with which they have no concern." Like Jefferson and Adams, Otis argued that emancipation should be a matter of individual conscience, not government decree. In the critical early years of the republic, few Bay Staters disagreed. Slavery remained not simply a southern problem but a personal problem; neither the federal government nor any individual state could legislate southern bondage out of existence without masters' approval. At best, then, abolitionist strategies were futile; at worst, they endangered the republic's stability.[51]

A PAS corresponding member, Virginian St. George Tucker, discovered Bay State apathy for himself in the 1790s. Seeking an abolitionist strategy that would surmount planter opposition and gain elite support in Virginia, Tucker wrote to some of Massachusetts's preeminent residents for advice. The Old Dominion's leaders, he noted, "feared every [legislative] attempt to eradicate" the institution of slavery. "To assist in removing this fear is my objective," he explained, "and having observed that slavery was wholly exterminated from Massachusetts, I wish to learn what methods are most likely to succeed in removing the same evil form amongst ourselves." Tucker asked a number of questions, such as "what was the exact mode of slavery's eradication," "how did white citizens react [to abolitionist court decisions]," "how did blacks contribute, if at all," and "what has been the result?"[52]

The Virginian received replies from Massachusetts jurists, ministers, politicians, merchants, even a historian. Though many wished him well, none were sanguine about Virginia's prospects for general emancipation; more importantly, none of the respondents believed that a government strategy could legitimately end slavery in the Old Dominion. A respected Salem physician commented that Virginia faced "difficulties which, if not absolutely insuperable, then very nearly approximate it," for the state contained too many slaves to be emancipated safely by any legislative decree. Another letter writer "heartily pitied the southern states," for, he predicted, they would never get rid of slavery without bloodshed.[53]

Without widespread abolitionist sentiment among planters and other influential figures, many of Tucker's correspondents agreed, "hard bondage" states such as Virginia could not declare slavery null and void, even by the most gradual abolitionist schemes.[54] Even Massachusetts's abolitionist decree had been a mistake, one judge asserted, for it robbed masters of their property rights and unleashed black paupers on white society. Though other writers took exception to this view, few disputed that free blacks now menaced the Bay State. Virginia, the correspondents agreed, would be better off shelving government abolitionist plans until some future period. Hoping to find a transferable abolitionist strategy from Massachusetts leaders, Tucker was left in doubt about his project.

Why did Massachusetts remain silent on the slavery issue until the 1820s and 1830s? One answer lies in the politics of union. Northern congressional figures routinely backed away from slavery to court southern concessions on northern economic plans. Another explanation derives from Bay Staters' racial fears. As John Adams suggested, the only reason Massachusetts courts could ban slavery in the first place was that the state contained a small number of slaves — roughly one thousand altogether, or barely one-half of 1 percent of the total population. Yet even this tiny emancipation decree generated concerns about racial confrontations between surly free blacks and angry whites. Finally, the state's political and business leaders may have refrained from attacking southern slavery and the slave trade for financial reasons. Bondage played an important part in the New England economy. Shipbuilders outfitted slave ships, financiers underwrote journeys to Africa and the Caribbean, and businesses (rum distilleries, trading houses) turned raw goods that came from the trade into products for both domestic and international markets. As one Rhode Island abolitionist remarked in 1789, the "mercantile interest" pervaded the New England states' politics and business.[55] Abolitionists would fight a lonely battle converting men "whose love of gain" ruled their lives.[56]

Subsequent generations of abolitionists would comment derisively on the refusal of Massachusetts political and religious elites to embrace national abolitionism. From Harrison Gray Otis in the 1790s to Edward Everett and Daniel Webster in the 1820s and 1830s, William Lloyd Garrison would announce, abolitionists could expect little support from Bay State leaders. Pennsylvania abolitionists noted the apathy of Massachusetts's leading men during the early republic, lamenting in their reports to the American Convention of Abolition Societies the opposition "northward" as well as in the southern states. At a time when Pennsylvanians sought to export their own abolitionist strategy (and gain elite patronage throughout the Union), prominent Massachusetts figures joined Virginians in defining slavery as a hands-off, nongovernmental concern. Without elite support in such critical states, the PAS wondered, how could abolitionism ever succeed nationally?[57]

ELITE OPPOSITION to its strategy perplexed the PAS. When men of property and standing lambasted PAS tactics as government "meddling" and PAS officers as "fanatics," the Pennsylvania society reemphasized its "weighty" membership and "honorable" strategy of gradually ending slavery via government action. Indeed, it argued, the PAS had broader white as well as black interests in mind, for unless the nation's elite conspired to destroy slavery, racial rebellion and political discord loomed. As good republicans and hopeful Union builders themselves, PAS leaders visualized a vibrant American nation for ages to come. Slavery tainted this vision and, on a more practical level, threatened the Union's very future. The PAS firmly believed that its government strategy offered America's best hope of averting racial disaster.

The group understandably despaired of abolition's failures, despite specific legal and political triumphs that put slavery on the defensive: termination of the overseas slave trade; the ending of slavery in Pennsylvania, New York, and New Jersey; and a host of successful black freedom suits involving African Americans from the Chesapeake states. Nevertheless, as a PAS report somberly put it in 1825, abolitionism should now be judged by its national successes or failures, not by particular triumphs. Unless southern slavery itself declined, or the nation's elites embraced the abolitionist cause, the group could not claim total success.[58]

These failures notwithstanding, the PAS never departed from its strategy. The society continued to appeal to "weighty" figures for support; continued its careful, if shrewd, legal and political work; and, not coincidentally, continued to hold other more "radical" strategists at bay, especially African Americans during the 1820s.[59] As a former PAS member recalled in 1839, PAS strategists deserved credit for shaking their republican world of the notion that slavery would wither without government interference. Even this correspondent admitted, however, that the group's strategy was "elitist" and that it became antiquated by the 1820s and 1830s.[60] To finally doom slavery, he insisted, abolitionists had to transcend the old-style republican strategy and tactics of the Pennsylvania Abolition Society and open up the movement to an array of democratic activists and egalitarian impulses. As the new-style reformers in Massachusetts argued by 1830, abolitionists had to revolutionize their own movement before they could finally revolutionize slavery in America.

CHAPTER TWO

Deferential Petitioners

The Pennsylvania Abolition Society in State
and Federal Government, 1790–1830

*To complain of injustice or petition for redress of grievances
cannot be mistaken for rebellion against the laws of our country.
Discretion will prevail in all of our proceedings.*
— PAS congressional petition, 1804

WHEN PENNSYLVANIA abolitionists drafted their first congressional petition in 1790, they drew on a sacred form of American political protest.
Long before the Revolutionary era, Americans used petitions to voice individual and collective concerns to their representative governments.[1] The
Pennsylvania Abolition Society (PAS) updated this tradition by focusing
the petition strategy on a single issue: slavery. "Promoting slavery's eradication," the PAS proclaimed in an 1809 missive to western abolitionists, required constant "applications to Legislatures for the enactment of [aboli-
tionist] laws." Only by "designing" such focused petition campaigns could
reformers turn abolitionist ideals into legislative reality.[2] "The agitation of
the slavery question in our government," one Georgia slaveholder remembered in 1860, began with a PAS congressional petition in 1790. "From that
moment onward, slavery has been under attack."[3]

Unlike the more well-known mass petition attacks of the 1830s, however, PAS memorials usually adhered to a conservative strategy. Respectfully
worded, carefully written, and bolstered by artful lobbying techniques of
prominent politicians, the group's documents looked to persuade subtly,
not to demand dogmatically. The Pennsylvanians rarely threw down gaunt-
lets or insisted on immediate abolition.[4] Their petitions thus illuminate the
very nature of radical protest, usually nonradically sustained.

BETWEEN 1790 and the late 1820s, Pennsylvania abolitionists petitioned state and federal government on a range of slavery issues: stopping the importation of Africans, banning the domestic slave trade between northern and southern states, prohibiting slavery's westward advance, and outlawing slavery in the District of Columbia.[5] Generally, the PAS used petitions to prod American leaders into confronting slavery. Political officials did not have to abolish bondage immediately, the group's memorials would continuously note, particularly in southern states containing the bulk of enslaved peoples. But governments must gradually impede slavery's operation. Through petitions, the PAS vowed not to let the founding generation of statesmen ignore America's slavery problem.

Petitions especially sought to influence the young republic's governing elite. As the PAS would variously assert, abolitionists had to enlist the support of powerful men; reformers could accomplish little without the aid of governors, legislative officials, and statesmen. The nation's governing elite alone could muster the diplomatic skill and the patronage to guide abolitionist laws through governments. The PAS thus looked to befriend "men [whose] character would add strength" to abolitionists' political "exertions," particularly the creation of laws to gradually destroy slavery.[6]

Flattery was one route to elite patronage. PAS congressional petitions routinely alluded to the "honorable" men in government office, those wise "patriots, philosophers and statesmen" whose benevolent support would offer incalculable aid to the abolitionist cause. As "one of the greatest and most dignified bodies the world has ever beheld," an 1826 memorial asserted, Congress would do honor to its already elevated reputation by eradicating slavery in the District of Columbia. "Our most respectful request" to the "benevolent" rulers of the land, another memorial stated in 1827, "is that Congress will be pleased to prohibit, by law, the [further] introduction of slaves into the Florida Territory." In other memorials, Pennsylvania reformers addressed state and federal legislators as "august," "most excellent," and "worthy" men whose legislative support would bring America's Revolutionary ideals to fruition.[7]

In searching for elite support, PAS petitions also stressed the respectable and "gentlemanly" character of their own petitioners. As an early appeal put it, the Pennsylvania society was an "honorable" organization through and through, with men whose "character" transcended the "vulgar prejudices" of slaveholders and other opponents of emancipation. Congressmen could respect these "Gentlemanly" petitioners, the PAS pointed out, even if they disagreed with them.[8]

The PAS could be apologetic about its petitioning strategy. "We hope our zeal in this business," an early federal memorial stated, "will not be regarded as an improper intrusion on your councils."[9] Indeed, "to complain of injustice or petition for redress of grievances," the society observed in 1804, "cannot be mistaken for rebellion against the laws of our country." Abolitionists, the PAS confidently pronounced, would remain cautious, requesting only constitutionally sanctioned doctrines from Congress. "Discretion will prevail in all of our proceedings," it assured the nation's rulers.[10]

The PAS wanted the good men of Congress, and the state assemblies, to devise legislation that would attack slavery without upsetting the American political order. "We dare not flatter ourselves with anything more than a very gradual work [of national emancipation]," the group announced in 1790, for "long habits die hard and strong interests are not overcome in an instant."[11]

To bolster its claims to respectability and moderation, the group usually affixed the signatures of eminent men to its memorials. Benjamin Franklin, as the PAS itself wrote, "deigned" to sign the group's first national memorials to the Constitutional Convention of 1787 and the inaugural federal Congress in 1790.[12] Even some antiabolitionist members of Congress paused before condemning a document signed by so "respectable" a man. In fact, the PAS worried that Franklin's death in 1790 would limit the organization's petitioning tactics, for he was a man of "eminent ability and character."[13]

Other estimable figures filled the void. James Pemberton, a leading Quaker merchant and PAS vice president, signed the group's petitions in the 1790s. Caspar Wistar, another prominent Quaker merchant and philanthropist, also offered his signature in Franklin's absence. In the 1810s and 1820s William Rawle, then head of the Pennsylvania bar, signed memorials for both the American Convention of Abolition Societies and the PAS. Abolitionist petitions on the District of Columbia and on the admission of new western states contained only the signatures of the well-known Rawle and the recording secretary at the time, "Dr. Edwin Atlee," son of a celebrated family of Philadelphia physicians.[14] In the late 1820s the group asked "our excellent fellow citizen, Charles Miner, esquire," a noted lawyer and political figure, and Thomas Earle, another eminent legal and political man from Philadelphia, to sign memorials to Congress. As one abolitionist wrote in 1828, the PAS had "a large number of respectable names" to affix to its petitions.[15]

Crafty and intensive behind-the-scenes lobbying of powerful men offered another route to elite support. The PAS took every opportunity to cultivate contacts with "influential individuals" in state and federal government.[16] Throughout the 1790s this approach worked with various national political figures based in Pennsylvania, including Tench Coxe, Albert Gallatin, and Thomas Hartley (Speaker of the House of Representatives during the First Congress). The group used these contacts to cultivate relationships with other powerful political figures during the early national period.

In 1790 the society drew on its contacts with John Adams in the Senate (who knew of the PAS through his association with Benjamin Franklin) and Pennsylvania's Thomas Hartley to present the first congressional memorials on the overseas slave trade. The Pennsylvanians looked to other "worthies" as well, including James Madison and President George Washington. Whereas Washington rebuffed the abolitionists, Madison vowed to support their attempts to ban the African trade. He wrote that "he had no idea [slave-trading] abuses were so deep." Although Madison later stepped back from this stand, the PAS remained flattered by his ostensible support.[17] In fact, the group corresponded with Madison during the Virginian's presidency. Hoping to curb abuses of the congressional slave-trading ban of 1808, which the PAS had been diligently tracking, Pennsylvania reformers asked Madison to push for stronger laws on the matter.[18] Once again he pledged his support but ultimately claimed that Deep South opposition tied his hands.

The PAS targeted other high-ranking officials as well. In the mid-1790s the Pennsylvanians asked Timothy Pickering and Oliver Wolcott, members of John Adams's administration, to prosecute foreign slave traders who used American ports in violation of a 1794 congressional law. Adams himself replied that any such action by the federal government would be inexpedient; the XYZ affair and the undeclared naval war with France remained higher government priorities.[19] During the Missouri Crisis of 1819–22, the PAS asked New York congressmen James Tallmadge and Rufus King to support abolitionist petitions against the admission of slave states.[20] Governors of various states, state assemblymen, and well-known jurists and lawyers received similar appeals before the 1820s.

In Pennsylvania, the PAS remained a consistent presence in the state capital of Harrisburg. After drafting petitions on various matters (from immediately banning slavery in Pennsylvania to protecting free black communities from kidnapping incidents) and forwarding them to state government, it routinely dispatched lobbyists to "stand in wait" of assemblymen. Once in 1819, the society even considered hiring a professional lobbyist to oppose a state assembly bill on fugitive slaves.[21] Every other time, however, the group relied on its own delegations. Far from small mobs of agitators, PAS lobbyists had specific tasks: they contacted individual legislators sympathetic to abolitionism and urged them to support certain abolitionist petitions; they distributed essays and reports providing fuller information to legislators on various issues (the extent of the domestic slave trade from Pennsylvania, for instance); and they reported on legislative debates for PAS reference. In 1814 and 1815, for example, the group sent Thomas Shipley and William Rawle to Harrisburg to oppose another proposed law restricting black emigration into the state. While Shipley circulated PAS memorials to lawmakers and collected unofficial opinions on the proceedings, Rawle urged legislative leaders to support PAS petitions.[22] On this occasion, the PAS could not preempt the antiblack bill from coming before the General Assembly. According to the proposed law, free blacks emigrating to the Quaker State had to register as resident aliens; if they did not, and they stayed longer then six months, they could be sold into slavery. Happily for the PAS, this bill too failed to become law.

As this incident suggests, the PAS often gained access to inside information from legislative bodies and committees. As early as 1793, for instance, it received draft copies of the first federal Fugitive Slave Bill from Pennsylvania congressmen.[23] The society then asked its legal experts to write abstracts of the proposed law's impact on northern black communities. If the group could not deter such harmful legislation (and according to PAS contacts, Congress was going to pass a fugitive law of some sort), then it could use advance information to prepare for distress calls from black clients.

Roberts Vaux, an eminent Philadelphia philanthropist, often obtained "previews" of new state and federal laws on slavery. Politicians in and outside of Pennsylvania respected the gentlemanly Vaux and often sought his opinion.[24] Through his political contacts, Vaux provided warnings about Maryland's plans to press for stronger fugitive slave laws in Pennsylvania. Maryland's masters fumed at runaways' success in Pennsylvania courts, and in 1823 the state asked the Pennsylvania General Assembly to crack down on black fugitives. Learning of a proposed meeting between legislators from the two states, the PAS quickly dispatched its own lobbyists to Harrisburg. Vaux privately worked his contacts for information on the meeting. As one correspondent informed Vaux, Maryland representatives had put Pennsylvania under tremendous pressure. The Quaker State would have to produce tougher fugitive slave provisions. Another elite contact, Pennsylvania lawyer William Meredith, explained that he and others had "worked against [such laws] at every stage of their progress, exerting [ourselves] to the utmost to defeat [them] altogether." Unfortunately, Meredith continued, "zealous friends" of slavery in both Maryland and Pennsylvania prevented a "smothering" of a new fugitive bill "in its cradle."[25]

Yet according to Meredith, "the new [fugitive slave] bill does not go a single iota beyond our constitutional obligation" to return runaways to southern states. In fact, he explained, abolitionists' lobbying efforts had yielded an important loophole. Because the new law required proof of a fugitive's identity prior to rendition, abolitionist lawyers might continually question the "identity" of accused runaways to foil masters' reclamation attempts. Vaux and the PAS used this insider information in exactly this fashion, to the continued chagrin of Maryland slaveholders.[26]

For PAS members no less than for other early national figures, the tactics of deferential politics and behind-the-scenes diplomacy became crucially important to the success of the cause. Currents of democratic rhetoric notwithstanding, the new republic's political world revolved largely around "men of standing," as the PAS put it. "Politicking" among the nation's governing elite, PAS activists would continually assert, provided critical access to the policy-making arena of statesmen and legislative bodies. Pennsylvania reformers could not imagine working outside this nexus of elite support.

THE PAS COUNSELED other abolitionists to follow its careful petitioning tactics: use only well-known signatories on abolitionist memorials, lobby and befriend political elites, emphasize the benevolent and worthy project of black emancipation, and never push governments too far on the abolitionist cause. "Be careful to join moderation to your zeal," the group warned abolitionists in southern Pennsylvania in 1789, and "proceed [only] with safety and usefulness" in mind.[27] The PAS realized that slavery remained a most sensitive issue in the new republic. Abolitionists could not demand action from a national Congress or needlessly arouse lawmakers to gain favorable legislation.

The creation and meaning of abolitionist laws, the PAS argued, depended on the constitutional and legislative latitude available to reformers. Abolitionist petitions should be adamant about seeking redress for black Americans, but only within legal and political limits at the state and federal levels. For example, the PAS did not and would not ask the General Assembly to nullify bordering states' fugitive slave provisions. Nor would it prevail upon Congress to outlaw slavery in the southern states (because the national

Constitution contained no explicit clause supporting domestic emancipation). In fact, abolitionist petitioners could not push any legislative body beyond "reasonable limits," lest the emancipation cause spiral out of control and threaten the Union's stability. PAS petitioners, as one memorandum asserted, had to adopt "patience and forbearance" as tactical mottoes. Since abolitionists belonged to the American "commonweal," one reformer announced, they could not recklessly prosecute their cause in representative assemblies.[28]

Because Pennsylvania's bill of rights protected "human freedom" regardless of color and gave the legislature power to act on behalf of all its "inhabitants," reformers felt secure in requesting strong abolitionist action from the state assembly. Enacting gradual abolition schemes in the 1780s signaled only the start of black emancipation, the society maintained. The state also had to prevent slaveholders from circumventing abolitionist laws, guard against the kidnapping of freed blacks, and ensure that even fugitive slaves from Pennsylvania and other states received fair legal and judicial treatment.[29]

The group's petitions had a hand in making Pennsylvania a "beacon of liberty" for black as well as white citizens. The effort began in 1790 with a PAS memorial to the convention meeting in Philadelphia to revise the 1776 state constitution. The petition strongly urged representatives not to limit basic constitutional rights to "white" citizens. Such a discriminatory doctrine, it warned, would establish a system of black subjugation tantamount to bondage. As one representative wrote the Pennsylvania society, its memorial helped prod the convention to drop the racist language from the new constitution. As the PAS victoriously proclaimed, the "just" state of Pennsylvania had put "a free black man on the same [constitutional] footing as any citizen."[30]

The PAS constantly utilized petitions to protect Pennsylvania's Gradual Abolition Act from assault. In 1793 it helped block a bill in the legislature that would have exempted from the act French slaveholders emigrating to the Quaker State from Haiti. The South Carolina and Maryland General Assemblies had already sheltered many of these slaveowners, asserting that "the laws of Justice and hospitality required" American governments to protect slave "property." When the Pennsylvania legislature rejected that doctrine, the PAS celebrated. "Our strenuous exertions," it noted, had kept Pennsylvania a land of freedom.[31]

Similarly, the group tried to bar congressional representatives from bringing their slaves into Philadelphia, where the new Congress temporarily resided during the 1790s. Learning of a bill that allowed "officers of the Government of the U.S. to hold slaves" while in Pennsylvania, the PAS hurriedly forwarded memorials denying immunity to federal congressmen.[32] Pennsylvania petitioners emphasized the General Assembly's legal and constitutional commitment to black freedom within the state. The PAS lost this battle, however. Federal representatives were permitted to bring their slaves into the Quaker State with full immunity from the Abolition Act.

Other important issues also prompted petition campaigns. As black complaints about kidnapping increased in the 1810s and 1820s, the PAS crafted numerous appeals to the General Assembly. Pointing to the alarming rise in the domestic slave trade between Pennsylvania and southern states, these memorials sought the "interposition . . . of legislative power" to stop the plunder of free black communities.[33] "It is the duty of the legislature," an early 1821 memorial claimed, "to protect [all of] its citizens from violence." According to the society's petitions, state power must "prevent the practice of man stealing" in Pennsylvania and thereby set a critical precedent for other states.[34]

Federal petition campaigns followed an even more cautious strategy. The PAS refrained from broad statements about blacks' constitutional rights or slaves' natural right to freedom. Indeed, Pennsylvania abolitionists conceded that the federal government could never interfere directly with masters' "private rights" to slave property. Thus their petitions merely sought to "enlist [federal] legislative support" in those areas of slavery that Congress theoretically could deal with.[35]

The group's focus on the overseas slave trade reveals the strict parameters within which the PAS operated. The society petitioned Congress on the issue at least ten times between 1787 and 1820. At first the PAS hoped to gain a constitutional ban on slave imports. When this failed, it strived for any congressional law that would "alleviate the sufferings" of blacks during the Middle Passage and restrict foreigners' involvement in the trade. After Congress banned the trade as per the Constitution in 1808, the PAS continued to petition U.S. lawmakers over the next decade on violations of the ban. Throughout, the abolitionists focused rigorously on the issue at hand, retreating to more moderate ground if their petitions proved too radical. Not once did they lecture Congress about its absolute duty to aid blacks, nor did they express exasperation with federal apathy.

PAS petitions initially sought to ban slave imports altogether. The trade had come under constant attack during the Revolutionary period, when many American leaders criticized the plundering of Africa and some American colonies-turned-states restricted the trade. By the late 1780s the PAS believed that many statesmen would support a "continental" ban on the African traffic. If slavery itself could not be abolished by any central government decree, then perhaps the slave trade might. James Madison, among other prominent officials, spoke of the PAS's laudable goal of ending the slave trade throughout America. Madison's colleague from the Old Dominion, George Mason, called the trade an "infernal traffic" and a "national sin" that should be prevented at the earliest possible time.[36]

The PAS petitioned the Constitutional Convention of 1787 to outlaw slave imports "at the very beginning" of the new federal era, for such a constitutional ban would be much more efficient than individual state laws. Tench Coxe, secretary of the PAS, forwarded the petition to Benjamin Franklin, the society's president and a delegate to the convention meeting in Philadelphia. With inside contacts and a spirit of Revolutionary benevolence on its side, the PAS hoped for firm action.[37]

Franklin pocketed the anti-slave-trading memorial, however, when the convention addressed the divisive slavery issue. While certain delegates from the North and Upper South discussed immediate bans on African imports, representatives from South Carolina and Georgia threatened to leave the convention and to reject any Union with such abolitionist goals. "The memorial [would probably] alarm some of the southern states," Franklin wrote, "and thereby defeat the wishes of the enemies of the slave trade." As John Rutledge of South Carolina announced, "if the Convention thinks that North Carolina, South Carolina and Georgia would ever agree" to join a Union that banned the slave trade immediately, "the expectation is in vain. The people of those states would never be such fools as to give up so important an interest."[38] In one of the small but significant compromises of 1787, the Constitution guaranteed African imports and put off congressional consideration of the slave trade issue until "twenty years hence." The new national Congress could not even consider banning the trade until the 1807 congressional year.[39]

Recognizing that it could not gain an immediate ban, PAS strategists looked to police the slave trade and relieve "as far as possible" its most excessive abuses. According to Article I, Section 9, of the U.S. Constitution, Congress could not "limit the importation" of slaves before 1808. But, abolitionist lawyers argued, Congress could watch over the slave trade in "limited ways." "Something may be done in the future," one legal counselor advised in 1790, to help "suffering" blacks. For example, Congress might prevent Americans from supplying slaves to foreign traders or dictate the conditions of passage for captured blacks. Neither of these tactics "banned" the trade. At the same time, the PAS believed that it could keep a small but important amount of pressure on Congress to act benevolently in Africans' behalf.[40]

But even this limited strategy proved controversial among Deep South lawmakers. In 1794 Congress passed a statute stipulating that American citizens could not sell captured Africans to foreign traders and that foreign ships could not be outfitted in American ports.[41] The diligent PAS found the law useful in federal court. Between 1795 and 1805, for instance, it tracked over fifty violations of the congressional law, many of which resulted in the prosecution of sea captains and masters as well as the release of enslaved Africans. Violators from South Carolina, New York, and Rhode Island felt the sting of PAS action.[42] Yet any victories were short-lived, the Pennsylvanians realized, for the slave trade poured around forty thousand new chattels into America before it was banned by Congress in 1808.

Only once did the PAS transcend its strict protocols on the slave trade. The first anti-slave-trading memorial to Congress—drafted in 1790 by a committee of such notables as Tench Coxe, James Pemberton, and Nicholas Waln—urged that body to reexamine its powers over the slave trade and, if constitutionally possible, ban the trade outright for broad humanitarian and religious reasons. Pointing out that the Pennsylvania abolitionists acted "from a regard for the happiness of mankind," the document essentially asked the federal government to ignore its constitutional limitations by "promoting the abolition of slavery" throughout America.[43] Indeed, although it focused on the overseas slave trade, the petition also encouraged Congress to consider outlawing domestic slavery itself "sometime hence." "From a persuasion that equal liberty was originally . . . a birthright of all men," the memorial explained, "your memorialists conceive themselves bound to use all justifiable endeavors to loosen the bands of slavery and promote a general enjoyment of . . . freedom."[44]

The 1790 petition then made a bold statement about federal power over domestic slavery: "[We] have observed with great satisfaction the many important and salutary powers vested in you for 'promoting the welfare and securing the blessings of liberty' to the people of the United States, and [we] conceive that these blessings ought rightfully to be administered [by Congress] without distinction of colour to all descriptions of people." In similarly expansive language, the PAS asked Congress to "step to the very verge of its powers . . . for discouraging every species of traffic in persons of your fellow men." The group would let Congress "devise [the] means for removing this inconsistency from the character of the American people." But its desire to have a strong federal government crack down on both the slave trade and domestic bondage was clear.[45]

Warned by luminaries in Congress that such radical claims for federal power would not only fail to end slavery but also might have disastrous political consequences in the new Union, the group quickly backed away. Moreover, the society's counselors established rigorous new guidelines for petitioning Congress on the slave trade. In fact, "the principle object" of future petitions, one circular to other abolition societies noted at the end of 1790, "would consist of a request that Congress . . . pass laws [only] to ALLEVIATE as much as possible the horrors of the slave trade," not to prohibit it or ban domestic slavery. The PAS admitted that its original strategy of citing "the unalienable right of all men to equal liberty" had done more harm than good in 1790. "It is indeed doubtful that Congress may interfere with the trade," William Rawle cautioned. The next PAS memorial merely asked Congress to work within its constitutional limits by regulating the conditions of the Middle Passage (if possible) and banning foreign involvement.[46]

The PAS asked other abolitionists to follow its now careful lead. As a circular put it, abolitionists should speak "in the same language" of deference and focus on the creation of narrow laws respecting the trade, not broad human rights or Africans' natural rights. As a further precaution, the group asked other reformers to "forward all memorials" to the PAS in Philadelphia for prior approval before submitting them to Congress.[47] Thus did "patience and forbearance" become the society's primary consideration when petitioning Congress. For instance, the group protested Missouri's admission to the Union between 1819 and 1822 but paid close attention to southern threats of disunion. Though the PAS believed that Congress had constitutional jurisdiction over federal territories (and thus could prevent the admission of new states if the lawmakers so desired), it decided to drop the matter for fear of pushing Congress too far.[48] In this manner, PAS memorials emphasized not just gradual abolitionism but moderate beginnings even for gradualism.

FOR DECADES, Pennsylvania strategists had urged the federal government to strike at slavery where it had the constitutional power to do so. According to PAS petitions of the 1820s, Congress maintained clear authority over one place if no other: the District of Columbia. Even the sober William

Rawle, adamant about not pushing for unwarranted uses of the federal government, believed that Congress could legislate slavery out of existence in "the small district." Indeed, by continually "urging the government to consider" the subject, Rawle asserted, abolitionists could set a crucial precedent for all subsequent national gradual emancipation efforts.[49]

The society's counselors formulated their District of Columbia strategy during the late 1810s. In December 1817 a special PAS committee advised the group to petition "the wise [Congress] of the nation" about banning the domestic slave trade in the District.[50] Two years later the same committee proclaimed the District to be one of the defining issues "for the advocates of humanity" in the coming years.[51] True to its own prophetic words, the PAS focused intensively on the District over the next decade. The group drafted several of its own memorials to Congress, petitioned the Pennsylvania General Assembly to support the District strategy, and took charge of national petition drives within the American Convention of Abolition Societies, drafting five separate memorials for that body between 1821 and 1829.

The District campaign coincided with a series of national events that produced new notoriety for slavery debates in the 1820s. First, Congress's three-year confrontation over Missouri brought sectional tensions to a head and renewed debate over the admission of slave states into the Union. (The PAS opposed the admission of Missouri as well as Alabama, Mississippi, and Florida.) Second, debates over colonization heightened concerns among many southern slaveholders about congressional interference in their property rights. Finally, Denmark Vesey's foiled South Carolina conspiracy had shaken masters' paternalist myths to their foundation. Vesey's claim to have been inspired by reprints of congressional debates over slavery appalled a new generation of southern representatives, who vigorously lashed out at the misguided abolitionist tactics of even the most gradualist reformers.

Lurking behind each of these issues was the broader question that PAS petitions posed: Could Congress touch slavery *within* the United States where it had constitutional jurisdiction? Southerners vehemently argued no — not even in the federally controlled District of Columbia. Because Virginia and Maryland, two states where slavery "existed full force," had originally ceded the federal territory in the 1790s, many southerners contended that Congress could not legislate on bondage there, either. As Aedenus Burke of South Carolina had noted as far back as 1790, he and other southern representatives would never allow slavery to be diminished in the nation's capital.[52]

DEFERENTIAL PETITIONERS

PAS petitions responded by citing article 1, section 8, of the federal Constitution: "Congress shall exert its control over the [capitol's] ten miles square." Using the baseline established in petition campaigns on the overseas and domestic slave trade, the PAS respectfully asked the national legislature to use this clear constitutional power to abolish slavery in the District. As an 1826 American Convention memorial succinctly put it, though the national government did not have "unlimited jurisdiction" over slavery's existence in America, "there is [still] ONE spot in which [the U.S. Constitution] invests Congress with an unrestricted privilege" to slay the institution of slavery: the District of Columbia. By eradicating slavery and the domestic slave trade in this admittedly small space, the memorial continued, Congress would make national emancipation a high priority, not to mention free the American capital from the stigma of bondage.[53]

Although the PAS concentrated on this issue throughout the 1820s, the District campaign peaked in 1829. In that one year, Pennsylvania abolitionists agitated simultaneously at local, state, and federal levels to break through legislative stonewalls in Congress: it pressured state officials to speak out on District emancipation, and it canvassed on behalf of Charles Miner's congressional resolutions in the House to smash bondage in the "ten miles square." Miner, a PAS member who relinquished his membership when he periodically returned to political office, utilized his congressional seat on this occasion to present "private resolutions" on slavery. Because the House was duty-bound to hear a fellow congressman's concerns, the PAS supported Miner in whatever way it could.[54]

Frustrated by the congressional tactic of burying abolitionist petitions in committees during the 1810s and 1820s, Pennsylvania abolitionists tried to capitalize on Miner's congressional privileges. The PAS helped Miner prepare his controversial proposals for submission to the House (fellow abolitionists critiqued his views and offered guidance on key constitutional issues). The society also lobbied hard to gain congressional approval of Miner's proposals. Finally, it reprinted and circulated Miner's work to abolitionists in other states, urging them to press their own representatives on District abolition.

"Mr. Miner's Proposals," as they were called, summarized a decade's worth of PAS plans for eradicating slavery in the District of Columbia. His preamble alone (which southern congressmen excised before it could even be considered in the House) distilled ideas previously set forth by Thomas Earle, Thomas Shipley, William Rawle, and other PAS members. Miner maintained that Congress had undisputed power over the District of Columbia. The Constitution's "words are full, clear and explicit" on the matter: federal power reigned supreme within the ten miles square. How could southerners deny such federal jurisdiction when Congress already exercised power over slavery in the District? Federal marshals, he explained, corralled fugitive slaves and housed them in federal prisons. Congress did not need individual states' approval of such action, illustrating once again the national legislature's power over bondage in the nation's capital.[55]

Slaveholders' rigid opposition, not controversial constitutional claims, remained the only obstacle to abolitionist action, Miner declared. This peculiar "sensitivity . . . ought not to prevail" much longer. Congress could, and should, abolish the slave trade and slavery in the District, if nowhere else. America's honor depended on it, and "many . . . citizens [were now] protesting" congressional apathy. With slavery growing numerically and expanding geographically in the South and Southwest, Miner concluded that abolition in the District would be a critical renewal of the Revolution's emancipatory promise.[56]

Southern representatives slammed the congressman's "abolitionist" resolutions in no uncertain terms. But nearly a year after the initial House debates on Miner's proposals, the PAS could still be found admonishing other reformers to read the speech "by our excellent fellow citizen, Charles Miner, Esq."[57] Other abolitionists took that advice, republishing Miner's resolutions in various forms over the next several years. Even Philadelphia's *North American Quarterly*, a journal highly skeptical of gradual abolitionism, approvingly published Miner's plans for the District.

For the PAS, years of lobbying and petitioning government seemed on the verge of paying off. Charles Miner's resolutions sparked new debate over slavery in the national legislature, reformers nationwide worked on a common strategy, and the abolitionist movement had a new sense of direction. The Pennsylvanians' tactics heralded a bright abolitionist future—or so they thought.

THE DISTRICT campaign galvanized a whole new generation of abolitionists, putting reformers "everywhere" into action. After a decade of petitioning the federal government to rid the "ten miles square" of slavery, the PAS detected a new abolitionist landscape on the horizon. African American activists promoted District emancipation in a publication called *Freedom's Journal*, the nation's first black-owned and edited newspaper. Reformers submitted congressional petitions from formerly apathetic areas, including

New England states, Virginia and Maryland, Ohio, Tennessee, and Michigan. Moreover, new leaders emerged to emphasize the significance of the District strategy, among them a young man named William Lloyd Garrison, coeditor of the *Genius of Universal Emancipation* in 1829.

After years of prodding the federal government to gradual action, the PAS appreciated this burst of enthusiasm from the youthful and fiery reformers. Working on a common abolitionist goal with an ascending generation, as Thomas Earle noted in 1826, would also "[re]commence the great work of emancipation," completing a "business which remains unfinished."[58] For a brief but hopeful period, the aging reformers cherished the opportunity of creating the next generation of abolitionist strategists in their own image.

Illusion gave way to a new reality in the late 1820s. The ascending generation did not endorse the PAS's traditional petitioning tactics or even its gradualist strategy. PAS leaders had to look no further than their own organization for outspoken critics. Arnold Buffum, Thomas Earle, Benjamin Jones, Abraham Pennock, and Edwin Atlee, among other recent members, had grown dissatisfied with the society's conservative congressional tactics, especially on District slavery. If abolitionists had such an ironclad constitutional case for District abolition, then they should demand (not request) action from Congress. Moreover, these critics complained, the PAS should not simply accept congressional apathy. They must mobilize anew. America's social and political world was rapidly changing, the PAS's emerging radicals argued, and abolitionists now must look for support beyond the ranks of the elite. In meetings, committee work, draft petitions, and private essays, the radical cohort made its dissenting feelings known.

Thomas Earle, a young Philadelphia lawyer who joined the PAS in the early 1820s, pushed his fellow abolitionists to craft more adamant petitions to the federal government. Earle urged abolitionists to think of the citizenry at large as a critical ally, for "the whole body of our fellow citizens" viewed District slavery as a "disgrace" to the federal government. Abolitionists must seize on popular ferment by circulating "citizen memorials" and by demanding government emancipation in the capital. Once federal emancipation proved both feasible and safe, Earle continued, abolitionists should press government officials for a further ban on slavery in all federally controlled territories.

Earle's radical views appeared in an 1826 congressional petition. His language was more emotional, his tone more urgent than anything previously drafted by the PAS or the American Convention of Abolition Societies. National abolition remained an "unfinished and important business," he declared, affecting not just America's honor but literally the lives of "thousands of the African race." Abolishing slavery in the District would free only a small portion of these tortured souls, men who were "purchased . . . in the surrounding country . . . and concentrated in the District." But it would liberate them nonetheless and strike a powerful blow for human freedom nationally. As it now stood, the petition went on, the unemancipated District was an eerie place "where the sounds of the clanking fetters [of slavery] mingle with the voice of American statesmen [supposedly] legislating for a free people." Abolitionists must tell Congress to "wipe away this foul reproach to the nation by fixing a period after which every child born of a slave in the District of Columbia SHALL BE FREE."[59]

Abolitionists should remain "respectful" of Congress, Earle wrote in 1829, but they could no longer accept congressional inaction on slavery, particularly where the federal government had the power to strike at the peculiar institution. In one essay Earle broached the subject of "immediate" abolition. But whether seeking gradual or immediate freedom, he concluded, abolitionists should escalate their petition campaigns annually. Only more forceful tactics, Earle insisted, would liberate blacks now held in the District.[60]

Earle's adamant tone found its way into a subsequent petition. Chiding congressional apathy, the 1829 memorial wondered why federal legislators refused to curb slavery in the nation's capital. "Why," the PAS asked, "should [abolition there] be so long postponed" when federal jurisdiction so clearly existed? As "the exclusive residence of the General Government," the District was "bound by no ancient or unalterable rules, exempted in no respect from the most absolute and comprehensive legislation which Congress may adopt." How, then, could "domestic slavery" and all of "its horrors" remain part of the District?[61]

Yet Earle's visionary tactics found only a temporary home. Many stalwart PASers distrusted his calls for a more radical approach. Older members like William Rawle and Roberts Vaux counseled cautious petitioning techniques, not even more numerous petition drives. Such radicalism would merely anger congressmen and hurt the movement's overall reputation. Rawle argued that without calm, "reasoned argument," abolitionist petitioners would reduce the cause to the "vulgar prejudices" that characterized slaveholders. Furthermore, abolitionists' few but significant legislative contacts would quickly back away from their inside support, leaving abolitionists without government sponsors. Finally, in the wake of the Missouri debates and fierce arguments over colonization, PAS stalwarts worried about stirring peoples' passions and playing on themes of sectional discord. Once they were aroused, abolitionists might not be able to control the emotions of new converts.[62]

Stalwarts did more than worry. On a few telling occasions, they shut down abolitionist tactics altogether. Rawle tabled even moderate PAS District petitions twice in the 1820s, citing his concern about pushing Congress too far on the sensitive slavery issue. In 1822, with one congressional contact poised to submit a new PAS petition on the admission of slave states, PAS leaders advised him to hold back, "the present time being injudicious" for further debate. In 1828 the PAS refrained from presenting memorials on the District for similar reasons: it would be "impolitic" to do so. In Rawle's eyes, abolitionists should never blindly agitate government; they too must worry about upsetting national unity. Abolitionists should continue to petition Congress on District emancipation, Rawle and his conservative cohorts would assert, but only after the country had settled down a bit after the Missouri debates and other divisive issues.[63]

"When will it be politic?" a newer member asked in 1828. "This cautious, timid disposition" must be questioned in the next several years, "and this calculating policy" of abolitionists "done away with." He continued: "Let us go to work—STUMP TO IT—and HOLD ON, whatever our antagonists may say or do. If there be much excitement among them, REGULATE your conduct according to the dictates of wisdom—but never cease from laboring to effect your object. NEVER ABANDON ONE INCH OF GROUND, AFTER IT HAS BEEN TAKEN.[64]

The District campaign of the 1820s had brought abolition's potential future alongside its past. For the present, the PAS could hold radicalism at bay—but the future was coming on fast by the end of the decade.

OF COURSE, even the PAS's relatively timid petitions had exposed slavery's potentially explosive nature in early federal politics. The mere presentation of abolitionist memorials brought howls of protest from southern congressman; there were occasional threats to ban abolitionist documents altogether from the federal legislature. Beginning in the First Congress, representatives from South Carolina and Georgia blasted the Pennsylvania abolitionists for "meddling in a business with which they had no concern." Sporadically over the next several decades, southern congressmen returned to this theme, disparaging reformers' attempts to stop the overseas slave trade, limit slavery's territorial expansion, and stamp out the institution in federally controlled areas such as the District of Columbia. "Abolition-ism has at one time or another been repeatedly pressed upon Congress," an 1829 House report engineered by southern congressmen concluded, "keep-ing the subject" dangerously "alive" before a powerful national Congress. Faced with such political tactics, slaveholders had good reason to oppose abolitionists' right to petition the federal legislature.[65]

Southern antipetition tactics stemmed from early sectional differences. Coming out of the Constitutional Convention of 1787, southern states beheld an institution of slavery that was far from dead; in a few key places, in fact, slavery enjoyed a resurgence. Throughout the 1790s the institution's social and economic impact intensified in key southern and southwestern areas: thousands of slaveholders poured into Kentucky and Tennessee at the same time that the number and percentage of slaveholders increased in the Lower South states of South Carolina and Georgia. On the wane in northern locales, bondage became a distinctly southern enterprise in post-Revolutionary America.

In a weak union of sovereign states, diverging northern and southern paths would have been no cause for concern. The Constitution of 1787, however, created a much stronger central government, and a majority of southern leaders immediately worried about slavery's viability in the new federal era. The national government, Patrick Henry warned Virginia's rati-fying convention in 1788, could dictate abolition without prior approval of individual states. Even died-in-the-wool Federalists like Charles C. Pinck-ney of South Carolina and George Washington of Virginia agreed with Henry's concern, arguing that southern slaveholders must remain eternally vigilant in the federal Congress. "Any interference with slavery," Pinckney warned, "would be considered a violation of our compact." With northern gradual abolition schemes ascendant and abolitionists' petitions already aimed at the powerful national legislature in the 1790s, southern lawmakers bridged various political and ideological divides to protect slavery in the South.[66]

The Union itself, southern strategists believed, hinged on slavery's pres-ent as well as future viability. Even abolitionist petitions on the overseas slave trade or other seemingly peripheral issues violated slavery's inherent protection. Indeed, they asserted, no slaveholder would ever have joined the Union in 1787 had he known that Congress would flirt with these "dangerous" abolitionist petitions. "All and every such attempt to influence Congress to pass laws" stifling slavery, one Maryland congressman noted in 1829, "would be an open violation . . . of the Constitution."[67] Even a limited precedent would be a bad precedent, southerners shouted over and over. Their federal Union could not countenance the political tactics of abolitionists.

Although Congress never enacted a formal gag rule before 1830, southerners routinely stifled early abolitionists' petitions. The Pennsylvania Abolition Society was not the only group rebuffed by slaveholders in the federal legislature. In 1791 Deep South representatives forced the House to return a Quaker petition because it made an "improper" request for federal intervention in the overseas slave trade. In 1797 southern congressmen persuaded their colleagues to dump the first black memorial on the same grounds: the petition allegedly assumed unwarranted constitutional powers to aid distressed black Americans. Pushing Congress to intervene on behalf of a group of reenslaved blacks from North Carolina, the memorial noted that "the great object of [the federal] government" was to institute "justice" via national "public policy." As North Carolina's Nathaniel Macon argued, however, the "general government" could not make "public policy" on slavery and therefore Congress could not even consider the blacks' petition.[68] "I did not think we were sent here to take up [federal] emancipation," a South Carolina representative proclaimed in 1800 before the House returned another petition by Philadelphia blacks.[69]

Congress technically received other abolitionist petitions but quickly passed them on to committees that never considered them. This policy, James Madison and other officials from the Upper South argued in the 1790s, shut abolitionists out of government without violating their petition rights — a critical point, Madison maintained, for American representatives always had to protect broader constitutional rights as well as slavery. Though initially slow to adopt this antiabolitionist tactic, other southern congressmen came to rely on it during the 1810s and 1820s. PAS petitions opposing the admission of new slave states and those requesting federal action against slavery in the District of Columbia routinely disappeared into the infamous Committee on the Judiciary.[70]

The First Congress set the tone for subsequent congressional repudiation of PAS petitions. Prompted by a PAS memorial against the slave trade in 1790, South Carolina and Georgia vigorously objected to abolitionists' right to petition government. Although the appeal was aimed at the overseas slave trade, they worried that abolitionist petitions had in mind wider views of government intervention in southern slavery. If not, the petitioners' made an unconstitutional request, given the fact that Congress could not consider a ban on the African trade before 1807. And even then, such a ban remained only a possibility. In short, Deep South congressmen proclaimed, PAS petitions must be returned to the abolitionists. Though moderates North and South accepted the petitions, they quickly secured a congressional report that prohibited "the general government" from ever legislating on southern slavery. According to South Carolinians and Georgians, the report actually meant that abolitionists could never petition the federal government. As early as the next year, the rest of Congress agreed, using the 1790 report to reject abolitionist petitions outright.[71]

Over the next forty years abolitionists would exploit personal contacts to bring petitions momentarily into the view of congressmen. But most of the time southerners convinced their congressional colleagues to restrict or prevent discussion on abolitionist memorials. To get beyond such informal gags in the years following the Missouri debates, abolitionists would clearly have to change their petitioning strategy and tactics.

DESPITE CONGRESSIONAL stonewalling, few PAS leaders supported more radical petitioning tactics. In fact, the acrimonious Missouri debates between 1819 and 1822 convinced many Pennsylvania abolitionists that even their own moderate petition campaigns could spur fearsome and regrettable discussion of the slavery issue. Abolitionism was "an event anxiously desired," the PAS reported, but the abolitionist movement could not press American leaders "beyond all reasonable measures." Moderation and "discretion" still guided reformers' tactics. "Conviction will spread," and abolitionist action would surely follow, the Pennsylvanians optimistically predicted, "but only when [men find] it [politically] safe as well as just" to support the cause.[72]

Thus abolitionist petitioners, sturdy PAS men such as William Rawle, Roberts Vaux, and Jonathan Roberts would increasingly insist during the 1820s, had to test the congressional climate before presenting new memorials, holding back if the political risks were too high for the American nation. "The present," Rawle argued in the early 1830s, "is precisely the period when increased [abolitionist] activity would be injudicious." Rawle's longtime associate Jonathan Roberts agreed, condemning the "fanatical" petition drives of the "modern abolitionists" after 1830.[73]

The PAS never wavered from its conservative petitioning strategy. No high-minded defenses of abolitionists' fundamental petition rights to break legislative gags; no rousing calls to the masses to overwhelm congressional apathy; no warnings to southerners that they would soon be buried by the superior organizing ability of free northern people—the PAS saw no need for any of these radical tactics. The group continued on its careful and deferential way, always believing that Congress would support abolitionists' call for legislative action at some future date. Those interested in more radical tactics during the 1820s, in other words, had to look elsewhere for organizational support. The society would not repudiate its principle of moderation.

This moderate stand derived from the PAS's elite guidance. In one sense, abolitionist petitioners and their congressional recipients were the same: white male political leaders, economic movers and shakers, and lawyers. PAS leaders continued to believe that through their well-placed contacts, abolitionists could push petitions before Congress and get some kind of hearing. The Pennsylvania elite never worried about its voice in government, and this imparted a less-than-urgent tone to the group's petitions.

Second-wave abolitionists would give due credit to the savvy Pennsylvanians for first using petitions as tactical weapons against slavery. Indeed, they had performed a signal service by challenging the founding generation of political leaders (at both the state and federal levels) to follow through on their Revolutionary commitments to black freedom. Yet Massachusetts reformers would also assert that the "old fashioned" tactics of the PAS needed to be radically updated. Petitions had to become the blunt instruments of a mass movement. All the behind-the-scenes lobbying and patient activism in the world would fail, newcomers would assert, since these tactics ultimately deferred to the power of the status quo. And the status quo supported slavery. In short, petitioners needed to become more than a nuisance. They had to become a force.

CHAPTER THREE

Creating Free Spaces

Blacks and Abolitionist Activism in
Pennsylvania Courts, 1780s–1830s

Our clients made us great.
— Jack Greenberg, NAACP Legal Defense Fund,
recalling the role black litigants played in civil
rights cases of the mid-twentieth century

IN SEPTEMBER 1836 the Pennsylvania Abolition Society (PAS) brought the case of Elizabeth, a runaway slave from Maryland, to trial in the state supreme court. Relying on loopholes in state and federal fugitive slave laws, the PAS argued that because Elizabeth's master had allowed her to visit "free" Pennsylvania, she could not be returned to enslavement in Maryland. Over vigorous objections from opposing attorneys, the judge agreed with the abolition society: "free" Pennsylvania could shelter slaves whose masters allowed them to leave southern plantations.[1]

Elizabeth's was just one of several prominent cases undertaken by the PAS in the autumn of 1836.[2] With a dedicated band of lawyers, the Pennsylvania society represented literally thousands of African Americans seeking legal aid during the early republic — from free blacks kidnapped into southern slavery and former slaves illegally held by their masters to southern runaways like Elizabeth seeking shelter in northern states. As one Maryland master complained, Pennsylvania abolitionists had erected such an annoying maze of legal obstacles that he and his fellow slaveholders found it difficult "to recover slaves" in the Quaker State.[3]

Legal strategies constitute one of the most important yet least studied aspects of early abolitionism. As the most pressing day-to-day activity of the PAS, legal tactics consumed much of the organization's energy and finances.

The group's legal docket thus offers a revealing portrait of early abolition-ism's inner workings and spotlights the impact of black social action on the growth of abolitionism. African American litigants continually sought legal aid in the Quaker State, compelling the PAS to assign more lawyers to black freedom suits and to increase funding for the mounting court cases. Put another way, Pennsylvania's leading role in the early fight against slavery evolved as much from African American struggles on the ground as it did from broad philosophical and religious trends circulating through post-Revolutionary American culture. In one sense, blacks' search for legal aid came as little surprise to white reformers. Although Pennsylvania had initi-ated a gradual abolition law in the 1780s, more than a few masters sought to circumvent it. The PAS promised to help endangered blacks whenever it could. Abolitionists were surprised, however, that so many African Ameri-cans outside of Pennsylvania tried to seek justice in Quaker State courts.

Beyond black social action, the PAS caseload provides a closer glimpse of the group's conception of activism. According to the Pennsylvania society, good abolitionists worked like good lawyers: they deferred to the law, they viewed learned jurists as their most important audience, and they main-tained an inherent respect for "the law of the land" — even if that law in-cluded slaveholders' property rights in man.

"WE HOPE TO subserve the cause," a PAS circular announced in 1789, by fighting masters "in courts of adjudicature."[4] In the decades leading to the Civil War, abolitionist litigation served as an important means of publiciz-ing immediatist ends. *Prigg v. Pennsylvania*, *Dred Scott*, *Anthony Burns* — such cases still resonate in the American consciousness. Yet whereas later antebellum legal strategists would use the courts to challenge slavery's very existence in American society, PAS tacticians merely sought to chip away at bondage's legal sanction in individual states. The group never sought to bring "test cases" to trial that, if successful, would render slavery null and void nationally. Rather, Pennsylvania lawyers worked on the margins, using loopholes, technicalities, and narrow legal opinions to liberate Afri-can Americans on a case-by-case basis. A steady buildup of narrow judicial victories, PAS strategists argued, would hamper slavery's operation as a national institution and compel even southern masters to support gradual abolition schemes.

This legal strategy had diverse roots. Since the founding of William Penn's colony in the 1600s, Pennsylvanians viewed their judiciary as a key arbiter of rights and liberties. Penn himself vowed to establish a court system "open" to anyone in search of redress. The state's Quaker population added to this pluralistic legal culture. Quakers played important roles in the legal profession and on the colonial bench, further highlighting notions of equity, tolerance, and justice for all.[5]

American independence revolutionized the law of slavery for African Americans, masters, and white abolitionists alike. State legislatures enacted a host of new statutes between the 1770s and 1790s involving such issues as emancipation, the rendition of fugitive slaves, and blacks' legal and constitutional rights. For example, Pennsylvania passed the Western world's first gradual abolition law in 1780.[6] Masters' challenges to such legislation and black freedom claims based on the law continually forced jurists to reinterpret the meaning of this statute over the next several decades. Could masters ignore gradual abolition plans? Did fugitive slaves have rights under such laws? Could blacks petition courts for redress of grievances?

Before the Revolution even Pennsylvania's open judicial culture denied blacks a fair hearing in court. Jailers, sheriffs, and justices of the peace often ignored black freedom claims, eagerly returning suspected fugitives to masters (for a fee) without the benefit of trial, or simply refusing to investigate black complaints about such practices as kidnapping.

Responding to the explosion of black complaints following the American Revolution, PAS lawyers established a legal aid system. Whereas before a trickle of cases flowed its way, by the 1790s the PAS received on average ten to fifteen new cases per quarter. As black freedom claims further increased, the PAS consistently added new legal counselors to its roster. Throughout the 1790s and early 1800s, in fact, PAS legal action paralleled black complaints in and around the Quaker State. In the 1810s, for instance, as black concerns about kidnapping grew (due, in part, to the banning of the overseas slave trade), the PAS became much more active on the matter in state and federal courts. And as fugitive slaves increasingly sought refuge in Pennsylvania during the 1820s and 1830s, Pennsylvania abolitionists devised new strategies to deal with them.

Legal work fell to the Acting Committee, consisting of six members elected by the society to track legal cases involving distressed blacks. According to onetime PAS president Isaac Parrish, legal counselors held several duties simultaneously. In addition to reporting on "all cases" concerning blacks, they had to "inform appropriate legal counsel of cases [coming to trial], to attend to trials themselves, to furnish means for procuring testimony [from black clients], and to see that the protection which the laws afford is extended to" African Americans.[7]

PAS counselors worked on a substantial number of black freedom cases between the 1780s and the 1830s. Indeed, the caseload of the PAS continually outpaced that of other abolitionist societies. As early as 1796, the Pennsylvanians had the largest number of pending suits among abolitionists at a national convention. An 1817 report noted that the PAS had taken on more than fifty-three such cases in the past two years, over half of which had resulted in freedom for African Americans. The group's hardest-working advisers could lose track of how many litigants they served in any given year. The usually indefatigable Thomas Shipley stopped keeping exhaustive records of his work after only nine months. Nevertheless, his notebook reveals that he had been called to over one hundred cases in one year alone and that he spent eighteen days on just one of these cases.[8] Other counselors reported similarly full caseloads. "I have attended to my duties for a fortnight," one adviser wrote, adding that he had spent nearly one hundred dollars of his own money. Counselors worked long, hard hours and usually pro bono.[9]

As the group hoped, PAS legal tactics pressured slaveholders in new ways. As one Maryland master exasperatingly wrote to his Philadelphia lawyer in 1829, "if I knew it would have been so difficult to recover [my runaway] slaves in your state, I would never have bothered with the expense of hiring you."[10] Other masters complained of legal obstacles erected by abolitionist lawyers.

On the other hand, African Americans celebrated the work of the Pennsylvania abolitionists precisely because it offered them new legal protections. "Numerous and respectable members of the people of color" residing in Philadelphia's black community honored Thomas Shipley following his death in 1836. Local papers estimated that over "3,000 people" attended a church service at which African Americans cited Shipley's "unwearied exertions" in court.[11] In a "Testimonial of Gratitude" in February 1841, the PAS's star lawyer David Paul Brown received an engraved silver-plated pitcher for "advocating the rights of the oppressed." "I present this pitcher," Robert Purvis shouted to an overflow crowd in Philadelphia's Bethel Church, "in testimony of our appreciation [for] those services which, without money or price, have never been wanting in you." Few Americans, Purvis proclaimed, did so much in "advocating the . . . liberties of the oppressed of this country." Brown, offering his own thanks for the "friendly and flattering terms with which you have noticed my services," replied that his "entire professional life" had been spent "facing down slaveholders" in court and that he would remain a legal advocate for the "colored community" until his dying day.[12]

The Pennsylvania society's lawyers mastered a plethora of laws, constitutions, and judicial opinions both nationally and internationally. They created a compendium of legal works and farmed it out to other abolitionists at every turn. The commentaries of Montesquieu, Blackstone, and other jurists on the operation of common law, constitutional law, and judicial precedents — this was the broader intellectual world that undergirded PAS legal work. The "Memoranda of Laws," as the group's legal compendium became known, contained information on Pennsylvania's abolition act, court decisions and laws, and opinions by PAS counselors on just about everything relating to slavery's legal status in American society. The "Memoranda" collated "slave codes" from such southern states as Louisiana, South Carolina, and Kentucky. When new "slave" states entered the Union (for example, Arkansas, Missouri, and Florida in the late 1810s and 1820s), the PAS quickly obtained copies of their constitutions and laws relating to bondage.[13]

Regardless of the case or the issue, PAS counselors knew the law. From "Dr. Taylor's ELEMENTS OF THE CIVIL LAW," for example, Pennsylvania reformers learned that slaves had virtually no rights in southern states: "Slaves are held pro-nulli, pro-mortuis, and pro-quadrepedibus — they have no head in the state, no name, title or register; they are not capable of being injured . . . they have no heirs and could therefore make no will . . . ; they could not plead nor be pleaded for but were excluded from any civil concerns whatsoever."[14]

The PAS remained acutely aware of legal developments in Virginia and Maryland, from which so many cases derived. The "Memoranda of Laws" had files on both states for quick reference: "The [Complete] Laws of Maryland in Regard to Slaves, 1715–1797" and a similar folder for the Old Dominion. Pennsylvania activists could thus discover that in Maryland, unlike Pennsylvania, "Free negroes are prohibited . . . from giving evidence against a white person, or . . . giving evidence to manumit any slave petitioning for freedom." Throughout the early national period, the PAS speedily obtained updates from Virginia and Maryland on such issues as the overseas slave trade, emigration of blacks to and from both states, and the rights of bondsmen as well as freemen.[15]

The PAS also paid particular attention to congressional laws on the international and domestic slave trade, black migration, and fugitive slaves. No sooner had the federal government passed the first fugitive slave law in 1793 than Pennsylvania abolitionists had commissioned a thorough analysis of its effect on both black communities and white reformers. Although slaveholders had a constitutional right to reclaim fugitives, William Rawle observed in a summary for other lawyers, the new law remained legally "objectionable." For one thing, he worried that the kidnapping of free blacks might explode because masters could file "affidavits" from out of state — they did not have to verify personally the identity of a suspected fugitive. This failure to protect black rights, Rawle informed his fellow members, "opens the door to severity and fraud." Moreover, the law threatened to penalize abolitionists for "OBSTRUCTING, RESCUING, and HARBOURING" black runaways. How, Rawle asked, would blacks even get a hearing in court if abolitionists faced fines as high as five hundred dollars for aiding suspected runaways?[16] Rawle's warnings helped abolitionists prepare for legal battles with masters throughout the 1790s and early 1800s.

Although legal acumen paid dividends, it prompted many Pennsylvania reformers to view the slavery issue in strictly legal terms. Second-wave abolitionists would strongly criticize the PAS for reducing bondage to legalisms. Yet as Rawle argued in the 1790s, bondage was a "legal and political creation"; therefore, abolitionists needed to formulate concrete legal strategies to attack the institution and, perhaps more importantly, remain "guarded" in front of judges, officers of the court, and other legal officials. "The total extinction of the most gross and shameful blot that has ever stained a nation is an event I would rejoice in," Rawle later observed, "but great caution should be used in the formation of any systematic plan . . . of effecting such a glorious result."[17]

Legal strategies and tactics imbued PAS activists with an inherently cautious attitude about fighting slavery. Lawyers refrained from making emotional pronouncements in court or preying on jurists' sentiments. Black narratives of suffering were routinely transformed into coherent legal arguments. The society warned its counselors not to be too "zealous" and not to take on an inordinate number of black legal cases. In 1804, for instance, a PAS memorandum advised counselors to work on only winnable cases. Not all blacks could be helped.[18]

Particularly after the formation of a stronger federal government in 1787, Pennsylvania abolitionists maintained their respect for property rights in man. "It is a prominent object of this Society," one reformer wrote, "to afford legal relief and advice to free negroes unlawfully held in bondage" and, in certain cases, "to assist persons seized as [fugitive] slaves on Pennsylvania soil." But the PAS could not, and would not, repudiate slaveholders' property rights. Thus, he continued, the group used legal tactics to pressure slaveholders and liberate "our fellow men" as far as legally possible. "But when [our legal tactics] could be of no avail," PAS president Isaac Parrish himself proclaimed in 1836, the society conceded "the stern decree of the law" and returned black "captives . . . to a life of bondage." In an 1816 case, for example, the PAS looked on helplessly as a black kidnapping victim was returned to his alleged owner in Virginia. The man, Peter King, claimed to have been born free in Pennsylvania during the late 1780s and then stolen into slavery while in New Orleans in 1815. Though black deponents from Philadelphia vouched for his free status, PAS lawyers could not locate King's free papers. Abolitionists felt that they had no choice but to deliver King to the Virginian master.[19]

Respect for the law of bondage did not stop abolitionists from manipulating various state and federal statutes to blacks' advantage. Nor did it prevent African Americans from seeking PAS legal aid. Nonetheless, the law limited the possibilities of abolitionist action against slaveholders. The law constantly reminded Pennsylvania activists of who they were (benevolent lawyers) and were not (law-breaking fanatics).

THE PAS'S CASELOAD revolved around black freedom claims. Black families approached the organization about relatives or friends who had been kidnapped. Black merchants, dock workers, and laborers offered depositions on the domestic and overseas slave trade. And black community leaders contacted white abolitionists on behalf of accused fugitives hundreds of miles away or relatives who had been reenslaved by devious masters in their own community. In short, a rich social foundation of black activism supported PAS legal work.

Black freedom claims usually took the form of oral complaints to the society's legal counselors. In one striking instance, Samuel Johnston, a free black man captured in Virginia and sold back into slavery by the British army during the Revolutionary War, literally "demanded his freedom" when interviewed by the PAS in the early 1790s. Detained in prison as a fugitive, Johnston listed several "free" relatives in Maryland and Virginia and told his white lawyers to substantiate his freedom claim in court, which they did.[20]

In the early 1800s the PAS heard the similarly distressing case of Bill

Coachman, a New Jersey slave who had bargained slavery-for-life down to indentured servitude. At the end of his seven-year contract, however, his master "sold Bill" back into slavery in Maryland. The PAS, brought in by members of the black community to secure Coachman's freedom, interviewed everyone familiar with the situation, including two free black neighbors, Peter Umfries and Nero Amessen. In sworn depositions, both men described Coachman's claim to freedom and his master's deviousness. Another deponent, Coachman's first master in New Jersey, told the PAS that Coachman himself had known "to the day" when his freedom would begin. A white female neighbor also reported that "freedom" to Coachman meant the ability to work for his own wages. In all, the society collected nine official depositions to establish Coachman's claim to freedom, including letters verifying that "Bill Coachman (a negro)" had been taxed "as a free man" by a New Jersey township. But on this occasion the PAS could not locate Coachman, whom deponents believed had long since been sold into southern slavery for life.[21]

The society's diligence in tracking such cases impressed local blacks. In 1797 PAS lawyers worked with family members and neighbors to liberate a Philadelphia man from a master who refused to honor an indenture agreement. The case went to trial in district court only after the man's family sought abolitionist support.[22] Similarly, pleas from family members in 1788 led to four successful freedom suits for a group of Pennsylvania blacks originally emancipated during the Revolutionary War and then reenslaved.[23] The list went on. The PAS secured writs for the freedom of five black men illegally reenslaved between 1796 and 1798. In 1800 it worked with black and white contacts in Winchester County, Virginia, to free Abraham, whose mistress had "detained him . . . after his declaration" because, as she testified in court, she "hath a right so to do . . . [for] under the laws of this commonwealth he is my slave." Abraham rebutted this story and asked his abolitionist lawyers to call witnesses in his support. The evidence proved that she had freed him, and the court released Abraham.[24]

African American women exhibited the same "freedom consciousness" as men. Over a third of the PAS's cases in the early national period revolved around women's claims to liberty. More importantly, some of the biggest cases involved female clients. A 1797 state supreme court proceeding, which examined how Pennsylvania's abolition act might affect slaveowners from Maryland and other southern states, derived from the freedom claims of two black women on the run; so did an 1815 lawsuit that freed the children of a fugitive mother from Maryland. In the 1820s the PAS represented several black women fleeing southern bondage or helping sisters and daughters caught in the domestic slave trade.[25]

In 1825 Mary Frances Argine brought her daughter's plight to the PAS's attention. A native of Port-au-Prince, Argine had moved to Pennsylvania with her master's family, the Dumases, in 1803. She subsequently had five children, one of whom, Frances, eventually worked on the Dumas estate. From Virginia, Frances wrote her mother that she feared she was about to be sold into slavery. In her deposition to the PAS, Mrs. Argine stated that "[my] daughter was never bound . . . to any person whatsoever, and was born . . . after I had acquired my freedom [in Pennsylvania]." Therefore, she argued vigorously, Frances was absolutely free. The PAS worked with the mayor of Philadelphia and abolitionist contacts in Virginia to return Frances to Philadelphia and freedom.[26]

The Pennsylvania society's legal aid system acquired a strong reputation among African Americans nationally. Between 1790 and 1820 blacks contacted the PAS from a number of southern and southwestern states, including Georgia, Mississippi, North Carolina, Tennessee, Kentucky, Alabama, and South Carolina. As the head of one black community in Cuba wrote the organization, the PAS was "well known [even] here."[27] Some of these contacts claimed freedom as former residents of Pennsylvania; others asserted that they had been promised freedom by masters before being sold South. All of them requested PAS legal assistance.

In 1804 a black woman transported through Tennessee claimed her freedom as a formerly free resident of Pennsylvania. The woman pleaded with a local constable to write to Pennsylvania officials for proof of her freedom. The sheriff contacted someone who, as he remembered, was "a member of an abolition society in Philadelphia." The constable asked his contact to retrieve and forward the appropriate documents to prove the black woman's "claims [to] her freedom." The PAS discovered that the woman had, in fact, been previously emancipated; after it secured her manumission papers, she was returned to freedom. The society worked on two other freedom claims involving blacks taken to the border states of Kentucky and Tennessee. In the first case, a young black man who had agreed to leave Pennsylvania "voluntarily" sued his master for freedom when he was sold in Kentucky. In the second case, a woman who had been transported to Tennessee argued that her master had "released her from bondage at a certain period"; the master denied ever having made such a promise. On the advice of her PAS attorney, the woman agreed to serve the man "during his life." "But if he should die," the agreement stated, "she is released." In 1821

Justice of the Peace John Henderson of Rocky Springs, Mississippi, informed the PAS that a man had arrived in his small town with "3 colored persons," each of whom claimed their freedom. They were all "born free," he explained, but were stolen by slave traders and therefore had no proof to support their appeals. Henderson stated that he would hold the blacks until the PAS could obtain either free papers or some other proof of their freedom. After the PAS forwarded the appropriate documentation, Henderson freed the detained blacks.[28]

The PAS forged a particularly impressive reputation regionally. Of the group's self-identified fifty most important cases prosecuted during the early republic, over half derived from the Chesapeake states of Maryland, Virginia, and, to a lesser extent, Delaware. Between the 1780s and 1820s, Virginia and Maryland accounted for over half of the PAS caseload. This profile matches Helen Catterall's compilation of *Judicial Cases Concerning American Slavery and the Negro* in and around Pennsylvania. Southern masters knew this all too well. In fact, depositions show that during the early national period free blacks and thousands of fugitive slaves tried to reach Pennsylvania. To do so, these African Americans moved along early versions of the Underground Railroad: homes, churches, and taverns housing sympathetic whites as well as free blacks. If they were seized by slave catchers or unsympathetic northerners, the PAS offered what legal assistance it could, provided black pleas for help made it to the society.[29]

Case derivations show the PAS's geographic influence extending southward from Philadelphia to the Maryland shore to Richmond, Virginia. To the PAS, the caseload reflected a revolving door on Pennsylvania's southern border: though blacks tried to reach safety in Pennsylvania, many more became kidnapping victims. Indeed, from the PAS's point of view, kidnapping grew at an alarming rate in the 1810s and 1820s, as southern demands for domestic slaves increased in the wake of America's slave-trading ban of 1808. The PAS caseload demonstrated this trend: at least a third of its cases between 1800 and the 1830s dealt with kidnapping victims. But again, the society estimated that for every case it solved, hundreds more blacks lost their freedom to the domestic trade.

In one of its most important roles, the PAS served as agent for southern runaways who wished to bargain their enslavement down to indentured servitude. In dealing with runaways, masters often agreed to either a cash payment in exchange for the slave's freedom or a contract with the escapee that converted slavery-for-life into indentured servitude, provided he or she would not flee again. As Billy Smith and Stephen Whitman have recently shown, runaways became a serious economic threat to slaveholders, especially in Maryland. In Baltimore, perpetual runaways forced masters to shift to contract labor, which provided a better return on investment and eliminated the headache of chasing fugitives. As one Maryland owner put it, indentures "avoided [the] trouble" of chasing down black fugitives again and again.[30]

Yet black fugitives also discovered how dangerous and unreliable contracts with masters could be. In the absence of legal representation, whites often forced African Americans to accept a gentleman's agreement: blacks would be freed at a specified date on the master's honor. According to various black deponents interviewed by the PAS, however, many slaveholders ignored these oral agreements, or worse, sold blacks into southern slavery before their bargained-down terms expired. For blacks who made it to Pennsylvania, the PAS narrowed the possibilities for fraud and violence by offering legal services to individuals and communities. In 1820, for instance, the society took the case of "Pricilla," a Maryland slave who had fled to Philadelphia and married a free black man. When her master sued for her return, the PAS secured a deed of indenture proving that the master had previously agreed to manumit her. The judge released Pricilla, but the slaveholder's attorney vowed to retry the case. "In the meantime," the PAS counsel recorded in his notes, "the friends of the girl interfered, and purchased her freedom, the husband binding himself to pay the account."[31]

Almost every year between 1790 and the 1820s, the PAS handled indenture transactions between southern masters and black fugitives: in 1791 a Maryland escapee bargained his slavery down to a six-year term of indenture with PAS support; in 1794 a fugitive slave from Baltimore used the PAS to negotiate with his master's lawyers for an indenture; in 1799 the PAS worked out a four-year indenture between a black man, who claimed he had already been freed, and his alleged Maryland owner. In certain cases, the society financially guaranteed an indenture, as in 1791, when Thomas Harrison of the PAS mediated a contract between Auqa and her master: she would serve for thirteen years, until "age 28," when the owner had "to set her free." If Aqua ran away again, however, the PAS agreed to compensate her former master.[32]

With great trepidation, the society sometimes paid outright for a slave's freedom. Although some members objected (on grounds that such purchases reenforced slavery's legal standing), many others placed a higher premium on immediate freedom for a detained African American. In 1810 "friends of certain detained blacks" in Loudon County, Virginia, asked the PAS to aid a freedom suit. After discovering that "they could not prove their freedom," PAS counselors "thought it was best to bargain for [the blacks'] . . . liberty" and helped raise six hundred dollars for that purpose. In the Quaker State, Rudolph Boice utilized PAS legal services in 1792 to bargain for his own freedom. Boice had fled his Baltimore-area plantation sometime in the 1780s and made it to Philadelphia; his master's son, after finally tracking him down, claimed Boice. However, as PAS depositions indicate, "a proposed accommodation was made by . . . two members of the Pennsylvania Society for Abolishing Slavery" in conjunction "with said Boice" and his former master: Boice was granted "his full freedom and liberty from bondage" in exchange for forty-five dollars, paid out "in three equal installments." In September 1829 a master who had traveled to Philadelphia to retrieve a fugitive black woman informed another PAS counselor that he "was anxious to recover something" for her. The two men agreed to a price of "100 dollars" for the woman's freedom, as well as one further condition written into a contract between the master and his former slave: that the women be "restricted . . . from coming back into the state" of Maryland and enticing her brethren to flee.[33]

The PAS set rigid guidelines for indentures between whites and blacks, distributing its code to abolitionists nationally. In addition, the society kept a master file of its indenture contracts for future reference.[34] This collection helped several blacks to promptly gain their freedom from devious masters. John Bassa informed the PAS that his wife "Tina is now unlawfully detained and held as a slave" by her former Maryland master. The group's Isaac Hopper brought the woman's indenture contract to the attention of local constables, who quickly drafted a writ for Tina's release.[35]

By assisting distressed African Americans, Pennsylvania abolitionists sometimes faced legal battles of their own. In September 1805, for instance, South Carolina's Pierce Butler sued Isaac Hopper for aiding his slave Ben. Butler, a former congressional representative who occupied a summer retreat in Philadelphia, claimed in court that the PAS had persuaded Ben to sue for his freedom. As a onetime member of Congress, Butler claimed immunity from Pennsylvania's abolition law, which allowed slaves to sue for freedom if they were kept in the state for longer than any six-month period). As the PAS argued in court, Butler had not served as a federal official for years, and so his suit against Hopper had no legal basis. A Pennsylvania jury found Hopper innocent on the same grounds. Other suits worked against the PAS, however, for which the organization paid heavy monetary damages to slaveholders.[36]

The plethora of legal work undertaken by the Pennsylvania Abolition Society illustrates the many links between black activism and white abolitionism. As Philip Schwarz argues in his book on the law of bondage in Virginia, African Americans continually shaped the meaning of the Old Dominion's slave laws. One cannot understand why certain laws were passed, and what those meanings were, without examining black actions.[37] As PAS members discovered too, their own legal tactics stemmed from African American protest. By claiming their freedom as residents of "free" Pennsylvania, by running away from southern plantations and forcing masters to bargain slavery down to indentured servitude, and by consistently requesting white legal assistance, African Americans laid a rich "experiential" foundation of resistance for Pennsylvania reformers to tap into. And because white abolitionists had the legal expertise and financial resources to address black social needs, African Americans continually sought their help.[38]

IF BLACK ACTION provided a spur, abolitionist legal maneuvering added an important spin. For while Pennsylvania reformers worked rigorously within the American legal system for black justice, their shrewd tactics magnified the impact of black runaways in Virginia and Maryland. Of course, only a small percentage of blacks used the PAS to successfully sue for their freedom in Pennsylvania courts. The society did not seek to eradicate slavery in the South. But its use of loopholes and technicalities in the nation's slave laws could make a difference in the fate of some blacks. That potential to liberate even a tiny fraction of fleeing African Americans plagued border state slaveholders throughout the early national period.

To consider one of the most significant examples, the PAS constantly seized upon loopholes and technicalities in Pennsylvania's Gradual Abolition Act to free slaves within and outside the state. Originating in 1780, the act outlined the legal steps to black freedom in Pennsylvania: resident masters had to register their slaves by a certain date; all slaves born *after* 1780 who had been registered would then be manumitted at a specific age (for men, twenty-one; for women, eighteen). The act also addressed contingency issues. The fifth section stipulated that slaveholders who did not properly register their slaves could lose them if challenged in court. Another section stated that no person could bring slaves into the state for longer than six months, lest they too be freed in court. Still another section provided legal redress to masters tracking runaways.[39]

No sooner had the law been implemented than the Pennsylvania Aboli-

tion Society began prosecuting slaveholders. In 1784 Stephen Carpenter—
"a yeoman" residing in Philadelphia County—lost his slaves in a PAS lawsuit for not registering them "agreeable to the directions of [the Abolition
Act]." Almost twenty-five years later, in September 1814, the society helped
Jesse sue his owner for not "properly" registering him within six months of
his birth. In September 1789 PAS lawyers persuaded the state supreme court
to free three children because their master, a man named Moore, did not
register them "properly." The parents, who had "previously obtained their
freedom," now petitioned the court for their "children's freedom," so "that
they may . . . be under the care of the parents." Two lower courts had previously split on the meaning of the word "properly," leaving the children in
bondage. Did the word require masters to provide every detail when registering chattels, including a person's sex and other characteristics? Or did
slaveholders have to meet the general spirit of the law? Once again, the society pushed for a literal interpretation of the law: registration of slaves had to
meet an absolute standard of exactitude. Chief Justice Samuel McKean
agreed, noting in his decision to free the children that a slaveowner who
did not comply with every last detail of the Abolition Act would lose his
slaves.[40]

Abolitionists could not always convince judges to accept their legal arguments. In October 1801 one Pennsylvania Supreme Court justice returned
"negro Hannah" to her master despite an incomplete registration. "The sole
question before the court," the judge noted in his opinion, "was, whether
her registry was invalid," for the master had listed Hannah as a "slave"
without noting "FOR LIFE." PAS counsel argued that this technicality should
free Hannah at once. According to the judge, however, the word "SLAVE . . .
signifies a perpetual servant." The society did not prevail. Yet in September
1817 it persuaded two judges to free a black woman immediately because
her master forgot to specify her "sex" or "his own occupation" on the
registration form. "The construction should [usually] be liberal in favor of
the master," one judge asserted, but not in this case.[41]

The PAS's rigid interpretation of Pennsylvania's Gradual Abolition Act
affected out-of-state slaveholders, too. A Maryland man lost his slave John
in May 1799 because he failed to register him on settling in Pennsylvania.
When the society discovered the loophole, it immediately brought the case
to trial and won. In the same year a Virginian lost his slave Lucy after she
filed a freedom claim with PAS help. Lucy had been shuttled back and forth
between Pennsylvania and Virginia in the early 1780s, as her master tried to
avoid Pennsylvania's abolition law. When abolitionists brought the case to

trial, the master claimed that Lucy was actually another slave named Ruth, who had already been "duly" registered. The court refused "even to admit the [fraudulent] testimony." The PAS cheered as the judges freed their clients and lectured the master to "bear the consequences" of his deceit.[42]

The PAS's tactical repertoire also included seemingly mundane legal procedures such as writs. Writs had been a standard part of Anglo-American law for centuries. The society deployed them in a systematic way to protect black rights. After discovering the whereabouts of black fugitives or kidnapping victims, Pennsylvania reformers usually took out a writ requiring slaveholders or jailers "to deliver the body [of a detainee] before" a legal official. These documents, the PAS knew, signaled formal legal action by the abolitionists: they bore the signature of Pennsylvania's judicial officials and the state's insignia. No one could tear them up and claim that they had never received notice, lest they face further litigation. To the PAS, then, writs became a vital means of both tracking cases and gaining blacks' liberty.

Between the 1790s and 1830s Pennsylvania reformers relied on two basic writs: habeas corpus and de homine replegiando. Though in many ways similar—both required a jailer or master to deliver up a detained person—habeas corpus signified the beginning of a "legal inquiry" whereas de homine replegiando became a means for blacks as well as abolitionists to be released from custody pending the result of formal charges.

The PAS began using habeas corpus to track slave-trading vessels that violated a federal statute of 1794 whereby American merchants could not sell captured Africans to foreign traders. The society used what some officials thought would be an ineffective law to prosecute dozens of violators between 1794 and the full slave-trading ban of 1808. In one exemplary case of 1805, Isaac Hopper served a writ of habeas corpus to a "Mrs. Robins" of Philadelphia for selling African slaves to non-Americans. But as the PAS discovered, Mrs. Robins had fled before her court date with the PAS.[43] In 1806 the society's Isaac Sherman served a writ on a southern sea captain accused of picking up three hundred African slaves for foreign merchants. Sherman traveled to district court in South Carolina, the ship's originating point, to prosecute the slave trader and have the enslaved Africans "condemned" and thus freed. Many other slave-trading prosecutions began with the delivery of a simple writ.[44]

The PAS deployed writs to confront domestic slave traders, too. In 1790 it sued for the return of "Negro Silas," a former New Jersey slave who had been sold contrary to an indenture agreement with his master. After his family had located him, the PAS had "a writ of Habeas Corpus" drawn up for Silas's "release." The New Jersey Supreme Court investigated the matter fully and pronounced Silas absolutely free. In 1819 Isaac Hopper brought a writ of habeas corpus to a Maryland slaveholder on behalf of a free black man who claimed that his wife "is now unlawfully detained" on a former master's Maryland plantation. As Hopper informed the Philadelphia magistrate who eventually signed the writ, the PAS "prays that you . . . will [have] a Habeas Corpus directed to the said [slaveholder] *commanding* him to bring the body of said [woman] before you in order that right may done in the premises." After thorough investigation, a Philadelphia court freed the woman "forever."[45]

Slaveholders and judges often tried to quash writs taken out by the PAS. In 1819, for instance, Pennsylvania judge H. C. Tilghman retroactively suppressed a PAS writ releasing "Wright, alias Hall," a Maryland fugitive slave seized in Philadelphia and confined in jail pending "an investigation." Tilghman argued that neither the PAS nor the black man had enough evidence to sue for freedom, and so the writ had "been issued in violation of the Constitution of the US." Indeed, Tilghman went on, fugitive slaves could not expect the law to treat them as normal citizens: they were guilty until proven innocent. Since the society could not prove the man's claim to freedom, he was returned to bondage.[46]

LITIGATION BASED on loopholes and technicalities allowed the PAS to influence — if ever so slightly — slavery's day-to-day standing in Pennsylvania courts without exceeding the limits of the law. As one reformer put it, although the PAS lawyers "interfered" with slavery's operation in and around the Quaker State, they never repudiated outright masters' property rights; slavery remained a legal institution for reformers no less than southern masters. Nonetheless, abolitionist litigation strategies exposed a raw nerve among slaveholders: the fear that northern polities would not treat "this species of property" with the same respect that their own states did. Indeed, southern masters discovered that northern courts did not automatically defer to their demands. If their slaves fled North, southern masters now had to hire expensive lawyers to fight for their rendition in court. And even if they had solid claims, masters could still find themselves bargaining with abolitionist litigators for a slave's return. Finally, slaveholders themselves could face prosecution for not rigidly complying with certain abolitionist laws or for taking the law into their own hands (by kidnapping an alleged fugitive slave or illegally enslaving a person past an indenture deadline). Thus, although PAS litigation did not abolish southern slavery, it unquestionably put small dents in bondage's legal armor. For slaveholders who lost through the courts, even the smallest dent was undesirable.

Three important cases, from three different decades, illustrate more fully PAS lawyers' limited though adverse impact on southern slavery in Pennsylvania courts: *Respublica v. Blackmore* (1797), *"Kitty" v. Chittier* (1815), and *Green v. Brickell* (1825) (the latter two cases were not classified in the state's legal register, *Pennsylvania Reports*). Although each of these cases began with a technicality or loophole in a certain law, the PAS shrewdly used it to reduce slavery's smooth operation as a legal institution in the North.

In the first case, *Respublica v. Blackmore*, which went to trial in the Pennsylvania Supreme Court in 1797, former Maryland resident Samuel Blackmore lost his two female slaves because he did not register them properly under Pennsylvania's Gradual Abolition Act of 1780. Blackmore had prospected southern Pennsylvania land in 1780, moved to the state in 1782, and then failed to comply with the new abolition law. With the PAS's legal assistance, two of Blackmore's slaves sued for their freedom. When Blackmore appealed, the issue went before the state supreme court.[47]

The case initially revolved around technicalities. Could Blackmore lose his slaves because he missed a registration deadline? Blackmore's counsel claimed that the family thought it had migrated to Virginia in the early 1780s and therefore did not immediately register its chattels for emancipation. The southern Pennsylvania counties of Washington and Westmoreland, where Blackmore originally settled, had previously been part of the Old Dominion; they were acquired by Pennsylvania only in 1782 (inhabitants of the disputed territory were then allowed to register their slaves belatedly). When Blackmore realized that he was actually in the Commonwealth of Pennsylvania, his lawyers continued, he registered his slaves.[48] According to his counselors, then, Blackmore could not be deprived of his slave property because he had met the spirit of his adopted state's Gradual Abolition Act.

PAS lawyers countered that Blackmore's error in judgment notwithstanding, his failure to register his slaves before a state-mandated deadline entitled them to freedom. But they also claimed that Pennsylvania's constitution further protected the women from reenslavement, for Blackmore's slaves became "free citizens" the moment he failed to register them. "And once free they must remain so," PAS counsel John Ross shouted to the court. "Can the legislature," he asked, "by a law, declare a free person to be a slave, when the Constitution . . . declares all men free? It is no answer . . . that one used to be a slave . . . or that he is black." Why "boast of a constitution," Ross chided the court, if it drew distinctions based on color? He asked the court to interpret the state constitution "liberally" in favor of Blackmore's slaves, indeed, "to go as far as possible" in "construing in favor of [their] liberty." For, he explained, the concept of liberty must be applied to African Americans. "Strong indeed must be ANY leaning against liberty," Ross summed up. "If these were white women," the constitutional "construction [in favor of liberty] would certainly be liberal, and it must be so in this case."[49]

Subsequently a member of the U.S. Senate, Ross impressed even other abolitionists with his fierce arguments. The PAS member who had originally asked Ross "to take the trouble of arguing the case" wrote that he not only "did great honor to his profession as a lawyer" but "at the same time" helped "the cause of humanity gain ground." His legal arguments on behalf of "liberation" exceeded "many years of exertions." In fact, since Ross's "masterly and prevailing argument was heard, scarcely a syllable has been uttered against" helping "those unfortunate people."[50]

The PAS realized that its broader claims rested on a technicality. It did not argue that all slaves in Pennsylvania could now demand their liberty based on the state constitution. Yet the group also believed that the case raised a question that no state law addressed: did freed black Pennsylvanians have constitutional rights? According to the PAS, the two women had gained their freedom, thereby assuming the same constitutional guarantee to liberty as any other Pennsylvanian. Blackmore's lawyers objected to this reasoning: courts and legislatures, they declared, existed to protect private property, not black rights. "And that is the end of it," Blackmore's lawyer tersely stated to the court.[51]

The state supreme court sided with the PAS. Pronouncing the case "of great consequence to the community," the court issued a firm and "uniform" decision for the black women's freedom. According to the justices, Blackmore failed to prove that he had been a resident of the disputed southern Pennsylvania territories in the early 1780s and was thus not entitled to a delayed registration. As a result, his slaves Cassandra and Lydia became free after Blackmore's six-month grace period expired (in accordance with the Gradual Abolition Act). And once "Cassandra and Lydia [became] free women," the judges ruled, they could not be reenslaved. In other words, masters now had to suffer the consequences of not following northern abolitionist laws.[52]

Nearly two decades later, in 1815, PAS lawyers confounded a Virginia master in Pennsylvania courts. *"Kitty" v. Chittier*, argued in the Federal District Court for Pennsylvania, concerned the three children of a black woman named Kitty who had fled slavery in Virginia, settled in Pennsylvania, married a free black man, and then had children. When her former mistress finally located Kitty she claimed both mother and children under the federal Fugitive Slave Law of 1793. Kitty objected that her mistress had no right to the children, who remained "free born" citizens of the Quaker State. Kitty's husband asked the PAS to uphold the children's freedom when the case came to trial.[53]

The facts struck an emotional chord with PAS lawyers, but, they wanted to know, did the case rest on compelling legal doctrine? The society quickly asked six of its most able counselors for advice. According to each member of this expert team, no legal precedent existed to guide abolitionists: neither the federal Fugitive Slave Law nor Pennsylvania's Gradual Abolition Act said anything about offspring of fugitives born in nonslaveholding states or territories. Moreover, no state or federal court had yet ruled on such a case. Each of the lawyers thus turned to Pennsylvania's duty to secure the children's freedom.

"It was the good fortune of these children to have been born here," Peter Du Ponceau, a member of the Philadelphia bar since 1792, put it bluntly in his written opinion, for Pennsylvania had become a "free" state: slavery's gradual abolition law entitled "freeborn" blacks to the same constitutional protections as whites. Unlike Virginians, De Ponceau explained, Pennsylvanians believed that free blacks had basic rights and liberties. As a sovereign state, Pennsylvania "was not bound to enforce the slave laws of Virginia." In Du Ponceau's legal estimation, the children should remain free.[54]

Considering "Pennsylvania's laws alone," William Meredith wrote, "the children are free." But, he cautioned, abolitionists had to consider the impact of the U.S. Constitution, for its laws might be construed as "paramount to those of the states." The Constitution guaranteed that the federal government would return fugitive slaves to their masters. Yet, Meredith concluded, Congress could not intervene in this case because the Virginia mistress did not have the facts on her side: the children were not born in "slave" Virginia and could not be classified as runaway slaves. Like Du Ponceau, Meredith confidently supported the children's bid for freedom.[55]

Attorney John Reed determined that the children had a constitutional claim to freedom "on entirely different footing from the mother." For though the mistress could indeed claim Kitty as a fugitive, she could not "interfere with [the children's] personal liberty." They remained beyond the scope of Virginia's "slave laws" as well as the federal Fugitive Slave Law. William Rawle agreed, stating that Pennsylvania's "positive words" in favor of "freedom" forever protected the children's liberty, for the state's bill of rights asserted that "all inhabitants . . . [are] guaranteed their liberty and safety."[56]

The federal court upheld the children's claim. Although transcripts of the case have not survived, notes by PAS lawyers indicate that the justices followed abolitionists' legal reasoning: because the children were neither "fugitives" nor "slaves," they could not be extradited to Virginia. In fact, they enjoyed the same basic legal and constitutional protections as any white citizens of the Quaker State. The PAS celebrated its victory by underlining the strategic implications of the case. In a Quarterly Meeting of 1816, one legal adviser noted that the recent court decision "may be used with great effect" if similar cases arise.[57] The PAS took on an analogous case just a few years later, pushing another Pennsylvania court to uphold the freedom claims of a fugitive mother's children who had been "freeborn" in the Quaker State.

In 1825 the PAS pushed technicalities and loopholes a bit further to free a fugitive slave in *Green v. Brickell*. Marshall Green, a Maryland slave, had obtained permission from his master to go to Pennsylvania to search for his missing daughter. When Green found her, he claimed sanctuary in the "free" state. His master sued for Green's return, and the case went to trial in U.S. District Court in Philadelphia County.

PAS lawyers initially argued that because Green had received his "master's consent" to go into a neighboring state, he could not be classified as a fugitive slave. According to the society, the case could not even go to trial "under the provisions of" either the U.S. Constitution or the 1793 Fugitive Slave Act, which guaranteed masters the return of "escaped" slaves "from one state into another." PAS counsel David Paul Brown proclaimed that Green's "arrest was illegal under the [fugitive] ACT of CONGRESS!"[58]

Without the permission of his master, the PAS admitted, Green's freedom claim would have no legal basis. But the society also urged the court to use the state's "free" constitution to shelter Green. Citing a previous case in which a slave willingly brought by his master into Pennsylvania successfully sued for his freedom, the PAS argued that the Quaker State had to protect its "inhabitants' liberty" in certain crucial instances. To make this argument, the society had to distinguish carefully among various types of fugitive slaves. Those who fled to Pennsylvania without their masters' prior approval had no claims to freedom, for "the law of the land" protected southern masters from "constructive flight": the conscious attempt to escape slavery. On the other hand, Pennsylvania's constitution could protect the freedom of African Americans who (by trickery or luck) gained their masters' approval to leave slave states and enter "free" Pennsylvania.[59]

Persuaded by the PAS's legal reasoning, the federal judge struck down Green's reenslavement. "I have carefully considered" the Fugitive Slave Law, he remarked, "and am clearly of opinion . . . that [a master] must prove that a negro escaped or fled from one state into ANOTHER." The judge favored "a strict — perhaps a literal — interpretation of the Constitution and [the Fugitive Slave] Act": a master must prove that his or her slave left the plantation to secure freedom in the North. "In the present instance, the negro Green came into . . . Pennsylvania from Maryland by the COMMAND or PERMISSION of his alleged master." Green could not be classified as a fugitive and therefore attained his liberty.[60]

But *Green* was the exception, not the rule: Master's claims more often trumped slaves' claims, both in courts of law and in disputes that never made it to the courts. Fugitives from Maryland and Virginia were often returned home before they ever reached the Quaker State. In any event, the PAS would not push such claims on a regular basis, for they knew most masters would not grant slave requests to cross state lines on any pretext (searching for family members, for example).

The exception of the Green case thus actually proved the rule: PAS legal tactics always operated in a controlled climate of judicial precedents, constitutional constructions, state and federal laws, and technicalities and loopholes. Only under the right legal circumstances would Pennsylvania reformers enlarge their arguments for black freedom in court — and only then would those arguments have implications for slavery's existence north of the Mason-Dixon line. As the PAS asserted in *Blackmore* in 1797, freed blacks had essential constitutional rights in the Quaker State (if no other) that no judge or former master could ignore. Moreover, as it argued in *"Kitty"* v. *Chittier* in 1815, Pennsylvania jurists did not have to automatically comply with the "slave laws" of Virginia when determining the fate of its black citizens. And as the society proclaimed in 1825 in *Green*, certain types of fugitive slaves from the South could seek legal sanctuary in the "free state" of Pennsylvania. But the legal conditions had to be right for the PAS to make such claims.

PAS court action would not topple southern slavery in one fell swoop. But its day-to-day legal tactics emphasized to southern masters and blacks alike just how much northern courts diverged from their southern counterparts on African American justice. As a PAS legal adviser familiar with judicial systems throughout the Chesapeake wrote at the close of the 1790s, "in Pennsylvania *at least* it will not be thought fanatical to protect a man though black . . . [while in Virginia and Maryland] the response is, 'But it is a violation of property rights!' "[61]

SOUTHERN SLAVEHOLDERS worried about the influence of abolitionists on northern courts. As one South Carolina congressman remarked in 1790, a southern "gentleman can hardly come to this place [Philadelphia] or New York without having his servants induced to flee" by "meddlesome" abolitionist lawyers.[62] Between 1790 and the early 1800s, when Congress temporarily resided in Philadelphia, several other South Carolina representatives lost slaves in Pennsylvania. Indeed, Virginians and Marylanders even lodged official complaints about the connection between runaways and abolitionist legal work.

Maryland slaveholders pressured their state legislature to crack down on the growing association between fugitive slaves and abolitionist legal tactics. If not a flood, the petition warned, the trickle of fugitive slaves who received sanctuary in northern courts threatened bondage's stability all the same. The legislature followed through by forwarding an unprecedented petition to the Pennsylvania General Assembly in 1823. "Our citizens are experiencing great difficulty in recovering fugitive slaves from [your state]," the memorial announced. Alluding to the impact of abolitionist legal aid to blacks in the Quaker State, Maryland demanded stronger compliance with the national Fugitive Slave Law and the creation of harsher state laws to prevent abolitionists from representing black runaways.[63] Maryland masters' continued pressure produced a meeting between the two states' legislative delegations in 1826. Pennsylvania representatives promised to study the problem, although they never established laws to fully protect southern slaveholders in northern courts.

The celebrated jurist William Tilghman — a Marylander by birth and a Philadelphian by legal trade — offered an interesting perspective on this issue. Tilghman apprenticed in the Maryland bar, served in the state legislature, and then abruptly moved to Philadelphia in 1793 to practice law. Through a relative's recommendation to Governor Thomas McKean, he became Pennsylvania's chief justice in 1806. Tilghman maintained his Maryland plantation and slaves. A professed opponent of slavery in the abstract, he waited several years before instituting his own gradual emancipation plan.

Tilghman found Pennsylvania to be a haven for fugitive slaves—and Pennsylvania abolitionists a troublesome presence in his courts. Furthermore, fugitive blacks remained a personal concern, as several of his own slaves fled at one time or another. Moreover, he constantly received letters from slaveholders in Maryland, Virginia, and South Carolina requesting his help in recovering fugitive slaves destined for the Quaker State (see Appendix 1).[64] One Maryland master wrote Tilghman that although he had located a fugitive in Philadelphia, he worried about fighting abolitionists in court. Other correspondents complained of the money and time fugitives had cost them; one slaveholder called his problem a "rash of runaways."[65]

Unreturned fugitives affected plantation discipline, southern masters angrily explained to Tilghman. "I expect the whole of [my slaves] will go off if I can't recover those who are [now] out," yet another Maryland slaveholder stated after six men fled his estate. Some runaways remained in contact with their cohorts on southern plantations, one master observed, hoping "to entice [all of] them away from me." For this reason, he and other Marylanders vowed to "spare no pains of expense" to retrieve runaway slaves.[66]

From Tilghman's perspective, day-to-day disputes between southern masters and Pennsylvanian abolitionists augured ill for the Union. He believed firmly in the concept of comity: the assurance of "good-will" among states with different legal cultures and social and economic concerns. The PAS's success in Pennsylvania courtrooms, in his eyes, punctured interstate comity on the slavery issue. Tilghman thus padded many of his judicial decisions involving either the PAS or fugitive slaves with broader arguments about slavery's national sanctity and legitimacy, especially in states—such as Pennsylvania—where bondage had been all but abolished. In an October 1813 case, for instance, Pennsylvania's highest-ranking jurist returned a fugitive slave to a Maryland planter with a strong admonition to the PAS: "whatever may be our ideas of the abstract right of slavery, that relation is recognized by most of the states, and is tolerated in this government."[67] A few months later, in January 1814, Tilghman made a more elaborate pronouncement when returning a fugitive slave to Congressman Langdon Cheves of South Carolina: "We all know that our southern brethren are very jealous of their rights . . . on slavery, and that their union with the other states could never have been cemented without yielding to their demands on [fugitive slaves]. Nor is it probable that the legislature of Pennsylvania could have intended to make a law [like the abolition] act, the probable consequence of which would have been the banishment of the Congress from this state."[68]

Through obiter dicta, other Pennsylvania judges tried to quell the potential implication of abolitionist legal tactics. Even when a trial seemed to turn on facts — Could a black person claimed as a fugitive slave produce a certificate of freedom? Did a southern master correctly take out a warrant for a fugitive slave? — some Pennsylvania judges might, like Tilghman, stress the need for comity between "free" and "slave" states. In October 1821, for example, Judge J. Duncan decided in favor of a Maryland slave-owning family that had sued in Pennsylvania courts for the return of a runaway named Charity. The family visited a spa in Pennsylvania several times each year; on one occasion, Charity ran away. PAS legal counselors claimed her freedom on a technicality: that her masters' sojourns into Pennsylvania had altogether exceeded six months (a violation of the Gradual Abolition Act).

Judge Duncan rejected Charity's freedom claim by citing the need for comity in a Union now clearly divided into "free" and "slave" states. "It was well known to the framers of our . . . Abolition Acts," he opined, "that southern gentlemen with their families were in the habit of visiting [here] . . . with their domestic slaves"; those noble Pennsylvanians surely did not mean to repudiate southern slavery. Freeing runaway slaves in court would amount to "a denial of the rights of hospitality" between northern and southern states.[69] Neither jurists nor lawyers, another Pennsylvania judge asserted in an April 1833 fugitive slave case, should "indulge [their] feelings" on the slavery issue, for "the law of the land . . . recognizes the right of one man to hold another in bondage." And the law of the land meant absolute protection for southern masters in northern courts.[70]

Yet other jurists sided with the PAS. In 1822, for instance, Judge Washington reversed the conviction of an abolitionist for aiding a fugitive slave. Whereas opposing attorneys wanted the man convicted of "obstruction" under the federal Fugitive Slave Law, the judge countered that "obstruction" meant physically intervening in a capture, not offering legal aid to distressed blacks.[71]

AFRICAN AMERICAN leaders condemned the PAS's racism in not embracing black activist tactics and in not admitting black members until the 1830s. Yet, despite their criticism, blacks would remain indebted to the organization's lawyers through the Civil War. As James Forten asserted in

1813, Pennsylvania "is the only state in the union wherein a black man is put on the same [legal] footing as a white man." PAS lawyers, Forten's son-in-law Robert Purvis continued, should be thanked for their hard work.[72] From the black perspective, of course, there was a tactical reason for such nods. Whereas later abolitionists prosecuted only high-profile cases, the Pennsylvania society continually addressed blacks' everyday legal needs, representing accused fugitives, kidnapped blacks, and others in distress. In Pennsylvania, on the border of southern slavery, such legal aid remained an all-too-real concern for African Americans. Even William Lloyd Garrison would have kind words for the PAS's gritty legal work. A close friend of the indefatigable Thomas Shipley starting in the late 1820s, Garrison called the Pennsylvanians as "thorough going reformers" as existed before the abolitionist revolution of the 1830s.[73]

That revolution occurred in part because second-wave reformers like Garrison, Amos A. Phelps, and some of the PAS's brightest activists (including Shipley) opposed the society's cautious legal strategy. Technicalities, loopholes, and individual victories, they would charge, left unanswered the most important question: Did some men have the right to hold other men as property? In Phelps's view, early abolitionists embraced a "false doctrine": the "wicked" belief that "slavery can ever be remedied on principles which assumed the legitimacy" of masters' property concerns. At its heart, slavery was not an amorphous legal creation but, as Garrison proclaimed in the "Declaration of Sentiments" in 1833, an evil institution that reduced "more than two million of our fellow people" to the status "of a marketable commodity." Second-wave abolitionists therefore would have to embrace a new founding creed: "no man has a right to enslave another."[74]

Other second-wave activists spoke in harsher tones. "The question is not whether or not we should offer legal help," Lewis Gunn, a young Philadelphia lawyer and self-described "ultra" abolitionist "of the Garrison variety," argued in 1837, "but what principles we should adopt?" For by buying individual slaves' freedom or returning fugitives to their masters, "we sanction the institution which we fight." In other words, abolitionists must not concede man's natural right to freedom on the altar of political expediency. Abolitionists should move away from narrow legal attacks and focus on slavery's legal sanction throughout America.[75]

Tactically, Gunn wrote, abolitionists should push for trial-by-jury guarantees for all fugitive slaves, so that the people themselves might stop slavery "in their own village or town." Moreover, each trial should be publicized for maximum effect. For example, when a New Jersey judge returned a fugitive to a southern master, Gunn challenged abolitionists to "publish an account of the case in handbill form, and to distribute it, saying, 'here is what you people of the north have to do with slavery. Will you permit it?' These handbills should be thrown into every house, into thickets before elections . . . so that hundreds who never read a law on the subject would learn the wrongs inflicted on their fellows. Sympathy would be awakened, public opinion regenerated, and slavery destroyed." As for the PAS's strategy of slow, "piecemeal reform," that, Gunn observed, was "spurious benevolence" indeed.[76]

Pennsylvania reformers conceded many of these points. As William Meredith, a well-known legal and political figure in Pennsylvania between the 1810s and 1830s, asserted, PAS lawyers would always be torn between the formal boundaries of legal codes and the desire to secure outright justice for blacks. "If it were in my power," he wrote from the Pennsylvania legislature to the PAS in 1822, "I would declare without hesitation that every fugitive slave setting foot on the soil of Pennsylvania should be free and emancipated at once. Born and educated in Pennsylvania, these sentiments are so deeply rooted in my heart that they can never be . . . shaken." But, Meredith quickly added, the American constitutional and legal order prevented such emotion from overtaking reformers. "Under the Constitution of the U.S.," he explained, "we have not the POWER to do what our hearts would prompt us to on this subject." Legally and constitutionally, fugitive slaves had to be rendered up to their owners — unless abolitionists could devise legal arguments against their return.[77]

On any number of other issues — unsubstantiated black freedom claims, faulty indentures with masters, hiring out contracts, binding agreements — the PAS would follow Meredith's dictum. In "a government of laws,"[78] abolitionists had to see the law as a guide to activism. The PAS certainly proved to be a formidable legal opponent for all who came in its way. But for abolition's second wave, reformers had to push laws further than ever before.

CHAPTER FOUR

An Appeal to the Heart

The Black Protest Tradition and
the Coming of Immediatism

If you love your children, if you love your country,
if you love the God of Love, clear your hands from slaves,
burden not your children or country with them.
— Richard Allen and Absalom Jones, "Address to Those
Who Keep Slaves and Uphold the Practice," 1794

WILLIAM LLOYD GARRISON uttered perhaps the most ironic words in antebellum American history when he proclaimed in 1831, "I will be heard." For though the young Massachusetts printer had only recently announced his fiery abolitionist strategy of "Immediatism," black activists had long demanded that Americans end slavery. As the Reverend Charles C. Gardner, a black abolitionist from Philadelphia, told the American Anti-Slavery Society (AASS) in 1837, "let me tell you that when Garrison was a schoolboy, the people of color in the different parts of the country" had already mobilized against slavery as a crime against both God and man. Indeed, Gardner blasted, although "William Lloyd Garrison has been branded as the individual who . . . set the blacks' hearts afire," black activists instead inspired Garrison and his white cohorts to attack bondage even more fiercely.[1]

Gardner spoke for many African American leaders who believed that earlier black abolitionism defined the new immediatist antislavery societies sweeping the nation during the 1830s. Although happy to see "Americans becoming more determined on the subject of slavery," Philadelphia's James Forten lamented that many white citizens "hardly noticed" the decades of black activism that influenced new strategies and tactics.[2]

Indeed, from Richard Allen and Prince Hall in the 1790s to David Walker and Maria Stewart in the late 1820s, African Americans developed an arsenal of strategies and tactics that diverged sharply from the learned and dispassionate legal/political activism of white abolitionists. Black abolitionists injected moralism and emotionalism into the fight against racial oppression. They called bondage a "monstrous evil," slaveholders "man-stealers," and, increasingly by the early nineteenth century, apathetic Americans "hypocrites" for not swiftly ending an institution that violated whites cherished creed of freedom for all. The "only remedy for such an evil," one group of black Philadelphians wrote in the 1790s, was to attack "slavery morally as well as politically."[3]

As black activists in Philadelphia, Boston, and New York City asserted, everyday Americans needed to see bondage's horror, understand its chilling effects on individuals and families, and feel a sense of collective guilt for its continued practice. Whereas white reformers used learned arguments to "persuade the liberal mind" of the elite, blacks sought to stir the "feelings" of a broader American public by means of literary tactics like pamphleteering. In 1813 one black author called his work "an appeal to the heart." He hoped that white Americans would recognize the authenticity and saliency of the black jeremiad in its various forms. More than a distinctive style of black abolitionist activity, however, African Americans turned a perceived tactical limitation into a strength.[4] Told by white reformers that they could not perform many of the essential duties of early abolitionism — in particular, arguing legal cases before judge and jury — African Americans were forced to fight slavery in the public realm. They wasted little time in doing so. In myriad narratives, public speeches, and essays, black tacticians sought to convey the "authentic" experience of racial oppression and thereby rouse the American nation to act against slavery once and for all.

BLACK RESISTANCE to slavery debuted with the first transatlantic slave-trading vessels.[5] Black colonials continually resisted slavery and racial injustice throughout the seventeenth and eighteenth centuries. Yet African American protest entered a new phase during the American Revolutionary era, as blacks sought to seize the political creed of freedom for all.

New social institutions enhanced black abolitionism.[6] Black Americans started autonomous churches, benevolent societies, debating clubs, and self-help organizations.[7] Much of this organizational activity occurred in the North (especially in large towns and cities like Albany, Boston, New York, and Philadelphia), where free black populations swelled in the wake of state-backed abolition schemes and private manumissions.[8] As the Boston "Free African Society" declared in 1787, its members "pledged to benefit each other" by forming an insurance association to "protect the needy of this society." Hundreds of miles away in Philadelphia, another group formed "for the mutual benefit" of the local African American community.[9]

Even in slave states, African Americans carved out autonomous institutional and cultural space, particularly in urban centers such as Richmond, Baltimore, and Charleston. As Douglas Egerton writes, Gabriel's Rebellion of 1800 owed much to the political and religious organization of free blacks in post-Revolutionary Virginia. In Charleston, South Carolina, a group of "free browne [sic] men" established a mutual self-help society in 1790, pledging to "relieve the wants and miseries" of their people and to "promote the welfare and happiness of each other." At roughly the same time in Savannah, Georgia, Andrew Bryan opened the first African Baptist Church in the United States.[10]

Paralleling these social developments, post-Revolutionary African Americans displayed an overtly political mindset on broader issues of slavery and civil rights. According to Shane White, black Americans now planned marches, election-day celebrations, and other public events to "proclaim to a skeptical and hostile white audience that blacks . . . were American citizens" with the same rights as anyone else. Black activism throughout the Chesapeake states, Philip Schwarz writes, became more confrontational during the early national period. White officials in Maryland and Virginia witnessed an increase in "freedom" crimes: insurrections and small-scale rebellions for black liberation. Virginia's Gabriel Prosser asked his band of revolutionaries to strike a blow for black freedom — or die trying.[11]

Working within this broader social and political context, the first generation of black abolitionists sought to join the white fight against slavery. But white abolitionists did not accept black members: neither the Pennsylvania Abolition Society (PAS) nor the New York Manumission Society, the two most important groups of the period, admitted blacks. Thus, despite the fact that the PAS hired Absalom Jones and Quomony Clarkson as schoolteachers, the organization kept them at arm's length as activists. (James Forten's son-in-law, Robert Purvis of Philadelphia, would bristle at the PAS's segregationist membership policies before the 1830s.)

Unable to join the white abolitionist organizations, early black reformers nonetheless tried to use PAS-style petitioning tactics to aid the broader abolitionist cause. In 1780, for instance, black Bostonians presented a memorial to the Massachusetts legislature requesting state-financed educa-

AN APPEAL TO THE HEART

tional facilities.[12] Four North Carolina freedmen who resettled in Philadelphia petitioned Congress in 1797 to ban the domestic slave trade. In perhaps the most interesting example, over seventy members of Philadelphia's black community asked Congress in 1800 to end both slavery and the slave trade. Telling federal representatives that blacks only "desired the birthright of the human race" and that slavery mocked Americans' Revolutionary heritage, the memorialists wanted Congress to undertake a plan of "national emancipation."[13]

White officials, including one PAS member, frowned on this request, debating for two days African Americans' right to petition the federal government. One Massachusetts lawmaker complained that white abolitionists had used blacks to bait southern slaveholders, as the memorial "appeared to be subscribed by a number of individuals who were incapable of writing their own names, or reading the petition, [or even] . . . digesting the principles of it." "To encourage a measure of the kind," he continued, "would have a terrible tendency, and must be mischievous to America very soon [for] it would teach [blacks] the art of assembling together, debating, and the like, and would soon . . . extend from one end of the union to another." Congressmen from South Carolina and Georgia charged that the petition contained a plethora of "lies" about black injustice. Did the Constitution protect black political protest, one Georgian asked? Obviously not, he concluded, for the preamble alone — "we the people" — does not include "them." Congress ultimately agreed, voting 84 to 1 to return the petition to its African American presenters.[14]

Facing such hostile responses in state and federal assemblies and a cold shoulder from white reformers, black abolitionists devised literary tactics such as pamphleteering to try to bring about racial redress in America. Print culture offered a powerful means of engaging the public's attention, early writers agreed. Pamphlets, newspaper articles, and other written forms of communication could reach many more people than petitions. And this broader public, once moved by stories of injustice and oppression, might compel their political leaders to liberate African Americans. Speaking in 1828, Philadelphia's William Whipper challenged black activists to master the literary arts and sciences. Literature not only represented knowledge and erudition, Whipper observed, but also, if wielded correctly, power. "The orator and the writer" could sway "an audience" to his side with one speech or essay. But, he admonished, the publicist "must display a pomp of words, a magnificence of tropes and figures."[15]

African American writers had already acted on Whipper's words. Between the 1790s and early 1820s, black publicists vied for the nation's attention in politically conscious writings of varying kinds: personal narratives from Venture Smith and James Forten, reprinted speeches from Prince Hall and Richard Allen, and polemical essays from Absalom Jones and Lemuel Haynes. During this first phase of literary activism, black reformers mixed rationalistic (even deferential, PAS-style) language with more forthright (and emotionally laden, non-PAS-style) challenges to white Americans. Of course, any public challenge coming from a black man's pen could cause a stir. Slaveholders repeatedly articulated fears about blacks' ability to use words to foment racial upheaval. In 1790 South Carolinians forced a newspaper editor who printed the appeal of "Yambo, an African" to pledge not to publish black men's words ever again.[16] In 1817 North Carolina editors admitted to white abolitionists their fears that "slaves can read"; they vowed not to publish anything that could stir black resistance or even rebellion.[17]

In fact, black abolitionists' shift toward literary tactics carried implicit as well as explicit messages to white citizens: African Americans were not the passive, inarticulate underlings that Enlightenment taxonomy often projected.[18] Even before the appearance of David Walker and William Lloyd Garrison, black abolitionists used words to mobilize public opinion. "We beseech your attention," a group of North Carolina blacks importuned in a 1797 petition on kidnapping. Though "we cannot claim the privilege of representation in your [political] councils, we trust we may address you as fellow men." Would liberal men allow the domestic slave trade to rip families apart? Would true Americans idly watch black suffering? The petition hoped to stir action with these direct questions.[19] Similarly, Richard Allen (co-creator of Philadelphia's black-run African Methodist Episcopal church) used his eulogy of George Washington as an emancipatory call to Americans in 1800. By publishing his address, which praised the late president for releasing his slaves, Allen hoped that "the whole of the American people" would gain "an . . . observance of . . . [my] short expressions," thereby "greatly promot[ing] the cause of the oppressed." Thus did readers in New York City and Philadelphia papers see Allen's challenge: "May a double portion of Washington's [emancipatory] spirit rest on the officers of the government of the United States and the whole of the American people."[20]

Essayists remained a fraction of the free black population. In many ways, these activists formed a black elite in terms of education, occupation, and social contacts with white communities. Yet as James Forten explained, early black publicists voiced the concerns of their people — free and un-free — throughout the United States. As Forten wrote of a black memorial to Congress in 1800, "700,000 of the human race are concerned in our petition."[21] Those whose voices could be heard through print culture or political debate had a duty to speak for the black community. And speak they did.[22]

Many pamphleteers benefited from independent clubs and societies that underwrote printing costs and held educational sessions about writing and public speaking. In 1808 Absalom Jones's Philadelphia church published over three hundred copies of his essay on the slave trade "for the use of the congregation." New York activist William Hamilton commented in an 1809 speech to New York's African Society for Mutual Relief that its expressions of thanks for his talk "do much pleasure to my feelings," though "your request for the publication of my address is a higher compliment." Publication, Hamilton proclaimed, would allow him to confront opinions "that Africans are inferior to white men in the structure of both body and mind." It would also permit him to speak bluntly to the masses.[23]

By reaching out to a broad audience with pamphlets and public essays, African American activists challenged white stereotypes throughout American society. More than a few white writers would have agreed with Thomas Jefferson's comments in *Notes on the State of Virginia* that "a black had [never] uttered a fact above the level of plain narration," nor "as far as I have heard, has a black excelled in any art, any science." Even Phyllis Wheatley's "compositions," he added, "are below the dignity of criticism."[24] Black writing shattered such myths. In 1790, for example, a New York City writer named "Africanus" debunked a white journalist's view of blacks' supposed inferiority. "Before we can form a clear idea upon [abolition]," the offending white correspondent (named "Rusticus") observed, "we must first acquaint ourselves with the name, nature and circumstances of the thing. . . . Thus I was compelled to travel over large philosophical and historical grounds, to find the place of the wool hairy negro in the order of nature." Rusticus's ultimate conclusion was that the African was somewhere between apes and men in nature's order, making slavery a thoroughly justifiable institution.[25]

"I am a SHEEP HAIRY negro," Africanus replied, "the son of an African man and woman,

> who by a train of fortunate events . . . was left free when very young . . . received a common English school education, and have been in-

structed in the Christian religion. [I am] a master of a trade . . . and am encouraged by several spirited, noble and generous Americans who are pleased to praise me for employing my time so much more rationally (as they say) than most white men in the same station of life. And please don't consider me as the link in the creation by which the monkey hangs to the gentleman.

"I hope the penning of my thoughts shall appear worthy," Africanus observed, "as an opponent to the Philosophic Rusticus." His own set of essays refuted Rusticus's claims that blacks' occupied the lower rungs of nature's grand ladder. "I will conclude by answering the last question of Rusticus," Africanus summed up: "The American and the African are one species — the law of nature declares it. And I, a sheep hairy African negro, being free and in some degree enlightened, feel myself equal to the duties of [any] spirited, noble, and generous American freeman."[26]

Other black publicists utilized print culture to inject something missing from white abolitionist discourses on slavery and racial subjection: an authentic or personalized view of bondage and oppression. An ex-slave interviewed by Pennsylvania abolitionists in 1790 illuminated this concern in a simple stanza:

> I cannot read nor use the pen
> But yet can think with other men.
> A clerk to pen my thoughts I have,
> that you may read my narrative
> I have a wish that you should see,
> The effects of Aristocracy.[27]

Interested in telling his life story, and thereby giving a true picture of slavery's horrors, "LundonDerry" released his thoughts for white Americans to see.

James Forten referred to his pamphlets as "Appeals to the Heart." "Judge what must be our feelings," he wrote to a congressman in 1800, "to find ourselves treated as a species of property . . . and think how anxious we must be to raise ourselves from this degrading state." For this reason, Forten concluded, "unprejudiced persons who receive [our] documents" — black writings and speeches — "will acknowledge that we are . . . humane people who wish our situation alleviated." "Justice to our colour demands . . . these [strong] remarks," Richard Allen and Absalom Jones proclaimed in a 1794 pamphlet that "addressed . . . those [Americans] who keep slaves and those who approve the practice." "If you love your country . . . and if you love God," they chastised Americans, "[then] clear your hands of slaves, [and] burden not your children or country with them."28

Russell Parrott, a young Philadelphia printer-turned-minister, preyed on readers emotions in two pamphlets on the slave trade published between 1812 and 1816. Parrott wished "to point to the fatal influence slavery has had" on blacks in compelling language and images. Describing the transcendent benefits of the slave trade ban and northern emancipation schemes, Parrott asked his readers to conjure up "scenes of distress" that still characterized many black lives: the Middle Passage, whose "stuffed slave ships" carried multitudes of "emaciated inhabitants" to lands of un-told sorrows; slave-trading auctions in the Americas, where blacks faced "the indelible shame — TO BE SOLD! TO BE SEPARATED FROM THEIR PART-NERS IN WO!"; and finally, life on "the plantation," that "field of sorrow."29

Parrott filled his pamphlets with other powerful phrases and descriptions not seen in PAS writings. Black Americans were not simply "oppressed," he asserted, they "groaned with agony and bled with profusion" because of the "licentious" work of white civilization. "When the philanthropic mind con-templates [emotional] scenes like these, the sympathetic tear finds vent, and the soul, alive to sorrow, exclaims . . . what have they done to merit this?" American citizens could transform scenes of distress into scenes of triumph, Parrott concluded, but only if they used black complaints to end slavery once and for all. For in "this land of liberty and rights," "the wrong of slavery is sanctioned" by the people as a whole.30

Perhaps most importantly, African American essayists used literary tactics to legitimize blacks' claims to universal freedom and equal citizenship. Pam-phlets routinely invoked transcendent political principles. George Law-rence, a New York city activist, asked Americans in 1813 "if [they] are ignorant of their own Declaration," which proclaimed all men naturally free. If not "ignorant of it," he challenged, then "they must enforce" the Declaration's words (by completely and speedily abolishing slavery), for "this government is founded on principles of liberty and equality." Those "noble sentiments 'we hold these truths to be self evident,'" the Reverend Peter Williams commented in an 1808 pamphlet, "[must be applied] to the bleeding African," who still pleads to Americans, "am I not a man and a brother?"31

Black Philadelphia and Boston leaders became especially prominent pamphleteers. Although David Walker made Boston's black community famous in the late 1820s, Walker himself represented a culmination of decades of African American struggle and protest in the city. From Prince Hall and Lemuel Haynes to Thomas Paul and William Nell, a succession of pamphleteers challenged white Americans on their own political terms. Prince Hall often used the African Masonic Lodge, formed in 1778, as a vital center for black speakers and publicists. In 1796 black Bostonians established the African Society, which hosted abolitionist speakers and published black tracts for public distribution.

In 1808, for example, the African Society printed one black activist's celebration of America's slave-trading ban. Much like David Walker decades later, the orator (who called himself "Brutus" in the pamphlet version of his talk) seized on the contradiction between American ideals and black subjugation. Also like Walker, Brutus warned that black people might be willing to die for freedom if white Americans did not eradicate slavery soon. "Men sacrifice their time, their property and . . . their lives in pursuit of [liberty]," Brutus declared. "Yea, I say there is something so dreadful about slavery that some had rather DIE than experience it."[32]

No less angry speeches and essays issued from Boston's black religious and cultural centers. Offering sweeping analyses of America's racial ills and the problem of slavery, black activists focused less on specific legislative proposals and more on the broad meaning of "freedom," "liberty," and "justice for all" to blacks. "Freedom is the theme of our contemplation," another black Bostonian wrote in 1809. "Did not Americans think freedom a privilege truly to be enjoyed when . . . [England] was about to invade her? Well, if so desirable to America as that, why then are Americans not willing to have it universal?"[33]

Slavery and racial subjugation, Lemuel Haynes observed in his book, *The Nature and Importance of True Republicanism*, represented the harshest form of "despotism" in the world. Indeed, he charged, white Americans should consider racial slavery the worst "attack on the rights of man." True republicanism required universal emancipation, Haynes concluded, not excuses about political expediency or blacks' inferiority. America would be defined by its ability or failure to destroy slavery.[34]

Black Philadelphians issued similarly fiery political challenges to white Americans in public speeches, pamphlets, and essays between the 1790s and 1820s, when Richard Allen, Absalom Jones, James Forten, Russell Parrott, and other activists broadcast their views on abolitionism and civil rights. In a pamphlet describing blacks' contributions to the sick and infirm during Philadelphia's horrendous cholera epidemic of 1793, Allen and Jones hoped to "excite citizens' attention" to the disease of slavery. "How hateful slavery is in the sight of that God who hath destroyed Kings and Princes for the oppression of slaves," they declared. "Will you," they chided readers, "plead our incapacity for freedom, and our contended condition under oppression, as a sufficient cause for keeping us under the grievous yoke?" Americans must prevail upon their countrymen to enact national abolition laws. "God himself hath pleaded [our] cause," Allen and Jones concluded; Americans would be wise to follow His call for broad emancipation.[35]

James Forten's 1813 pamphlet, *A Series of Letters by a Man of Color*, was perhaps the most fully articulated attack on racial prejudice and slavery in the early republic. Written to protest a proposed Pennsylvania law that forced black émigrés to register in the state's localities (lest they be seized and sold into southern bondage), Forten's essay appeared in both the *Pennsylvania Freeman* and in pamphlet form. It remained a seminal document for subsequent generations of black activists, including Frederick Douglass. In 1827 *Freedom's Journal* reprinted the entire series of letters to regenerate black activism nationally.

Forten took America to task for rolling back its Revolutionary promise of liberation to all. The Declaration of Independence, the Pennsylvania constitution, the very notion that all men were created equal—surely, Forten argued, these were expansive not restrictive doctrines, "embracing the Indian and the European, the savage and the saint . . . the white man and the African." "Whatever measures are adopted subversive to these inestimable privileges," he boldly stated, "are in direct violation of the letter and spirit of our Constitution and subject of the animadversion of all." Indeed, Forten protested, American declarations seemed even further removed from African American realities. Even "free" states like Pennsylvania threatened blacks' constitutional liberties. "This is the only state in the union wherein the African race have justly boasted of rational liberty," he proclaimed, "and shall it now be said that they will be deprived of protections by the laws?" "All men are born equally free," and the "motto of our state legislature ought to be: 'the law knows no distinction.'" Pennsylvania lawmakers seemed to have "mistook this sentiment, and do not consider us men." The future looked bleak, Forten observed, if even "free" states like Pennsylvania degraded black rights.[36]

Despite Forten's exasperation, he felt that literary tactics could still turn the tide. "An appeal to the heart is my intention," he concluded, "and if I have failed, it is my great misfortune not to have had a power of eloquence sufficient to convince." Forten, like activists in Boston and other areas, believed that a strategy of public protest would be the best route to large-scale black liberation. The angry words of African American pamphlets, black publicists claimed, provided an emotional edge and moral compass that could engage the "whole of the American people." Taking this black abolitionist call to the masses, not restricting abolitionism to the elite few, would lead all Americans to the promised land.[37]

EMPHASIZING A STRATEGY of moral confrontation and swift redress of racial grievances, and utilizing literary tactics such as pamphleteering, African American reformers established a distinct protest tradition within the broader antislavery world. Although black strategists would remain largely segregated until the 1830s, they did become part of mainstream debates over slavery and abolitionism in the 1820s — ironically, on an issue that sought to send them further away from white Americans: colonization.

Founded in 1817 in Washington, D.C., the American Colonization Society (ACS) proposed a strategy for ridding the country of its black problem. By gradually exporting free blacks to African settlements, the ACS hoped to encourage slaveholders to liberate their chattels, who would then be exported under the group's guiding hand. Funded largely by private donations and vowing never to coerce masters into emancipating their slaves, the ACS thrived in the Upper South and North alike during the 1820s. Though Deep South states such as Georgia and South Carolina remained wary (if not hostile) to the plan, almost every other state in the Union had colonizationist auxiliaries: by the 1830s over two hundred local groups pledged allegiance to the ACS. In addition, slaveholder statesmen of the highest rank supported the plan — among them James Madison, James Monroe, John Marshall, Roger B. Taney, and Henry Clay. "The concurrence in every part of the country to strengthen and establish [the ACS]," the society wrote in its first annual report, "leaves no doubt that . . . the philanthropist will be satisfied with the success of [this] issue."[38]

Colonization proved to be a key transitional topic for both black and white abolitionists. The refusal of white activists to publicly and forcefully condemn colonization as a strategy for redressing racial slavery in America left a void in the broader antislavery community. The very failure of the Pennsylvania Abolition Society to attack the American Colonization Society pushed black reformers into the national spotlight.

Although the Colonization Society's formation generated immediate concern, the PAS consistently backed away from confrontational stands in the 1820s and 1830s. In 1829, for example, both the PAS and the American

AN APPEAL TO THE HEART

Convention of Abolition Societies reported that they would refrain from "any opinion favorable or adverse to colonization" for fear of offending well-meaning philanthropists still in favor of the plan. Some of the most respectable pastors, physicians, and public figures in Philadelphia supported the ACS by 1830. The parent society noted that residents had raised a large share of one annual sum, newspapers announced meetings and offered essays advocating the scheme, and a young men's branch was created early on. Though Philadelphia's colonizationists professed that they would not forcibly expel free blacks, their antiblack tone was ominous. Thus the black community not only mobilized itself but also looked for white allies. As one PAS member admitted in an 1819 essay, colonization's popularity spoke to white northerners' fear of racial "intermixture, to which many are averse." Except for individual dissenters (the PAS's Thomas Shipley, as usual, shined in blacks' eyes for his adamant denunciations of such racism), America's premier abolitionist organization remained silent.[39]

In fact, black activists stood virtually alone in their public condemnation of coerced expatriation. Nevertheless, their rigid defense of their rights WITHIN the United States established a critical line of dissent for future generations of abolitionists in America, white as well as black. More importantly, the colonization debate forced African Americans to coordinate their tactics nationally in the 1820s and to seek new alliances with white abolitionists who agreed that colonization threatened the very ideal of the antislavery cause. Finally, the prospect of exportation elicited an angrier, more confrontational tone among black writers. In 1829 David Walker's famous *Appeal* put an exclamation point after this decade of anticolonizationist black activism, pointing out that the African American masses had to fill the gaping void left by chary white abolitionists and statesmen. The word "immediatism" was never used by black reformers in the decade leading to Walker's warlike call. But the message that Americans had to end slavery at once came through more loudly and clearly than ever. "Behold . . . thou vain, bloated upstart worlding of a slave-holder," one black activist proclaimed in the 1820s, "know on thee we pronounce our judgement": the oppressed "shall prefer" death to "suffering under thy slavery." If national emancipation did not come soon, "the voice of imperative justice, however harsh," will be heard by groaning whites![40]

According to a host of black reformers writing in the late 1810s and 1820s, friends of the African American community had to promote heated condemnations of plans to export blacks overseas. John Russwurm and Samuel Cornish, coeditors of the first black-owned and edited newspaper,

Freedom's Journal, highlighted this concern in editorials throughout the late 1820s. With colonization societies growing at a brisk rate in many northern communities, black abolitionists called on white abolitionists to take a firm public stand against expatriation. For "the ACS has been zealous and successful in imposing on the public," one editorial began in August 1827, "the foolish idea that we are all longing to emigrate to their land of milk and honey." It was "high time," Russwurm and Cornish continued, that all Americans "should know the truth of the matter": blacks demanded the abolition of slavery and broader civil rights protections WITHIN America. "Can the JUSTICE of God tolerate so much INIQUITY AND INJUSTICE?" they asked. Unrepentant slaveholders and white supplicants of colonization would surely find out when they met with Divine Redress in the afterlife. But in the here and now, black and white philanthropists must confront the American Colonization Society.[41]

Boston and Philadelphia were the entrepôts of black anticolonization in the 1810s and 1820s. Philadelphia's African American community mobilized against the ACS from its inception. Drawing on a strategy that had long emphasized blacks' civic equality in American society, African Americans in the City of Brotherly Love expressed their outrage in a succession of mass demonstrations, pamphlets, and petitions. No sooner had the ACS formed than black leaders petitioned the biennial meeting of the American Convention of Abolition Societies meeting in the city in 1817. Presented by Prince Saunders, secretary of a community action group dedicated to fighting the ACS, the memorial asked white reformers to begin "a careful examination of" expatriation plans "imposed upon us" by slaveholders and wily politicians. Pennsylvania abolitionists, Saunders's document pointed out, had a long history of providing legal aid to distressed blacks; they should now move to the front of the anticolonization battle. In short, black activists wanted the "first abolition society in the world" to mount a blistering attack on a proposal that surrendered the moral high ground of abolitionism and legitimized whites' worst racial assumptions.[42]

The petition also urged white abolitionists to try to understand blacks' "interests and feelings" about expatriation. White reformers needed African American activists, black Philadelphians explained, for they provided an authentic voice of outrage and pain. "[You] could only reach" the broader black community "through us," the petitioners admonished the American Convention. The time had come, in other words, for white reformers to take seriously the work of black activists. The convention patiently accepted the blacks' memorial but did not act on it.[43]

Black Philadelphians unleashed their own public attack on the ACS. In a forceful display of solidarity, city leaders staged a mass meeting in 1817 in Bethel Church to condemn colonization as a virtual declaration of war on African Americans. Chaired by James Forten and Prince Saunders, the assembly attracted nearly three thousand people and generated publicity for the anticolonization cause in local papers. The Philadelphians issued a pamphlet blasting the "stigma . . . attached to the free people of color" by the ACS. Colonization, the pamphlet declared, would actually ensure slavery by separating free black activists from their enslaved brethren. Philadelphia's free black community proclaimed that its members would "NEVER separate . . . voluntarily from the slave population" nor end their vitriolic public condemnations of racial injustice in America.[44]

Throughout the 1820s black leaders held similar public protest meetings in and around Philadelphia. Richard Allen, John Gloucester, James Forten, and others lectured their brethren about the need to remain vigilant defenders of blacks' essential rights in American society. They also emphasized the white community's lackluster efforts in condemning colonization. Responding to slaveholders who maintained that colonization would benefit black as well as white Americans, Allen issued several public appeals that captured the fury of black reformers. "We were STOLEN from our MOTHER COUNTRY and brought HERE," he wrote angrily in a public letter to *Freedom's Journal* in 1827. "The land we have watered with our tears and our blood is now OUR MOTHER COUNTRY," Allen concluded in a stirring appeal to racial equality. Blacks would stay and fight for "their RIGHTS." Would whites join them? he wondered.[45]

In the late 1820s another prominent group of black activists organized "a Committee . . . to express our indignation at such [schemes as colonization, which] will be injurious to our brethren." Composed of six men, including William Whipper, Francis Webb, and James Cornish, the committee pledged to publicly combat all "scurrilous" propositions relating to people of color. In 1828 the group issued a pamphlet entitled the *Philadelphia Report*. Ostensibly a response to an "injurious" story about black inferiority appearing in the *United States Gazette*, the report attacked Americans' inherent racial prejudice. No wonder colonization was so popular, it charged, when white Americans did not challenge "the vulgar expatriation of the people of color." "We have as strong claims to residence IN this country" as anyone, the report emphasized. If white reformers and citizens would not confront them, then pro-colonizationists "will have to CONTEND WITH THE COLORED POPULATION" at every turn. "And," the pamphlet concluded, "WE SHALL CONQUER" those who claim blacks are a "lazy race" better left enslaved or shipped overseas.[46]

Black Boston matched this anticolonizationist fervor. From the late 1810s through the 1830s the city's "African" debating societies and black churches publicly protested the ACS. Indeed, as support for colonization exploded in New England, black groups organized the only formal challenges in Massachusetts. Capping years of informal activity, dozens of activists met in 1826 to form the General Colored Association (GCA), an umbrella organization dedicated to securing black freedom and racial justice in American society. The GCA earned a national reputation for its adamant protests against colonization, and many important activists, including David Walker, James Barbadoes, and William C. Nell, cut their protest teeth in the association.

David Walker became perhaps the most important black activist in the 1820s. He remains best known for his 1829 work, *Appeal in Four Articles: Together with a Preamble to the Colored Citizens of the World*, which challenged Americans in visceral and confrontational language to reread both the Declaration of Independence and the Bible before defending slavery or expatriating free blacks. But Walker was no one-hit wonder. Between 1828 and his mysterious death in 1830, he proved to be an energizing force both regionally and nationally. In addition to his used-clothes business in Boston's Fisherman's Wharf section, Walker served as correspondent and agent for *Freedom's Journal*. He continually spoke at public gatherings of various sorts, earning a reputation as an orator of considerable power and eloquence.[47]

Walker urged his fellow Bostonians to stand up as never before against racial injustice. In a period when colonization gained strength as a remedy to the country's racial ills and white reformers shied away from condemning the ACS, Walker challenged African Americans to become the vanguard of a new national abolitionism based on transcendent religious and political principles. Like his cohorts elsewhere, he realized the value of existing abolitionist societies and the legal services they provided. But Walker worried that these groups did not have the "correct" view of America's racial problem — its psychological depth and pervasive impact on institutions of government and law.[48]

According to Walker, the rivers of American racism ran deep; the popularity of colonization offered only the most recent example. White reformers who viewed slavery in objective legal terms — bondage as a degraded legal status — did not seem to understand this. For blacks, Walker shouted to a Boston crowd celebrating the visit of African prince Abduhl Rahman, bondage and racism amounted to a harrowing daily reality of "derision, violence and oppression." Worse than hypocritical, Walker called Americans "evil" on matters relating to racial complexion. Thus, abolishing racial subjugation required more than mere legal tactics or gradual emancipation schemes. True freedom, he argued, necessitated a thorough moral interrogation of the white psyche — something that African American activists could supply in abundance.[49]

To impress these harsh views upon the broader white culture, Walker told blacks not just to publish and publicly protest but to organize the masses. "A general union" of blacks was "a necessity." African Americans had already laid the ideological framework for a new era of protest by "exhibiting our miseries" in speeches and pamphlets. It was time to initiate a subsequent phase of national organization. "Now I ask," he observed on one occasion, "if [free black activists alone] were united . . . and resolved to aid and assist each other to the utmost of their power, what mighty deeds would be done by them for the good of OUR cause?" With "two and a half millions of colored people in the United States" behind them, black liberation would not be so far from reality.[50]

The General Colored Association, in Walker's eyes, already offered a model for such organization, for its "primary object . . . is to unite the colored population . . . throughout the United States" and to publicly interrogate white racism. By "forming [such] societies" in other cities, each with an eye toward educating, uniting, and mobilizing new groups of community activists, Walker hoped that African Americans would build a public protest movement to overwhelm white apathy. "That we should stand as neutral spectators" while white colonizationists mobilized their own hateful societies would be unconscionable, he concluded in another speech. Black activists had to become mass organizers, "not withholding anything which may meliorate our miserable condition."[51]

Walker was not a lone voice within the GCA. Other members, such as James Barbadoes, became pivotal anticolonizationists for both black and white Bostonians between the mid-1820s and mid-1830s, particularly after Walker's death. Barbadoes helped persuade William Lloyd Garrison to turn against colonization and to embrace Walker's strategy of confrontation. In 1831 Barbadoes cowrote an important anticolonizationist tract with other members of the GCA that reproduced Walker's harsh views on white hypocrisy. Although colonization brought new attention to slavery, Barbadoes argued, Americans seemed to be focusing less on getting rid of bondage and more on getting rid of blacks. "We are sensible," he stated, "that a moral disease, SLAVERY, is in America, and not in Africa." Framing the address in terms of "an appeal" to the American public, Barbadoes told Americans to confront this racial sickness before it killed their supposedly democratic society. If, however, white citizens considered colonization the only practical remedy to the racial problem, then grim consequences might follow. "We remind many that the blood of Abel is beginning to be heard"; it might soon unleash in the form of massive black rebellion.[52]

Like Walker, too, Barbadoes called slavery a crime in the eyes of both God and man. Yet Americans could atone for this sin by resolving to end bondage. "Let him who stealeth, obey the word of God and steal no more," Barbadoes offered. On a more practical level, American citizens, legislators, and reformers could end slavery by demanding justice for blacks. "The clergy," he announced, "with their mighty influence," could tell slaveholders to release their bondsmen, lest they risk eternal damnation. Similarly, newspaper editors could cite America's founding creed of universal equality as license to end bondage. "Then will be done away with this horrible traffic in blood."[53]

Outside of the GCA, black Boston's female activists also began agitating against colonization. Maria Stewart, a religious reformer and women's rights activist of increasing prominence in the early 1830s, picked up the mantle of Walker and Barbadoes. Working against what her biographer Marilyn Richardson calls "a backdrop of religious, militant activism" in antebellum Boston, Stewart issued urgent calls to black action in public speeches and pamphlets. Colonization, she commented at one point, represented a horrid retreat in the battle against slavery and racism. With white reformers shrinking from the challenge, black activists would have to be the heart and soul of a new abolition movement in the United States. "Why sit ye here and die?" she asked her brothers and sisters in 1832. If colonization succeeds and blacks are sent back to Africa en masse, many "will die"; if blacks remain idle in America, "many will die" as well.[54]

To rouse her cohorts, Stewart suffused her public appeals with Walker's fire. "I feel [so] strong a desire" to fight for justice in the world, she proclaimed, that "I would willingly sacrifice my life for the cause of God and my brethren." Linking her activism to black Boston's proud lineage of reformers, she noted that many sons of Africa had already suffered in the fight for equal rights, and "many [more] will suffer for pleading the cause of oppressed Africa." But Stewart challenged black activists to remobilize by recalling that "most noble, fearless, and undaunted" abolitionist, white or black, David Walker. "I shall glory in being one of [his] martyrs" to the cause of black freedom. Stewart hoped that the "many powerful sons and daughters of Africa . . . [would] arise" with her and demand "their rights" anew. "If refused," she warned, "I am afraid that they will spread horror and devastation around."[55]

In her own public challenges Stewart brought black Boston's political activism to life. "This is a land of freedom," she shouted on one occasion, "and according to the Constitution of these United States . . . all men [are] free and equal." Why, then, she wondered, "should one worm say to another, 'Keep you down there, while I sit up yonder, for I am better than thou.'" If they did not act, Americans would eventually suffer eternal wrath under God's all-knowing eyes. "The oppression of injured Africa has come up before the majesty of heaven," she commented; but Americans could still achieve grace by ending the sin of racial subjection. By favoring colonization, however, they snubbed God and man — and they would suffer themselves in the hereafter.[56]

The colonization debate forced the black protest tradition to evolve and forced black abolitionists to think more about coordinating their tactics nationally. In the 1820s black communities throughout the Northeast and Midwest established anticolonizationist organizations, as well as other action groups that worked to end slavery and racism. Moreover, black leaders began to speak of forming national organizations to protest racial injustice. The black convention movement of the early 1830s provided a formal foundation for these twin strategies of anticolonization and black abolition, as African American leaders from around the country met for the first time to discuss strategy and tactics. Fittingly, the first meeting of the American Society for The Free Persons of Color was held in Philadelphia in 1830. Hosted by black dignitaries such as Richard Allen and James Forten, the American Society announced black activists' "firm and settled conviction" that redressing the nation's racial ills could only occur on American soil.[57]

To do this, black activists vowed to raise the "moral and political" attention of blacks and whites alike. "What caused the abolition of the slave trade," a correspondent in *Freedom's Journal* asked, "but the glowing language and vivid colouring given to its abominations" by black activists and a small band of white reformers? So should African Americans become a vanguard of a new era of national protest against colonization, domestic slavery, and racial injustice. Black activists in Boston and Philadelphia, as well as in New York, *Freedom's Journal* would note again and again between 1827 and 1829, had already taken the lead in this regard, using the colonizationist issue to promote greater action against slavery and racism in America. Perhaps the rest of the nation would soon catch up. When it did, blacks had to maintain their position as national protest leaders.[58]

White Lady, happy, Proud and Free, Lend awhile, thine ear to me;
Let the Negro Mother's Wail Turn Thy Pale cheek yet more pale.
— "A Negro Mother's Appeal," quoted in the *Abolitionist*, 1833

WHITE ACTIVISTS such as Elizabeth Heyrich of Britain and William Lloyd Garrison put a name on the strategy of ending slavery at once: "Immediatism." Yet precisely because immediatism symbolized much more than a timetable of reform, black activists played a crucial role in the coming of a new abolitionist era during the 1830s. The Age of Immediatism signaled a new urgency in the fight against slavery, a ferocious and angry declaration that Americans had to confront the moral and emotional horrors of bondage (not downplay its significance or gradually export the problem overseas).[59] Slavery had to be attacked, white as well as black reformers now argued, by appealing directly to the American conscience, by challenging Americans to see the hypocrisy of holding slaves in the land of the free, by turning abolitionism itself into a moral crusade among the masses. "Slavery is a crime," Garrison proclaimed in 1833, and abolitionists "cannot surrender this great fundamental principle." "Anything which serves as a substitute for the immediate and absolute abolition of slavery," his organization, the New England Anti-Slavery Society (NEASS) asserted, referring particularly to colonization, "is delusive, cruel, and dangerous."[60]

Early black activists' strategy of moral confrontation clearly influenced the new immediatist abolition societies. As Garrison himself noted, black activists helped convince him and many of his contemporaries to embrace their angry tradition of reform, eschewing the still-deferential tactics of both gradual abolitionists and colonizationists. Garrison spoke of incorporating blacks' "enthusiasm" and "authentic" outrage even before he had started the NEASS in 1832. Black tacticians' use of literary techniques — especially pamphleteering — to rouse sympathy and stir emotions segued smoothly into the early activities of the New England Anti-Slavery Society and the American Anti-Slavery Society. "Appeals," "Narratives," and documentary "Testimony" poured out of the abolitionist press, diffusing "slavery's truth" far and wide: the separation of families by masters, the flogging of men and women for minor offenses, the lie given America's "Declaration of Independence." As Garrison admitted, black reformers already "looked up to the press as the great instrument . . . of their restoration." They had been cultivating its tactical uses for decades prior to the *Liberator*'s advent.[61]

A host of black activists from Philadelphia, Boston, New York, Providence, and other areas joined the new antislavery societies. But the black presence went deeper still. Many white essayists including Lydia Maria Child, David Lee Child, and Amos Phelps simply appended black "testimony" to their harsh essays condemning bondage. "The apologists of Southern slavery are accustomed to brand every picture of slavery . . . as exaggeration or calumny," wrote Lydia Maria Child. "The facts stated in these sheets," she continued, "are capable of satisfactory and legal proof." Those who doubted her stories' authenticity need only consult the "office of the Massachusetts Anti-Slavery Society" for verification and documentation. Black narratives, according to another paper, publicized as nothing else could "such an array of horrible facts . . . such glaring scenes of damning iniquity as would astound the philanthropic beholder, crimson his cheek with the tear of blood and make the very hairs on his head stand on end." This "living commentary" literally flowed "from the victims of slavery" who now vented their anger through "authentic" narratives. "The voice of the oppressed [will be] heard!!"[62]

In the 1830s and 1840s Massachusetts abolitionists consistently underwrote "Narratives" of slaves, including the life stories of James Barbadoes, Solomon Northup, Frederick Douglass, and William Wells Brown. "This simple narrative of a native African," NEASS reprints of Olaudah Equiano's famous tract asserted in the mid-1830s, "will be found to contain much instructive matter . . . on liberty and slavery." It is "recommended to all the friends of the black man, who can learn . . . from his own ARTFUL pen" about black "intelligence" and the "brutality" of slavery.[63] At Garrison's beloved *Liberator*, letters from black authors filled the columns. In the paper's first year, the *Liberator* published nearly two hundred articles, approximately 20 percent of which came from black writers—a phenomenal number for the time, outdistancing nearly a decade's worth of blacks' letters in the *Genius of Universal Emancipation* from 1821 through 1831. So striking was the black voice in modern abolitionist documents that one antiabolitionist declared that Garrison was nothing but a white Negro.[64]

Although blacks expressed "confidence" in new reformers' tactics, many African American activists claimed to be hearing nothing new except that it came from a white mouth. "We have read your interesting and, TO US, invaluable paper," Baltimore activist William Watkins wrote in the *Liberator* in 1831. But, Watkins noted, "We recognize, in *The Liberator* . . . a FAITH-

FUL REPRESENTATIVE OF OUR sentiments and interests; and an uncompromising advocate of OUR indefensible rights." Whites were the newcomers to the more radical abolitionist strategy of declaring a moral war against bondage; black activists had been using it for decades.[65]

Early white abolitionists had no place for black activist strategies and tactics that would turn their dispassionate reform movement into a moral crusade. Many members of the Pennsylvania Abolition Society worried that statesmen and jurists, already wary of slavery's divisive nature in the Union, would completely back away from calls for immediate abolitionist action; blacks' emotional appeals might even threaten gradual emancipation plans. More importantly, groups like the PAS had no place for black activists. "So deeply had the ploughshare of despotism been driven into the human affection," wrote former PASer Edwin Needles in 1840 of one of the most "striking" differences between older reformers and "modern day" abolitionists,

> that equal kindness and civility [towards blacks] . . . was considered so totally incompatible with . . . civilized society . . . that very few even of the Abolitionists in those days, were free from the deep seated prejudice of caste; and thus suffered themselves to act incoherently toward their colored brethren, as though they really were an inferior race of beings, and not entitled to notice, further than was necessary to relieve them from the cruel bonds of slavery . . . But, anything like an approach towards equality with the whites seemed never to have been contemplated.

In activism, as in social interaction, another PAS member observed in 1819, early abolitionists thought it best to keep black and white "distinct."[66]

The "revolution" in American abolition's tactics in 1830 signaled a moment that black activists had been working for since the early national period.[67] Long hoping to shape white reformers' movement to end slavery, African American strategists finally projected their fiery agenda onto the national stage. It was no mistake that the broader abolitionist cause became a virtual war on bondage after 1830, for it was only then that black strategies and tactics found explicit acceptance in newly race-conscious organizations.

CHAPTER FIVE

From Pennsylvania to Massachusetts, from Colonization to Immediatism

Race and the Overhaul of American Abolitionism

> That hitherto strong-footed but sore-eyed vixen, prejudice, is limping off,
> seeking the shade. The [new] Anti-slavery society and the friends of
> Immediate abolition are taking a noble stand.
> — William Hamilton at the Fourth Annual
> Convention of the People of Color, 1834

WHEN THE NEW ENGLAND Anti-Slavery Society (NEASS) formed in January 1832, it announced radical departures from the American abolitionist tradition. The NEASS explicitly aligned itself with black activists, who comprised nearly 25 percent of the signers to its inaugural constitution.[1] The group also vowed to attack racial prejudice in a public and "hostile" way. Most famously, the NEASS unfurled the banner of "Immediate Abolitionism." No longer content to work for a gradual end to bondage, this inaugural "modern" antislavery society proclaimed to Americans that "all property in slaves should HENCEFORTH cease." Labeling slaves "countrymen" and "brothers," immediatists strove by all legal means to "smash" southern bondage.[2]

Although a well-known story among students of abolitionism, Massachusetts reformers' commitment to immediatism raises two important but unexamined questions about the evolution of abolitionist strategies in the 1820s and 1830s. Why did the NEASS overtake the Pennsylvania Abolition Society (PAS), America's inaugural abolitionist organization, as the leader of the national cause? And why did Massachusetts reformers, most of whom initially supported the American Colonization Society (ACS), repudiate colonization in favor of immediatism? At the heart of these twin dilemmas lurked the issue of race.[3]

Colonization's explosion as a reform strategy in the 1820s brought new national attention to the antislavery cause, particularly in Massachusetts.[4] But it also portrayed blacks (not just slavery) as America's enduring problem. "The rapid increase of the black population in some parts of our country," a pro-colonization group wrote from Boston in 1822, "is becoming every year more serious." Unless Americans solved this explosive threat, blacks would "predominate over those who hold them in servitude." Down the road, these growing black masses would threaten northern society, too. Expatriation was the vital answer to America's looming racial storm.[5]

Whereas African Americans fought colonization virtually alone in the 1820s, they were eventually joined by dissidents from both the ACS and the PAS. Looking for more "race-conscious" strategies than either of the two groups offered, these disparate reformers gravitated toward one another to establish a new antislavery society. Only by incorporating African Americans into the broader antislavery community, they came to believe, would abolitionists finally rout slavery. And only by inaugurating an age of *immediate* racial vindication could they destroy "unholy and vindictive prejudice against people of color" *everywhere* in American culture.[6]

PRIOR TO THE ADVENT of the American Colonization Society in 1817, Massachusetts contained no formal antislavery organization. In the 1790s the PAS had urged Massachusetts leaders to form an anti-slave-trading society, although Bay Staters continually backed away. The Reverend Jeremy Belknap, the prominent Boston reformer, balked at the notion of creating a society in Massachusetts to fight southern slavery. The very idea seemed "unconstitutional" to him, as slavery remained a state concern; it was completely out of the hands of northern reformers and the federal government alike.[7]

Nevertheless, some early national leaders in Massachusetts opposed slavery in the abstract. "Slavery is utterly unreconcilable with the principle that all men are free," a correspondent wrote to the *Massachusetts Centinel* in 1788. "Are millions of the human race to be doomed to a life of unmerited misery," he asked (referring to the Constitutional Convention's compromise with southern bondage), "in order to fill the bags of avarice?" "No man abhors that wicked practice more than I do," the Reverend Isaac Backus lectured the Massachusetts Ratifying Convention, although he conceded slavery's sanctity in the new American Union. Thirty years later, the Reverend John Kenrick of Newton, Massachusetts, produced a pamphlet entitled *The Horrors of Slavery*, which depicted southern bondage as a moral wasteland of sin and evil. Kenrick pleaded with American citizens and governing elites not to "overlook or deny" the country's slavery problem. "Such is the inconsistency of the white inhabitants of the United States," Kenrick complained, "that they would treat their brethren of a different color as PROPERTY, to be bought and sold like oxen and horses."[8]

The Missouri Compromise sparked a new wave of antislavery sentiment in Massachusetts. Fearful of slaveholders' growing congressional strength, politicians throughout New England held anti-Missouri town meetings and distributed pamphlets opposing slavery's spread into new territories. Missouri's admission as a slave state, Bay State officials asserted, would bolster the South's political power and threaten white liberties at the same time. "It is too obvious," one congressional representative wrote in March 1820, "that there is an unmanly jealously maintained by southern politicians against their brethren in the north and insidious attempts made to keep the eastern section of the Union [down]." If this continued, he sneered, "those from our quarter will have to bow to those who have slaves."[9]

Inspired by national debate on the subject, the Reverend Timothy Harris of Dorchester, Massachusetts (just outside of Boston), began collecting materials on slavery and the slave trade to use in sermons and letters to benevolent friends. "The very name of slavery is odious to the ear," began one of Harris's sermons, "and conveys the complex notion of everything that is humiliating, disgraceful and wretched." Celebrated clergymen William Ellery Channing also began focusing on the issue during the 1820s. "[Parson Channing] preached a sermon about slavery which was quite scandalous," a Boston woman wrote in the mid-1820s; his parishioners could not stop discussing it. With new attention being paid to slavery, some New Englanders felt that they should become more involved in antislavery activities. "With many others of the Northern people," a Maine reformer proclaimed, "I have long entertained erroneous views. I have supposed that slavery was an evil confined merely to the slave-holder himself, and that he might and ought immediately to manumit his slaves. But I am [now] convinced that slavery is a National sin!"[10]

Yet an old problem remained: how could northern nonslaveholders become active participants in a seemingly southern issue? "I regard domestic slavery as one of the greatest evils, both moral and political," Daniel Webster wrote, "but though it is a malady, I leave it to those whose right and duty it is to decide": southern masters. "This has been uniformly the sentiment of the North," he went on, "and must continue to be."[11]

Colonization offered the Holy Grail to Massachusetts citizens interested in ending bondage without hurting the South or the political Union. "It is some times said by the desponding," a young Isaac Knapp, soon to be William Lloyd Garrison's partner at the *Liberator*, observed in 1827, "that slavery is too great an evil to be gotten rid of." Expatriation of blacks offered hope to African Americans, masters, and the entire country that this "great, formidable evil of slavery could be expunged." By exporting free blacks and then slaves, colonization would inspire southerners to rid themselves of slavery voluntarily, thus joining northerners in this "great [national] project." The ACS, Caleb Cushing told the Massachusetts Colonization Society in the early 1830s, respected "the rights of the south" while simultaneously "encouraging a fair solution" to the slavery problem. Northern supporters of the ACS, Cushing soothingly observed, would thus not upset "the very fundamental conditions of the Union" or the Constitution.[12]

Although some slaveholders worried about colonization's links to a coercive central government, many Bay Staters made clear that they would not force the matter on the South. "What is to be done with the great moral evil of slavery? NOTHING, NOTHING! Out of the slaveholding states," a Boston colonizationist thundered on one occasion. While cheering for slavery's removal from the land of the free and supporting colonization as a means to this end, Governor Edward Everett also sought to sooth southern fears about potentially meddlesome northerners. Noninterference in southern slavery "is the law, is the duty, is the INTEREST of every northern man," he argued. "The principle of anti-slavery is right," the procolonizationist "Africaner" wrote, in a Portland, Maine, newspaper, but reformers must not invade states' "individual sovereignties" to rout bondage. "Let us not press usurpation into the service of humanity, for it will produce yet more evil." The *Springfield Gazette* favored colonization but not if it entailed coercive government. "Slavery is an evil," one editorial observed, "but the nation has nothing to do with it" short of providing moral and financial support to the ACS.[13]

Between 1817 and the early 1830s, the ACS gained increasing support in Massachusetts. A group of twelve Bostonians inaugurated the city's first auxiliary organization in 1823, pledging to work for the cause in and around the Bay State. In Andover, near the Maine border, a group of ministers started the Society of Inquiry as another auxiliary to the ACS. According to one of the society's early petitions, colonization would not only drain southern bondage but also "restore the African to his rights" by returning him to the land of his ancestors. Across the state in Springfield, local citizens created the Hampden Colonization Society, which would become one of the largest auxiliaries in Massachusetts. Testifying to their belief in the ACS, several members of the Hampden society offered personal donations of fifty, one hundred, and one thousand dollars each in one fund drive of 1830.[14] Well-known figures joined middling men as ACS supporters in Massachusetts. While, for example, prominent Bay Staters Edward Everett and Daniel Webster became national spokesmen for the ACS, the young printer William Lloyd Garrison advocated colonization "as a means to righting the wrongs that our slaves endure." "I am sick of our unmeaning declamations in praise of liberty . . . and the rights of man," he observed in a July 1829 lecture in Boston. "Establishing auxiliary colonization societies in every state, county and town" of America, he concluded, would finally put slavery on the path to total destruction. Amos A. Phelps, a Yale-educated minister who began his clerical career at Andover Theological Seminary (before taking over Boston's Pine Street Church in the early 1830s), called colonization "one of the most prominent if not the only effectual means of . . . eradicating [slavery and the slave trade] and restoring the African to his long lost rights." Joining the Society of Inquiry in Andover, Phelps helped draft ACS petitions and recruit new members to the cause.[15]

In addition to garnering popular support, colonization gained the sanction of the Massachusetts General Assembly. "The legislature views with great interest the efforts made by the American Colonization Society," an 1828 report began. "Eminently deserving the attention and aid of Congress," not to mention benevolent citizens everywhere, the legislature declared the ACS to be America's great antislavery hope.[16]

In its early growth and popularity, Massachusetts colonization exemplified what Garrison labeled the national "colonization mania" of the 1820s and early 1830s. Auxiliary groups exploded throughout the Union, as the American Colonization Society never tired of pointing out. From a single organization in 1817, the ACS spawned over two hundred local and state societies by 1831. Clergymen, newspaper editors, and politicians North and South praised the ACS for "labouring in the cause of humanity," and state governments passed formal resolutions supporting the society. "At no time since the origin of this institution," the ACS reported in 1828, "have the managers of the . . . Society . . . appeared before [the public] with such entire confidence in the ultimate success of their scheme."[17]

In fact, for the first time since the Revolutionary era, American leaders seemed confident that they would eradicate slavery. By encouraging the "spirit of emancipation" among all classes of people and in all sections of the Union, Caleb Cushing proclaimed at the July 1833 meeting in Boston, the ACS produced a national consensus about *how* to attack southern bondage. "There is not," a Vermont editor concluded, "another benevolent enterprise on earth so well calculated to secure the favorable opinion and enlist the hearty good will of all men, as is this, when its objects and hearings are fully understood."[18]

SEEMING CONSENSUS notwithstanding, Massachusetts colonizationists divided over one key issue by 1830: Were blacks the problem or was slavery? Many colonizationists argued that African Americans could not live peaceably with whites, that blacks were as much of a problem as bondage itself. Edward Everett called free blacks "ignorant and needy," two factors that led them "as a class" to, as he put it, commit a disproportionate percentage of crimes. Although they constituted only "one-seventy-fifth of the [Bay State's] population," he claimed that they accounted for nearly "one-sixth of its criminal offenses." Colonization, he argued, could solve both the North's and the South's racial problems.[19]

For many northerners, Everett had it right: free blacks represented a troubling presence. Gradual abolition schemes and emigration of blacks from slave to free states had produced palpable increases in northern black communities. That meant vexatious relations between black and white people. In Massachusetts, for example, black inhabitants increased sevenfold during the early national period, even though African Americans still comprised a small percentage of the total population.[20] "Much is said nowadays about the amalgamation of white and black, as though some folks would like to see the bars of distinction thrown down," a correspondent warned in a Plymouth, Massachusetts, paper. This "inexcusable disregard for caste" (a by-product of abolition) should not be tolerated in American society. If southern abolition occurred without colonization, one Massachusetts congressman worried, then "amalgamationist" trends would only worsen as emancipated blacks moved to northern states. "It will then be important that [our state constitutions] will have a DISTINCTION," he concluded, between the rights of black and white men.[21]

Even those Bay Staters who disliked such explicitly prejudicial statements agreed that masses of blacks could not live peaceably in white society. "It is impossible to deny that [free blacks] in the United States labor under disadvantages arising from color," Caleb Cushing declared at the 1833 Fourth of July celebration in Boston, "which no System of Laws, however just and equal . . . can remove." "Proceeding upon this incontestable fact," he continued, "the Colonization Society says to the freed colored inhabitants: 'We offer you a secure asylum in a land congenial to your physical Constitution, where you will be a dominant race . . . in the land of your fathers.'"[22]

Other northern colonizationists became increasingly restive about the panacea. Isaac Knapp, a member of the Hampden society in Springfield, claimed that colonization would be a "great [abolitionist] project" that would harm neither masters nor free blacks. Yet he also declared that reformers should not force any free black man to leave "his" country. Garrison rejected colonization after only a few months in the ACS's ranks. "My thoughts on [that] scheme can be summed up in a single sentence," he wrote later in 1832: "[The ACS] has an antipathy against blacks. They do not wish to admit them to equality." Amos Phelps had a similar epiphany, which led to serious disagreements with fellow members of the Society of Inquiry in Andover. Phelps tried unsuccessfully to get the society to condemn white prejudice as the root cause of black inequality. In his original draft of an 1829 "Report of the Colonization Committee of the Society of Inquiry," for instance, Phelps wrote that white "ignorance, prejudice and self-interest" had produced black oppression. The "enemies of African rights" erected tremendous obstacles to black uplift throughout American culture. Until white Americans addressed their psychological prejudices against color, racism and slavery would operate unchecked. The society excised Phelps's comments from the final report. Instead, "The Colonization committee . . . would direct your attention to the scheme of colonization, believing it to be the most promising . . . means of restoring to the African his rights." Like Garrison, Phelps was leaving his former colonizationist allies behind.[23]

Meetings with black activists in Boston, Philadelphia, New York, and Baltimore helped to transform disaffected Massachusetts colonizationists into advocates for total racial justice. As Garrison wrote in his celebrated pamphlet, *Thoughts on African Colonization*, "the mass of evidence" from "the people of color" convinced him beyond doubt that the ACS only intensified antiblack feelings in America. Garrison's attack on the society reprinted thirty-three pages of black anticolonization reports from over twenty different African American communities around the nation (collected for him largely by black activists James Forten and William Watkins). "This exhibition should kindle a righteous indignation" in the hearts of every freedom-loving American, Garrison observed, for it had profoundly affected him. "It is [now] the sacred duty of the nation to abolish slavery and to recognize the people of color as *brethren and countrymen*," he rousingly concluded.[24]

After becoming Benjamin Lundy's editorial assistant at the *Genius of Universal Emancipation* in 1829, Garrison was in constant touch with black activists. Following Lundy to the paper's home base in Maryland, he shared a rooming house with William Watkins, of Baltimore, with whom he discussed both colonization and abolitionism. Lundy also took his young protégé to Philadelphia, where the two sat in on PAS meetings. Garrison formed a friendship with Thomas Shipley, who put the young editor in contact with influential members of Philadelphia's black community, including James Forten. When Garrison returned to Boston to start the *Liberator* in 1830, he met James Barbadoes and Nathaniel Paul, read David Walker's famous *Appeal in Four Articles: Together with a Preamble to the Colored Citizens of the World* (1829), and began soliciting money and essays for the *Liberator* from black contacts in Providence, New York, Boston, Philadelphia, and Baltimore.[25]

Before inaugurating his own paper, Garrison's anticolonization editorials in the *Genius* revealed his new strategy of radical racial vindication. In brief comments on national events as well as replies to letter writers, he sympathized with black activists over and against colonizationists or slave masters. When, for example, "A Citizen of the District" wrote that the "complaints and declarations from every quarter of the country" illustrated the folly of manumission-without-extradition, Garrison fumed, "So much for the thoughts of a slaveholder!" Far from supporting black expatriation, he countered, Americans must condemn "the severe reproaches . . . heaped upon our free coloured population" by colonizationists and apathetic masters.[26]

With similar zeal, Garrison lashed out at white abolitionists who backed down from confronting colonization and praised those who were "UNCOMPROMISING in their opposition to slavery" and to "slanders" against free blacks. A congressional report denying the efficacy of abolishing slavery in the District of Columbia, reprinted in the *Genius* in January 1830, brought howls from Garrison. In response, he pointed to the report's "total destitution of sympathy for the oppressed," as well as the American government's hypocrisy for not immediately outlawing slavery in the nation's capital. Was there "no shame for inconsistency in [our] government," he wondered, for so clearly ignoring black pleas for justice?[27]

As he pointed out in letters, essays, and speeches, blacks became one of Garrison's primary sources of support and inspiration during the early 1830s. He called black activists like Robert Purvis "coadjutors" of a new abolitionist era. To facilitate plans for a national abolition society in 1832, Garrison "consulted" black reformers, attended black conventions, and printed black writers' essays in the *Liberator*. "The colored people begin to feel their strength and to use it," he wrote after a "stunning" meeting of black activists in Philadelphia. "The proceedings of this convention, when published, will command the attention of the entire country," he professed, "exciting" reformers everywhere. "Nothing encourages me more," he informed a trio of black Bostonians, "than to witness the singular unanimity which everywhere exists among my colored brethren [in support of immediate abolitionism]."[28]

Garrison admitted that black financial support kept the *Liberator* afloat. "It is good to know that [blacks] look up to the press as the great instrument . . . of their restoration," he wrote in 1832. Of the nearly 400 first-year subscribers, Garrison tabulated that three-quarters were black, with "my colored brethren" in Philadelphia and Boston providing over 150 subscriptions alone in the first few months of operation. For Garrison, immediate abolitionism had an undeniably black foundation.[29]

As another member of the New England Anti-Slavery Society who turned his back on the ACS, Amos Phelps spoke again and again of blacks' inspirational activism. Garrison's *Thoughts on Colonization*, with its striking black views, impressed Phelps no end. On lecture tours through Massachusetts, Connecticut, Pennsylvania, and Maryland, Phelps continually met with black activists (including James Forten, William Watkins, Robert Purvis, and James Barbadoes). Invited to attend a "convention called to organize a national anti-slavery society" in Philadelphia in 1833, Phelps spoke of "spirited" and moving meetings with the local black community. Returning to Boston, he dined with black reformers, spoke to communities north and south of the city, and published his own influential works on slavery and racial justice. By 1834, when Phelps wrote his seminal treatise on immediate abolition, *Lectures on Slavery and Its Remedy*, he would insist that modern abolitionists must pledge that "slaveholding is a heinous crime against God and man" and "recognize in every colored man a neighbor and a brother in the fullest sense of the terms."[30]

Phelps provided a natural law condemnation of American slavery that became a standard part of antislavery discourse after his book appeared. This definition, one abolitionist wrote, "enabled us to sweep away AT ONCE a whole brood" of antiabolitionists theories, comparing slavery to "the relationship between man and child [or] criminal and magistrate." Slavery was "a sin against God and a crime against man." Phelps's theory, "so simple as to exclude cavils," "was taken up by all the antislavery speakers." Few abolitionists who came to prominence in the early 1830s (white, black, female) were unfamiliar with it.[31]

Samuel May, one of the most ardent antebellum immediatists, also migrated from his colonizationist beliefs to a more racially conscious stand on slavery and black civil rights. In 1829 May had created a local colonization group in Brooklyn, Connecticut. "Although May opposed slavery," his biographer Donald Yacovone writes, "little evidence exists that he invested much energy . . . in combatting . . . American racial attitudes." In 1830, however, May heard one of Garrison's fiery attacks on southern bondage and American racism and vowed to support the cause. "It is OUR prejudice against . . . color . . . that makes US consent to the tremendous wrongs [blacks] are suffering" both in the South and in the North. In a "bombshell," May declared that bringing justice to black Americans should have priority over every other national concern, including a unified American republic.[32]

As leaders of the New England Anti-Slavery Society during the 1830s, Garrison, Phelps, and May went on to convert scores of other immediate abolitionists.[33] The strategy of seeking complete racial vindication inspired Americans who did not agree with the ACS but had no alternative. Immediatism inspired even the most skeptical locals in Massachusetts. "Why do you have that Garrison in your cause?" a woman near Concord asked a NEASS agent in 1835. "After more talk about the sacrifices of Garrison," the agent remarked, "she exclaimed, 'he ought to be canonized!'" So convinced was she of Garrison's racial righteousness, the woman vowed to subscribe to *The Liberator*, fight for blacks' rights in her village, and tell friends to join abolition societies. "Just a few minutes of conversation [about the new] anti-slavery cause," the agent bragged, had "totally revolutionized" her thinking.[34]

JUST AS MASSACHUSETTS colonizationists divided over the meaning of race in the American Colonization Society, a small but important group of dissidents raised the same issue in the world's inaugural abolitionist organization, the Pennsylvania Abolition Society. Why, dissidents like Thomas Shipley, Arnold Buffum, and Thomas Earle began to ask, did the PAS tolerate colonizationism? Why did it remain aloof while black activists in Philadelphia held public meetings condemning the ACS and demanding that Americans accept blacks everywhere as true equals? And why did the PAS refuse to consider black reformers as coworkers in the larger antislavery community?

In the 1820s and early 1830s Pennsylvania became a hotbed of colonization as auxiliary societies spread rapidly throughout the state. By 1831 Pennsylvanians had formed over eighty local groups, more than a third of all national auxiliaries. In addition, newspapers provided positive coverage of the ACS, and prominent citizens offered monetary support to black expatriation plans. Most importantly, perhaps, increasingly confident colonizationists put the PAS on the defensive by questioning the motives of even gradual abolitionists. "National Emancipation," the *Pennsylvanian* editorialized, would be unthinkable "without extirpating" blacks, for African Americans could never be full members of civil society. Northern communities would face hoards of migrating blacks if southern slaveholders relinquished their chattels — and northerners, the paper claimed, had enough concerns about free blacks already residing in the Quaker State. Indeed, Pennsylvania's gradual abolition experiment had produced a free black class of vagrants, drunks, and criminals.[35]

The only thing more foolhardy than gradual emancipation was immediate abolition, "a wild and visionary scheme that will set the Potomac on fire," in the words of the *Pennsylvanian*. Immediatism would force "every slaveholder to release his sable thrall and offer his throat meekly to the knife of the semi-savage, maddened with the possession of the Liberty he is incapable of appreciating or comprehending." After rampaging in southern white communities, black "semi-savages" would invade northern communities. No white citizen of America would be safe.[36]

Philadelphia jurist J. R. Tyson told the Young Man's Colonization Society of Philadelphia that "legal emancipation" had failed even in the North. While the original motives of the PAS should be respected, Tyson asked if "it is unfair to doubt the final result of emancipation" in Pennsylvania when (according to him) black crime, unemployment, and vagrancy rates exceeded that of the lowest class of whites? Free blacks, like their enslaved cohorts, suffered from a "low scale of moral virtue." Although a professed friend of "the African," reformers should no longer waste time or money on useless abolitionist strategies. "No, the facts cannot be reasoned against," Tyson concluded, "the moral inferiority of the black man" prevents his being integrated into white society. Colonization must be American reformers' new watchword.[37]

"Rational colonizationists" claimed to have the only sensible plan, for they "would drain off the [entire] black population gradually." As the Reverend Gregory Bedell argued at one local ACS meeting, colonization offered "the ONLY reasonable and unobjectionable method of freeing the land of the curse of slavery and free people of color." *Poulson's Daily Advertiser*, long friendly to the PAS, disavowed the ACS's attack on free blacks. But even its editor reluctantly agreed that colonization seemed to be the best solution for ending American slavery and racial discord.[38]

The PAS never publicly rebuked the ACS's antiblack stereotypes, as members of Philadelphia's African American community had hoped. Although the PAS conceded that America's "prejudices and customs . . . exclude [blacks] from . . . many of the advantages which whites possess," and that colonization mistook the nature of society's racial trouble, it nevertheless agreed that black Americans needed to become more virtuous. "What can or ought to be done," one PAS report asked, about white racism? The answer was "the moral and religious *education* and *instruction* of the rising generation" of blacks. Moreover, reformers should move blacks around, although not out of the country. "Scattering" black families and individuals WITHIN American society, the PAS claimed, would loosen "the bad examples" from their present settlements. Put "among neighborhoods of whites," African Americans "would gradually derive important hints in the science of living." In other words, the PAS thought that African American citizens should accommodate to whites fears and prejudices, not confront or interrogate them. Uplift not outrage was the answer.[39]

As for colonization itself, William Rawle, the PAS's venerable president, declared the scheme ineffectual and therefore unworthy of active opposition. From a "national point of view," he wrote in 1833, "all that has been done" in behalf of colonization, "will [not] be of much importance." Yet Rawle worried about offending potential allies who, when they did reject colonization as a strategy of reform, might join the PAS. Colonization had "so many ardent friends," he commented, that confronting it might actually hurt the PAS. Too much time would be taken away from the group's legal work and too much energy expended on a pointless fight against well-meaning (and well-connected) philanthropists.[40]

Other PASers had important friends in the colonizationist camp, including clergymen, politicians, and southern slaveholders. Jonathan Roberts corresponded with a Philadelphia philanthropist who professed that the ACS remained his only "faith and hope" for getting rid of slavery.[41] With such benign motives, Roberts felt that he could not critique ACS supporters.

Still other PAS members, such as Roberts Vaux and the Reverend Charles Milnor, became colonizationists themselves.[42]

Such PAS leaders betrayed a none-too-subtle racism. "As to the Project of colonizing the Free Blacks several serious objections occur," admitted one Pennsylvania abolitionist, "but one only seems now necessary to be mentioned: the Number of faulty Blacks should greatly increase among us." Some PASers sneered at black activists who tried to become involved in the broader movement. In 1837, for example, PAS member Lindley Coates strongly objected to black activists protesting at the Pennsylvania legislature. Coates, working against a law that rescinded black voting rights, thought blacks would "do more harm than good." They should "return home," he observed, and let white men do their bidding uninterrupted.[43]

A minority of PAS leaders dissented. Arnold Buffum, for example, grew increasingly dissatisfied with the society's shrinking response to colonization and black activists' demands for acceptance in the society. Though Pennsylvania reformers had done signal service in the cause of emancipation ("abolishing the legalized foreign slave trade" and "in seven out of thirteen states" helping to craft "decrees" of "universal emancipation within their respective limits"), their failure to confront racial prejudice hampered the cause's moral weight. The PAS had let "corrupted" public sentiment and "unshaken interest" fester, Buffum complained, and had not confronted prejudice among some of its own members. Abolitionists had to embrace people of color as never before, he concluded, forcing Americans to view racism and slavery as twin parts of a broader psychological dilemma.[44]

Thomas Shipley concurred. He was not surprised that southern slavery had grown stronger, since colonization degraded African Americans on a daily basis. A new generation of slaveholders and politicians had come of age in the 1820s believing that blacks, not slavery itself, were the nation's central problem. "The great body of slaveholders," he wrote in the 1830s, "are not [now] convinced of the inherent right of the slaves to freedom and the absolute guilt . . . in holding slaves."[45] Like Buffum, Shipley drew inspiration from black reformers who challenged white Americans in moralistic terms.

Such Pennsylvania dissidents believed that the PAS could rejuvenate itself by accepting black activists as "coadjutors" of the abolitionist cause. As Thomas Earle observed in an 1824 pamphlet for English reformers, white activists would only "form a correct estimate of the real situation of slavery in this or any other country" by ignoring "the planters" and listening to blacks. "We must learn to put our stead in the souls of the poor African," he wrote, "and taste and drink and feel his wrongs." It was Earle's desire that the PAS form closer relationships with (and learn from the tactics of) Philadelphia's African American community, whose activism against colonization, southern slavery, and northern racism deserved only applause. James Forten, Quomony Clarkson, Richard Allen—these names, Earle hoped, would now be part of the broader abolitionist movement, not segregated at its periphery.[46]

Thomas Shipley and Arnold Buffum gravitated toward local black activists as well as national reformers interested in integrating abolitionism. These and other former PASers had a hand in creating the nation's inaugural "Immediate" abolition societies in the early 1830s: the New England Anti-Slavery Society and the American Anti-Slavery Society (AASS). After meeting William Lloyd Garrison through Benjamin Lundy, Shipley brought the young Massachusetts printer to Philadelphia in September 1830 to give his first public lectures on the meaning of immediatist strategies.[47] Shipley introduced Garrison to leaders in the city's African American community. Buffum likewise helped Garrison acquire black contacts, particularly subscribers to the *Liberator*. Working with local African American canvassers (including James McCrummill), Buffum forwarded hundreds of names to Garrison in the mid-1830s.

"Modern" abolitionism, as it became known, offered PAS dissidents a more thorough strategy of fighting for racial justice. Groups like the NEASS were integrated, dedicated to ending slavery immediately, and unafraid to publicly condemn American racial attitudes. In Shipley's eyes, the new anti-slavery organizations focused not only on abolishing slavery and giving blacks political rights but also on "incorporating" African Americans into American culture. Indeed, the updated abolitionist movement made the phrase "universal freedom among men" a reality by accepting African Americans as coworkers. For Buffum, Shipley, Earle, and other former PASers, the constitution of the New England Anti-Slavery Society said it all. Massachusetts abolitionists "endeavored by all legal means to abolish slavery immediately and correct public opinion by obtaining equal civil and legal privileges with the white inhabitants of this land."[48]

DRAWING FROM THREE disparate strands of leadership—former Massachusetts colonizationists, a minority of former Pennsylvania abolitionists, and black activists—the New England Anti-Slavery Society created the world's first integrated abolitionist society in 1832. The NEASS's immediatist strategy sought not simply to end slavery "at once" but "to revolution-ize public opinion" about blacks' rights. As William J. Snelling told an NEASS meeting in 1833, "[Blacks] are not treated as free men . . . or [even] political equals." This was "our fault." Did white mechanics hire black ap-prentices? he asked rhetorically. "Do we admit [blacks] to our schools?" Do they "gain a convenient seat in God's Temple?" The *Abolitionist*, the official organ of the new NEASS, likewise accused *all* Americans of holding "very unsound opinions and unchristian feelings" about blacks. Americans' "in-veterate and unchristian prejudice," the paper declared, must be shaken at its core by vitriolic public appeals and harsh condemnations. By attacking white racism at its psychological source, the NEASS hoped that it would thoroughly "destroy prejudice" in America once and for all.[49]

NEASS auxiliaries sprouting up in myriad Massachusetts towns — Haver-hill, Salem, Lynn, Plymouth — ratified this broad strategy of antiracism. The seventy members of the Scituate Anti-Slavery Society, near Plymouth, spoke for many Bay State activists when they pledged not only to seek "the immediate removal" of southern slavery by "moral influence" but also to "endeavor to correct public opinion and fight oppression by obtaining equal civil and political privileges with the white inhabitants of the land." "We owe it to the oppressed," the Scituate constitution stated.[50]

Much in the manner that blacks had done since 1817, the New England Anti-Slavery Society and its auxiliaries attacked the American Colonization Society in unyielding terms. The NEASS's first major report literally copied out anticolonization resolutions from black communities nationwide. Cit-ing innumerable black conventions, the report argued that "Vindictive prej-udice" ruled ACS operations, "persecuting" African Americans more than attacking slavery. The new generation of abolitionists, recognizing that "benevolence and prejudice . . . are opposed to each other," would stop at nothing to vindicate blacks in the eyes of American citizens.[51]

The NEASS's northern tactics forced the state legislature to change certain discriminatory laws. In the late 1830s, for example, the group had Jim Crow policies outlawed in the state's transportation facilities. In 1840 Massachu-setts abolitionists forwarded over nine thousand petitions to the General Assembly seeking the repeal of an antimiscegenation law; the legislature soon banned the code. The next year, the NEASS began a multidecade cam-paign that would eventually end segregated public schools in Massachu-setts. As Amos Phelps remarked, the NEASS would not rest until northern blacks enjoyed the same rights as every white man.

Bay State abolitionists' race-consciousness manifested itself in another tactic: the integration of abolitionist organizations after 1830. The New England Anti-Slavery Society set the standard in 1832, admitting over twenty black abolitionists to its ranks. Other immediatist groups followed, from the American Anti-Slavery Society at the national level to the Amherst (Massachusetts) College Anti-Slavery Society at the local level, as well as a number of organizations in between: female abolition societies in Boston, state antislavery societies, county and ward groups. Surveying this new interracial abolitionist landscape in 1834, one black reformer spoke of the "revolution in racial relations."[52]

The revolution also involved a new coalition of black and white women. The Boston Female Anti-Slavery Society (BFASS), cofounded by local whites and blacks in 1834, encouraged American women to seek out "our colored sisters." "Without their sympathy and confidence," the group argued, northern abolitionism would fail as a reform cause. Abolition's "opposers" might "justly call into question our sincerity" if white reformers worked without black members. And white reformers would "almost certainly" have the wrong "state of mind" without the aid of black activists.[53] The national convention of antislavery women in 1837 pressed female antislavery organizations to "invite . . . colored people to join your society." "Let us urge upon you a total abandonment of prejudice against color," exhorted the *National Enquirer*. "How can we ask our southern brethren to make sacrifices if we are not willing" to welcome blacks into the antislavery ranks? No mere "shibboleth," the national paper emphasized that integration would prove "our sincerity and consistency" as racial reformers.[54]

The Amherst (College) Anti-Slavery Society, one of several white youth groups to organize an NEASS auxiliary, also adopted race-conscious membership platforms. Like female reformers, the college group told its members to seek out black citizens. Although relatively small and short-lived (with only a few black members out of seventy-eight adherents), the Amherst society created a furor for its "exertions" with and in the name of blacks. The group held integrated "monthly prayer meetings" in nearby Springfield, agitated faculty members to become immediate abolitionists, and publicly rebuked members of a campus colonization chapter. "Believing that the free people of color are unrighteously oppressed," the society's constitution declared, "and realizing that God hath made one blood of all nations," Amherst student abolitionists vowed to revolutionize their own racial sentiments while fighting southern slavery. Indeed, they wished to "effect the emancipation of the whole colored race within the US" by attacking "unholy prejudice against blacks" in any form.[55]

Massachusetts reformers hoped that this strategy of integration would have deep societal repercussions. If other Americans saw blacks and whites working together in a national cause, they might question their own racial assumptions. Even informal "intermingling" on the lecture circuit made an important statement about fighting northern prejudice. Conservatives were outraged. According to a newspaper correspondent for the Plymouth journal *We, the People*, integrated abolitionist meetings demonstrated a flagrant disregard for racial convention. "Colored people have been seen at anti-slavery meetings intermixing with whites," he wrote, "sometimes on the same seats!" This "disregard for caste" would lead to other forms of social integration, from "walking in the street together" to "talking to each other publicly" to intermarriage. While the writer fumed, immediate abolitionists beamed.[56]

In fact, lecturers took special note of their audience's racial composition. William Lloyd Garrison spoke to mixed crowds in Boston, Philadelphia, and New York City but addressed mostly "colored inhabitants" in Providence, Rhode Island; Portland, Maine; and Middletown, Connecticut.[57] Amos Phelps and Arnold Buffum addressed both integrated and predominantly black crowds on their lecture tours of the Northeast. In addition, local antislavery groups in the Bay State sponsored black speakers from time to time. Garrison thought Simeon Jocelyn would make a valuable agent in 1833 but could not afford to pay him. In 1837 members of the Mansfield Anti-Slavery Society in southeastern Massachusetts asked Hosea Easton to be a featured speaker.[58]

In proclaiming an "entire and everlasting emancipation" from racism, Amos Phelps admitted that Bay State abolitionists would encounter "a little fear about taking the bull by the horns." "But there is NO fear that our friends will stand firm on ALL our great principles." And there was great hope that antiracism would grow even more in the North.[59]

BONDAGE WAS A "sin against god" and "a crime" against man, Massachusetts abolitionists proclaimed, and should therefore be destroyed "at once." More than a strategy of timeliness, however, immediatism signaled a possible new alliance between northern reformers and southern slaves. According to the Bay State abolitionists, bondage was a daily battle between oppressed and oppressor, the enslaved and their so-called masters. Because black individuals, families, and communities suffered under "the yoke of oppression," abolitionists had to take clear sides in this conflict to remain true to their principles. As William Lloyd Garrison announced, immediatists had no other standard than that of "righting" the enslaved, "restoring him to himself." No longer interested in "faulty" gradualist or colonizationist schemes, the new generation of abolitionists declared that they would undermine "masters' control" of "our fellow countrymen" and accelerate the total emancipation of "TWO MILLION of our enslaved brethren."[60]

The NEASS constitution of 1832 made this strategy so clear that even some of its original (white) signatories worried about the implications of immediatist doctrine. Modern reformers must politicize the master-slave relationship, the document asserted, particularly its devastating impact on black families and black lives. Slavery should be immediately banned because black "children should belong to their parents," not to tyrannical white masters; because no one should be subjected to the "tremendous power which is now vested in every slaveholder . . . [and which is used] to a savage extent"; and because slaves too, once freed, had rights to "intellectual illumination," "just wages," and a place in civil as well as political society.[61]

Abolition must become a virtual war on slavery, Garrison's even more radical "Declaration of Sentiments" for the American Anti-Slavery Society proclaimed in 1833. Abolitionists, he wrote, now actively "strived" for the liberation of "one-sixth of our countryman," people who "enjoy no constitutional or legal protection" from "murderous outrages" committed on them daily. Slaves, not simply free blacks, had the "inalienable rights of man": "a right to [their] own bodies . . . to the products of [their] labor . . . and to the common advantages of society." Slavery should be abolished, the AASS constitution went on, without *any* compensation to masters. Compensating slaveholders with money would only "surrender the great fundamental principle that man cannot hold property in man." If anything, money ought to be directed to "the outraged and guiltless slaves . . . not those who plundered and abused them." In short, immediate abolitionists saw masters' theory of property rights as immoral.[62]

Bay State activists attacked gradual abolitionists for respecting masters' property rights. Although the PAS would defend fugitive slaves to the limited extent of the law, immediatists charged that its lawyers could never conceive of a political alliance with *all* bondsmen, much less declare a moral war against slavery. William Rawle was delighted to be guilty of this charge. Disavowing property rights, he said, would frighten slaveholders and threaten abolitionist plans. In addition, such a strategy would encourage a virtual torrent of runaways to the North, overwhelming abolitionist legal aid systems. Most alarmingly, declaring explicit alliances with southern blacks might encourage servile war against whites in the South.[63]

This attitude, Amos Phelps would argue, hampered abolitionism, as PAS reformers allowed masters to keep slaves without a sense of guilt. "Slavery can never be remedied by schemes of gradual emancipation," Phelps wrote, because they were "built" on an understanding of "masters' duty" as much as "slaves' rights." This "false" and "wicked doctrine," he continued, "respected ASSUMED rights and IMAGINED interests of the master, in preference to the REAL rights . . . of the slave." If "either party is to be favored," Phelps proclaimed, it "MUST BE" the slave. Unfortunately, groups like the Pennsylvania Abolition Society had given enslaved blacks a "secondary importance"; their freedom from daily oppression took a back seat to masters' legal rights and the nation's political expediency. Immediatists, on the other hand, would make slaves' claims to freedom "the primary standard" of the abolition movement. Phelps condemned those gradualist tactics that did not explicitly sympathize "with the slave" or work for an immediate end to his or her captivity. They were "inefficient" and illusory, for they "did not lift a finger in breaking the rod of the oppressor."[64]

Whereas some Massachusetts abolitionists could slip into "romantic racialism" (a view of southern slaves as Christ-like innocents in desperate need of abolitionist redemption), many Bay State reformers idealized the enslaved as America's last true patriots: oppressed men and women whose fight for liberty should inspire the world.[65] Both Amos Phelps and Arnold Buffum, two of the NEASS's most indefatigable traveling lecturers, depicted southern blacks as a potent protest group. In his speeches to communities throughout Massachusetts in the early 1830s, Phelps portrayed fugitive slaves as political activists very much like himself. "Look at their efforts to escape," he pointed out, and slaves' "efforts to get their friends free." These heroic actions evinced a "general disposition" to be liberated from tyranny, a far cry from the picture of black apathy and contentment projected by slaveholders. Abolitionists, Phelps thundered, had to politicize this "inadvertent testimony" of runaway slaves, for it offered convincing proof that blacks — like any human being held down — longed to be free.[66]

Buffum echoed Phelps, telling his audiences that black slaves would leave their masters were it not for the constant threats of physical violence. Southern slaves, like the Haitian rebels or American Revolutionaries themselves, acted on the same "liberal principles" that animated revolutions throughout the Western world. William Lloyd Garrison linked America's historic struggle for freedom with southern slaves' valiant fight. "What kindled the fires of Seventy-Six? Oppression! What has infuriated the southern slaves? OPPRESSION!" Slaves, Garrison wrote, knew the words of the Declaration of Independence as well as anyone: "'All men are created equal, and endowed by their Creator with certain inalienable rights: among which are life, liberty, and the pursuit of happiness!'"[67]

Unlike previous generations of chary reformers, modern abolitionists would use black resistance to undermine bondage, "the most flagrant violation of every principle of justice and humanity." One traveling lecturer told a Philadelphia crowd that even returned runaways served a vital political function as "missionaries or apostles to the poor slaves, for they carry with them the knowledge of freedom. . . . For every one carried back into slavery," he went on, "many, many, very many, [will] learn how to become free themselves." Working with reclaimed fugitives, abolitionists could indeed "break every yoke" of slavery by encouraging black dissent from inside the South itself.[68]

Black activists stories of the emotional, physical, and psychological effects of bondage helped Massachusetts abolitionists portray southern slaves as freedom fighters. James Bradley, a former Alabama slave who purchased his own freedom and then worked with northern reformers, wrote a brief narrative for Lydia Maria Child, who recounted the story in her own writings. "Liberty is all the slave thinks about," Bradley observed, "why would anyone think differently."[69] Isaac Knapp published Olaudah Equiano's slave narrative (unpublished by American printers for decades) to provide what Charles Burleigh called a "black man's" vantage point of bondage.[70] David Lee Child appended actual depositions of kidnapped blacks to his 1833 pamphlet, *The Despotism of Freedom* to illustrate the inherent violence done to slaves by southern masters. In one document, James Barbadoes recited the story of his son's abduction in New Orleans. Not only was he "handcuffed and chained" as a suspected fugitive slave, "but [also he was] often severely flogged" for claiming "that he was free born." Almost given up for dead, the younger Barbadoes had the incredible good fortune to be put in a cell with another "free black man" (who had also been taken from "this so-called paradise of freedom"), who communicated the son's whereabouts to his parents in the North. After gaining his son's freedom, James Barbados circulated his story for abolitionist purposes.[71]

Child used the account to raise northerners' ire. He told an audience in South Reading, Massachusetts, that white citizens must look across the color line and understand the paradox of "the republican slave." Would whites endure oppression and violence without seeking redress? Of course not, Child answered. Then why, he asked, did they permit the slavery of black men to go unchecked? "The annual number of colored people who come to an untimely end in consequence of 'due correction' or 'moderate whipping' must be beyond any conception which we have formed on the subject," he observed. "A single such instance permitted by a community to go unpunished ought to arouse the attention and excite the active exertions of the whole country," Child went on. "But no such condition exists in this republic. I have never heard of a white [master] being impartially punished for the murder of a colored man."[72]

Immediatism's all encompassing ideology provided a solution: give southern slaves the same liberties that any white citizen would demand, including trial-by-jury guarantees, the protection of all civil and penal laws, and the right to participate in elections and governance (once freed). According to Child, rights and liberties knew neither geographic nor racial distinctions. White citizens of the republic *must* be made to see this as a truism.

The remedy for Child and his colleagues at the NEASS thus was to give all blacks immediate citizenship: southern blacks by emancipation, education, and integration into civil and political society and northern free blacks by social and political integration. Let white Americans remember that "the mass of our ancestors were once slaves," Child finished. "In this they were like southern slaves": no property rights, no political voice, no protections to life or liberty. Total emancipation succeeded with whites; so, too, must it succeed with southern blacks.[73]

With the master-slave relationship depicted in such combative terms and with abolitionists now taking a public vow of allegiance to none other than southern slaves, thoughts of violence seeped into the minds of some Massachusetts reformers. But most of them repudiated that solution. Garrison himself declaimed violent means at the outset of the immediatist era, rebuking David Walker's allusions to insurrection in his short review of Walker's *Appeal*. "We shall advocate immediate abolition," the *Abolitionist* asserted in 1833, though its readers "should not startle at the words." Explaining that slavery contradicted both God's will and man's natural rights, the paper pointed out that immediatist reformers did not seek "to excite the slaves to insurrection." "[Articles] with such an object in mind," the piece sternly warned, "will find no admission in *The Abolitionist*, and receive from it nothing but reprobation."[74] Amos A. Phelps, Samuel J. May, Arnold Buffum, Charles C. Burleigh — nearly every leader to emerge during abolition's transitional period between 1830 and 1835 — disavowed violence.

Yet some Massachusetts leaders accepted the slave's right to use extreme force. Because bondage itself was so violent and horrifying, some white activists admitted that slaves might have a theoretical right to revolt or to respond to physical violence in kind. "The Constitution of the American Anti-Slavery Society contains the usual pledge that we will NOT countenance the SLAVES in a resort to force," Ellis Grey Loring of Boston wrote to famed New England cleric William Ellery Channing, "yet you cannot deny their abstract right" to self-defense. "There is no question that the chains of American slavery must be broken," an essayist in *Plymouth, We the People*, asserted. "And if [this] cannot be done by high and noble sacrifice, it will be done by VIOLENCE in some form."[75]

Part of the dilemma for modern reformers stemmed from their commitment to natural rights principles as embodied in the Declaration of Independence, which valorized liberation of the oppressed. Even Benjamin Lundy, who consistently opposed violent means from his debut as an abolitionist editor in the 1820s onward, felt compelled to reexamine the Declaration in the wake of major slave revolts, admitting that he found nothing to condemn in Denmark Vesey or Nat Turner. Similarly, Arnold Buffum recalled a public debate at which he had an epiphany about violence by slaves in the abstract. As Buffum wrote to Garrison, a supporter of colonization accused modern abolitionists of encouraging servile insurrection by claiming that slaves had the same natural rights as whites. "Suppose slaves aboard a ship" adopted the immediatist banner, Buffum's colonizationist opponent shouted to a Massachusetts audience, "that all slaves had a right to freedom"—would not they "murder the [white] officers and . . . drive the boat to the bottom of the sea?" "I almost exclaimed," Buffum wrote, "'then joy to the tempest that whelms them beneath and makes their destruction.'"[76]

Garrison himself straddled the line of violence, rejecting it as a broad strategy and simultaneously sympathizing with the enslaved who resorted to extreme measures. "We are horror struck at the late tidings" in Virginia, Garrison editorialized in the *Liberator* following Nat Turner's uprising. But now that Turner's armies had been "killed and routed," he asked Americans to "remember" the violence and harm done to *all* slaves in the first place: "In our fury against the revolters, who will remember their wrongs? the catalogue of their sufferings, their lacerated bodies. Is it enough that the victims were black—that circumstance makes them less precious than dogs?" Why would Americans criticize any "black brutes [for] pretending to be men?" Because, Garrison answered (mimicking whites), "God made them to serve us! They are black."[77]

"Ye patriotic hypocrites," he fumed, "ye fustian declaimers for liberty! Cast no reproach upon the conduct of the slaves, but let your own lips and cheeks wear the blisters of condemnation." Abolitionists wrote nothing "to justify the excess of the slaves," for oppressed blacks "need no incentives at our hands." Any horrified American should reexamine his own Revolutionary tradition, which venerated freedom fighters. Southern slaveholders need look no further than the paradoxes surrounding their own plantations, where slaves' "emaciated bodies . . . toiled" near men whose "fathers have fought for liberty" and who themselves cited "liberty . . . in [their] speeches, pamphlets and newspapers. . . . Surrounded by such influences, and smarting under their newly made wounds, is it wonderful that they should rise to contend—as other HEROES have contended—for their lost rights?"[78]

Garrison did not think slave rebellion altogether "wonderful," but he wanted Americans to understand that southern blacks, like any oppressed peoples, longed for freedom. Race made no difference, he cautioned, for just as white Americans would want speedy relief from tyranny, so too did blacks. "Immediate emancipation," he pleaded, "alone can save [America] from the Vengeance of heaven and cancel the debt of ages." In a tone eerily reminiscent of David Walker, Garrison warned: "wo to this land, unless she speedily repents her evil doings! [For] the blood of millions of her sons cries aloud for redress."[79]

In speaking of slavery in violent language, in confronting slaveholders as "criminals," tyrants, and hypocrites, and in explicitly aligning themselves with "the slave-restoring him to himself," abolitionists conveyed the importance of immediate action against a "cruel and despotic" institution. As Amos Phelps prodded his audiences, Americans should ever think of slavery as "a robbery of human rights! A ROBBERY OF THE WORST KIND!"[80]

THE ADVENT OF immediatism in the early 1830s represented a divergence in core abolitionist strategies about northern racism, about southern slaves, and about the struggle against slavery itself. Whereas the early movement emphasized "conscientious emancipation" (working in slow but sure legal ways to destroy bondage), the later movement revolved around broad concepts of social justice for all blacks, slave as well as free. Indeed, for the first time in American abolitionism, white reformers publicly embraced northern black activists and southern slaves. As the NEASS announced in 1832, immediate abolitionists fought "for the enforcement of that clause in the

Declaration of Independence which asserts 'that ALL men are created equal, that they are endowed by their Creator with inalienable rights, among which are life, liberty, and the pursuit of happiness.'" This translated into "the instant recognition of EVERY American-born citizen, as a countryman and brother!"[81] For black and white activists alike, immediatism provided the strategic outlook needed to eradicate racial injustice from the American polity and create a multiracial democracy.[82]

Thomas Shipley tried unsuccessfully to bring the PAS into this multiracial immediatist age in the 1830s. Tabling motions to alter the society's constitution, a PAS Quarterly Meeting resolved that it would be "inexpedient" for Pennsylvania abolitionists to embrace immediatism in any way, shape, or form. In the PAS's eyes, immediatism signaled not simply "immediate attacks" on bondage but unacceptable new tactics: politicizing fugitive slave cases, using black narratives of bondage to sway public sympathy, even empathizing with black revolutionary action in Haiti![83]

Garrisonian allies in Pennsylvania, such as Lucretia Mott, excoriated the PAS as "half-way" abolitionists. The venerable group may have inaugurated organized abolitionism in the Revolutionary age, but Pennsylvania reformers remained stuck in a bygone era: they refused to work with black reformers or to embrace confrontational tactics on blacks' behalf. According to Mott, African Americans knew who "the real Philadelphia abolitionists" were: immediate or "thorough" reformers.[84]

Befitting a romantic age of absolute commitments, Massachusetts reformers declared a metaphoric war on bondage. The PAS, much less the American Colonization Society, could never sanction such a tactic. Second-wave abolitionists most assuredly could—and that was what immediatism was all about.

CHAPTER SIX

The New Abolitionist Imperative

Mass Action Strategies

We have met tonight in this obscure school-house; our numbers
are few and our influence limited; but mark my prediction,
Fanueil Hall shall ere long echo with the principles we have set forth.
We shall shake the Nation by their mighty power.
— William Lloyd Garrison after the founding of
the New England Anti-Slavery Society, January 1, 1832

[The most recent abolitionist petition has 65,000 signatures on it and]
is three feet in height. . . . When John Quincy Adams stands up
[to present it], it is a foot above his head. . . . The southern members . . .
consider it an international insult.
— Massachusetts congressman Leverett Saltonstall to his wife, Mary,
February 22, 1843, on the presentation of the Latimer Petition in Congress

ALTHOUGH IMMEDIATISM garnered most of the headlines, Bay State
reformers inaugurated another important strategy in the 1830s: mass action. Whatever tactics they employed, whatever arguments they made,
Massachusetts abolitionists hoped to rouse the people to end slavery. "To
mount up the Abolition heat," Henry Stanton proclaimed, "[we] must
warm up . . . the people. . . . Our speeches, our publications, our Societies,
our Conventions and our prayers are kindling up a sacred fire that shall
cause the public mind to glow . . . and our public servants to feel its
warming influence." For the first time, abolitionists sought to make their
movement one of the people, by the people, and for the people.[1]

In this first mass democratic age, Bay State abolitionists became supreme
organizers and agitators. Starting with the twelve original members of the
New England Anti-Slavery Society (NEASS) in 1832, their two hundred

auxiliary societies mobilized thousands of supporters in Massachusetts over the next decade. Sending dozens of lecturers to every city, town, and village possible, gathering tens of thousands of petition signatures, and diffusing hundreds of thousands of pamphlets, they "awakened the country" to the evils of slavery as never before.[2] A popular revolt against slavery, modern abolitionists predicted, was at hand.

But how could these numbers attack southern bondage? "My fellow citizens," David Lee Child lectured one crowd, "'We the people' might AMEND the Constitution," or force Congress to ban slavery in the federally controlled District of Columbia, or compel northern legislators to bar southern masters from reclaiming fugitive slaves.[3] Other Bay State activists agreed. Far from being mere "moral suasionists," they would mobilize the masses to slay bondage.

SAMUEL MAY'S comments captured William Lloyd Garrison's place in the pantheon of nineteenth-century heroes. Speaking at Garrison's funeral in 1879, May observed that most reformers would simply say that they were "glad to have walked the earth when he did."[4] Garrison was the first white abolitionist who spoke adamantly about turning abolitionism into a forceful public movement. As he proclaimed on one occasion in 1829, the American people must be made to "come alive" on abolition.[5] In that way alone, politicians, lawyers, and public officials would be forced at long last to reconcile slavery and freedom in American society. In short, Garrison startled other reformers by arguing that the general public, not the legal and political elite, could become the nation's liberator.

Garrison's mass action strategy initially took shape at Benjamin Lundy's *Genius of Universal Emancipation.* Although Garrison spent less than a year as coeditor of Lundy's paper (then headquartered in Baltimore), he gained invaluable lessons and inspiration. Setting the weekly pages of the *Genius* in 1829 was like printing a map on abolition's current state as well as its future possibilities. Garrison could see, for instance, that Pennsylvania abolitionists' deferential petitioning strategy had failed to break congressional apathy on the slavery issue. He could also see that women and blacks, excluded from existing abolitionist societies, had begun forming their own antislavery organizations. Furthermore, he could visualize the fight against slavery fragmenting into hundreds of tiny pieces, each with its own strategy, none with an overarching direction.

Mass action provided the antidote. By creating a grassroots, unified national movement, abolitionists could agitate efficiently and effectively. Everyone would work on similar goals: ending the domestic slave trade, banning slavery in federally controlled territories, pressuring slaveholders to support abolitionist legislation. "The Friends of the cause must go to work," Garrison counseled, by circulating "petitions and remonstrances" to fellow citizens, disseminating "facts and arguments" about slavery's horrors, and encouraging a popular movement aimed at southerners. Mobilizing the masses, he predicted, would create a potent "public sentiment." The people could then dictate abolitionist action.[6]

The potential for turning petition campaigns into weapons of an organized mass movement struck Garrison like a thunderbolt. Reporting on one occasion in 1830 that "twelve petitions had been sent to Congress from one county in Pennsylvania," he challenged his *Genius* readers to exceed this number: a groundswell of memorials must confront Congress. "Let the tide of public opinion continue to swell on the subject [of slavery]," he wrote, until people "from one end of the country to another" flooded the nation's capital with abolitionist protests. Garrison praised the Philadelphia man who had "gone and got [petition] signatures" from his own neighborhood. He admonished his audience to do likewise.[7]

Benjamin Lundy, Garrison's mentor at the *Genius*, differed. Adopting the abolitionist ethos of the Pennsylvania Abolition Society (PAS), to which he belonged, Lundy told activists to *hold back* their exertions from time to time. Heeding politicians' warnings about slavery's political volatility, he advised them to consider "both interest and safety." For instance, they should never arouse public resentment against southern masters, for that would make abolition even less tolerable. "Justice is slow in its progress," Lundy concluded. Although "every exertion is necessary, and every practical method should be adopted, to promote the great and important work," abolitionists must maintain a certain moderation.[8]

How different from Garrison, who already condemned any scheme that would not lead to full-scale abolition! Abolitionists could not waste more time worrying about slaveholders' reactions or about political expediency or sectional discord. Mass action must abolish slavery, not win friends. "The more information we collect on slavery," he observed in 1830, and the more emphasis reformers put on mobilizing the masses, "the more efficient will be OUR efforts to overthrow [slavery]." "Oh that my countrymen would look at things in their true light," Garrison protested on leaving Baltimore in July 1830. "Oh that they might feel as keenly for black skin as for a white one! Oh that they might think 'only of the poor slave.'" If every American vowed to become an abolitionist, then "popular sympathy" would become a weapon, and "two million valuable and immortal souls" would speedily be saved from slavery.[9]

WILLIAM LLOYD GARRISON was not the sole architect of abolition's mass action strategy between 1830 and 1835. Be it Samuel May urging citizens to protest in every northern community or Maria Weston Chapman hailing abolition as a social movement, Massachusetts abolitionists spoke collectively of "the people" as the new agents of reform.[10] As the Boston Female Anti-Slavery Society (BFASS) put it, abolitionists must engage "EVERYONE" in the fight.[11]

Among the new popular activists, two strategists stood out: Amos Phelps and Margaret Chandler. Both emphasized mass action early in their careers, impressing Garrison, among others, and both illuminated modern abolitionism's radical break from the past. Elizabeth Margaret Chandler preceded Garrison at Benjamin Lundy's *Genius*. Chandler, who shared editorial duties with the young printer until she moved to Michigan, struck Garrison as inspirational. "[There is not] a female in the United States who has written so copiously in the cause of the oppressed," he wrote. "The effusions of her pen are chiefly found in the *Genius*, [although] she has contributed to the columns of *The Liberator*, which have obtained a wide circulation. She was a prodigy in literature and philanthropy."[12] Although a reclusive person, the young Philadelphia Quaker proved to be a key transitional figure for women's abolitionism, in particular, and American abolitionism more generally. Her poetry and prose impressed scores of reformers throughout the 1830s. "She employed her pen," one admiring writer commented after her untimely death in 1834, "with power and elegance . . . throwing her whole moral being against a system which sanctions the crime of slavery. Her works ought to be on EVERY TABLE IN THE LAND."[13]

Although a Philadelphian, Chandler ignored the Pennyslvania Abolition Society. Instead, she joined a local female antislavery group in the late 1820s and made a more powerful impact in the abolitionist movement as editor of the "Ladies Repository" section of *Genius*. No sooner had she assumed her duties at the paper in 1828 than Chandler began demanding that women become "active" participants in a mass movement against southern slavery. Like Garrison, she argued that "the people" must form the core of a new national abolitionist cause. Like Garrison too, Chandler diverged strikingly from their mentor Benjamin Lundy on the future of abolition.[14]

Lundy and Chandler especially differed on female activism. Lundy's own "Ladies Repository" essays urged women only to be republican mothers. By nurturing sympathetic attitudes about race and antislavery, he hoped, mothers would instill abolitionist views in America's youth. But Chandler emphasized female activism outside the home, particularly signing petitions and organizing antislavery societies. "It is hoped that by devoting a portion of this paper expressly to themselves," Chandler's first full-fledged editorial announced in September 1829, "the minds of our females, in general, may be awakened to a more lively interest" in abolitionist activism.[15] Over several years Chandler used the "Ladies Repository" to push women into the broader abolitionist movement and thereby remake it.

Packing the column with information on women's abolitionism around the nation and around the globe, Chandler hoped to foment women's "active opposition" to southern bondage. Titles such as "Our Cause" and "Female Exertions" stressed women's potential as activists. True, "exerting" a moral "influence in the minds of your off-spring" would help the cause. But, she pleaded, "you can do a great deal more — you can give it your active exertions, and you must do so if you would ever behold the day when the cry of the oppressed shall no longer be heard." "Do not remain sunk in guilty apathy," Chandler admonished, for "lifelessness" and "apathy . . . are the most dangerous enemies to the cause of emancipation."[16]

Chandler urged women to "form yourselves into societies for the opposition of slavery," publicize the wrong done to "our colored population," "diffuse" abolitionist information far and wide, and convert "friends" to the cause. In every instance, women must point "their efforts . . . [toward] the public mind." Chandler realized the radical nature of her call. "Women will impinge upon men's sphere," she predicted. But if female exertions "cooled," she worried that abolitionism itself would wither.[17]

Chandler's vision of women's activism emerged just as female reformers in the North began to assert themselves in the public sphere. In the late 1820s and early 1830s women in Massachusetts, New York, Ohio, and Pennsylvania started a variety of benevolent organizations, testing the boundaries of social convention. Chandler asked women to concentrate their reformist energies on the singular issue of slavery, swelling abolition's ranks by their inspiring example. In her eyes, abolition would succeed only if women became organizers and agitators.[18]

Amos Phelps, the Yale-educated minister who joined the New England Anti-Slavery Society after taking over Boston's Pine Street Church in the early 1830s, provided another coherent view of what he called abolitionism's new "Design." His lectures, articles, and books sought to mobilize the American people as the sole means of destroying bondage. "It is obvious," he observed in 1834, "that the only way the people of the non-slaveholding states can operate effectually on the subject of slavery is through the medium of public sentiment." Phelps then turned public sentiment into a "weapon of warfare." His 1834 *Lectures on Slavery and Its Remedy* served as a manifesto of mass action. After explaining the differences between gradualism and immediatism, the pamphlet focused on how American abolitionists could mobilize against bondage. Far from being simply a legal or political problem best left to the experts, or a matter of individual conscience best left to sinning slaveholders and their God, slavery was a "collective" issue for the American people. The American popular "community" could and should confront slavery in "a collective capacity."[19]

Because slaveholders would perennially resist abolitionism, as would politicians worried about the Union's well-being, Phelps argued, nonslaveholding citizens had to fight slavery en masse. As he put it, citizens "should BEGIN at once, in every lawful and practicable way, to enlighten the public mind, to change the tone of public sentiment, to organize and concentrate their energies" on destroying southern slavery. By "spreading light [via] the pulpit AND the press," by asking individuals to "speak out clearly and distinctly," and by creating a grand "design of action," abolitionists could originate "an enlightened public sentiment that shall DEMAND" abolition of its governments and "MAKE our representatives afraid NOT TO ACT." Suspicious of mere "talk," Phelps proposed "a national society . . . to superintend this great movement." Abolitionists had to develop not only "moral suasion philosophies," but also practical goals and organizations to implement immediate emancipation. Thus, the national organization would plan petition campaigns, diffuse abolitionist literature throughout the polity, and propose constitutional amendments banning slavery.[20]

According to Phelps, a mass movement would begin with a thousand individuals revolutionizing their own consciousness. But these individuals must then unite to overthrow slavery. The new wave of abolition societies made sure that "the individual [would not be] adrift" in a world of chaotic and evil impulses; he or she would enter "a community" of activists with clear-cut objectives (signing petitions, reading the *Liberator*, publicly protesting slavery). For Phelps, connecting individuals en masse and channeling their energies into public protests was the essence of the cause.[21]

Phelps outlined the various ways that "individuals" could become political activists, locally and nationally. "Take an abolitionist newspaper," he advised, but do not stop there: "read it," "lend it to your neighbor," "send it . . . to friends at the south," and make sure "they know it is from you." "Supply your minister, the lyceum, the reading room, the public house" with abolitionist papers. Use your prayer time to attend interdenominational "prayer meetings" or to pray with the "family," with "a social circle"—with anyone interested in the problem of slavery. Prayer was not simply a personal or even spiritual affair. It became a form of community vigil about ending slavery. Phelps again provided guidelines for would-be activists: pray about "slavery," the condition of "free people of color," as well as "all those who despise" them; and direct these prayers to "Slaveholders," "Legislators and those in authority," "those who plead publicly . . . and devise measures for [black] relief," and finally, pray for "the Nation—the entire people."[22]

As Phelps summed up his view of mass action, reformers must do the Lord's work against slavery "in conjunction with the people." Everyday citizens had to become organizers, congressional petitioners, and avatars of the new national movement to destroy southern bondage. The cause was too important to be left to lawyers, politicians, and statesmen alone.[23]

THE NEW ENGLAND Anti-Slavery Society incorporated mass action strategies into its organizational framework. "Slavery is maintained by the people and the government of the United States," stated its first annual report. Thus, "it is right that the people of this country, and especially New England . . . should understand abolitionists' motives, principles and purposes," for they must be the key arbiters of change. The people (like their "rulers") could manifest a "base" disinterestedness in the plight of slaves, but once enlightened and compelled to recognize the evil, what "individual . . . [would be] hostile to the liberation of slaves?" By stirring America's collective "soul," every citizen "would exclaim, 'I am for the rescue of two-million enslaved countrymen!'" A collective push for national abolitionist legislation would soon follow.[24]

The NEASS spent most of its funds on traveling lecturers and the dissemination of publications far and wide. In 1837, now called the Massachusetts Anti-Slavery Society (MASS), it noted that its lecturing agents had spread the "claims of our enslaved countrymen" to "many thousands of citizens of Massachusetts" and "scattered [publications] unsparingly throughout the land." That same year the American Anti-Slavery Society reported that Bay Staters had organized nearly two hundred local societies, each attracting about forty members. Every day, the MASS bragged, "this number multiplies." While masters fumed and northern politicians worried, the abolitionists vowed to continue speaking publicly, distributing essays, and disseminating their message until they had reached every citizen.[25]

But just who should and would join the people's movement? The new abolitionists "came from every sect, and class and party," Maria Weston Chapman announced, from "every age and sex and color." According to Bay Staters, by the 1830s the "people" included new groups of activists, not simply white males. "We consider the anti-slavery cause as the cause of philanthropy," one NEASS resolution declared, "in which all human beings, white men and colored men, citizens and foreigners, men and women, have the SAME DUTIES and THE SAME RIGHTS." Boston minister Amasa Walker hailed the NEASS's heterogeneity as a defining characteristic of modern abolitionism. Whereas previous reform movements had attracted "a formidable array of great men" to their ranks — including "judges, governors, congressmen and lawyers" — new-wave activists would draw support from a kaleidoscope of ordinary Americans.[26]

In the minds of Massachusetts reformers, African Americans formed a critical base of support. Indeed, calls for excluding black activists from "our antislavery proceedings," Charles Follen pointed out, would not only render the cause anemic (for abolitionists would be hypocrites) but would also "deprive ourselves of faithful fellow laborers." Arnold Buffum raved about his work with black activists in Philadelphia, who, he maintained, surpassed the canvassing efforts of many white activists. "There is an excellent spirit among the colored people here," Buffum observed, "and I should not be surprised to have one thousand new subscribers [to the *Liberator*]" after he and his black coworkers (James McCrummill and Robert Purvis) made their rounds. Amos Phelps cited his important personal experience with black activists in Massachusetts, Pennsylvania, and New York. After a series of public lectures in Philadelphia in 1834, Phelps called the city's black abolitionists unsurpassed agitators.[27]

With his African American contacts numbering well over one hundred in the early 1830s, William Lloyd Garrison built a foundation on black abolitionism. By the mid-1830s, he considered using black lecturing agents in Massachusetts. Hosea Easton was one riveting black orator favored by Bay State reformers. "One great truth is acknowledged by all Christendom," he exclaimed in a series of speeches in 1837, "God hath made of one blood all nations of men." Other African Americans served as guest speakers at local antislavery rallies, particularly Charles C. Gardner and James Forten.[28]

Women formed another critical component of mass abolitionism. "Whose influence is so potent as woman's?" Garrison asked Harriott Plummer of Boston in 1832. Women could persuade husbands and friends to support abolition, he continued, but they could also organize female abolition societies, attend antislavery conventions, and circulate petitions against slavery in towns and cities all over the nation. By becoming full-time antislavery activists, women "may set an example which shall not be powerless." Indeed, female reformers would bolster the national ranks. "Our opponents sneer at [female] cooperation," the Massachusetts Anti-Slavery Society proclaimed in 1836, "but we welcome and are grateful for it." "Our American Revolution was not achieved by men alone," the society stated; neither would the revolutionizing of American abolitionism.[29]

Women saw themselves as potent activists. Not only would they engage in moral suasion ("talking kindly but earnestly to slaveholders" and "the women of the South"), but also they vowed to be just as committed and active as men. Bay State woman established over forty female antislavery societies in Massachusetts alone before the end of the 1830s and played a key role in forming the National Convention of Anti-Slavery Women in 1837. "Sisters," Mary Parker of the Boston Female Anti-Slavery Society enjoined, "will you not USE the power God has entrusted to your hands for good?" "Visit every house," she challenged women everywhere, "ask every individual" to sign abolitionist memorials to Congress, persuade other women to "join societies," and confront men as well as women who oppose abolition. By the mid-1830s Boston women bragged that they had proved themselves "more valuable auxiliaries" than many men. "The cause had over-leaped the graceful feebleness which the age cherished as an ornament in the female character," Maria Weston Chapman wrote in 1836, for "women were peculiarly active" as petitioners and shapers of "public opinion." These "politicians in petticoats," as one southern master sneered, proved especially meddlesome over the next several years.[30]

The rise of youthful activism offered yet another foundation of mass action. "The sentiment of . . . our young men is of the highest importance," Joshua Coffin wrote to Boston's Samuel Sewall in 1835. Already, Coffin noted, abolitionist organizations had formed "in all colleges" in New England. "This means that the pulpit, the bar, the bench" — nearly every public and governing institution — would "soon be filled with abolitionists."[31]

Garrison could not help but admire the youthful activism taking shape at Amherst College in Northampton, Massachusetts. In the fall of 1835 he contrasted Boston's "sinking apathy" with Amherst students' rising activism. "We have some excellent materials . . . in that institution," Garrison cheered as one acquaintance informed him that the student abolition society had routed the student colonization society. Colonization at Amherst, Garrison rejoiced, was "dead — dead — dead!"[32]

One student petition from Amherst declared that abolition in the District of Columbia was "loudly called for by the VOICE OF HUMANITY." Collecting petition signatures in the community at large, planning public lectures and debates, holding public vigils, posting broadsides, forwarding editorials to newspapers, establishing "antislavery" libraries for the public, and confronting skeptical faculty members, the students brought abolition alive in western Massachusetts. Their "public agitations" so disturbed the Amherst faculty that the administration banned the student abolition society in 1835. Before closing the campus chapter, however, the young men made a declaration that excited Garrison: "While we can no longer be an Anti-Slavery Society, we will now and forever BE ANTI-SLAVERY MEN!" Such "youthful exertions," Garrison proclaimed, served as a metaphor for the people "coming alive" on abolitionism.[33]

BUT EXACTLY WHAT could the abolitionist masses do? "WE would MAKE Congress use its powers over the District of Columbia and the Territories," Amos Phelps thundered, or "we could seek an amendment" to the Constitution repealing the fugitive slave clause. Organizing "whole communities" of citizens, William Lloyd Garrison proclaimed, would mean little without "mak[ing] a demonstration of their strength" to state and federal governments. "We know that a growing party has the power to produce MIRACULOUS changes in society," he warned John Quincy Adams in early 1832. Though abolitionists' objective "was not a political one," Garrison lectured Adams, the very "nature of [our] enterprise unavoidably brings me into contact with you as a political representative of the nation." Reformers would not start their own party or run candidates for political office. But they would pressure the people's servants into passing abolitionist legislation, supporting blacks' constitutional rights, and pressing southern masters themselves to emancipate their slaves. Adams's refusal to present a petition from "the people" (which had advocated immediate liberation of slaves in the District of Columbia) upset Garrison and his ranks; unlike previous generations of reformers, however, he would not let Adams's move go unchecked. Indeed, abolitionists would force Adams and his political colleagues to present their petitions on slavery.[34]

Arnold Buffum agreed with Garrison. "In a republic where the people choose their rulers," Buffum wrote, "the character of government is but an indicator of the character of the nation. If the people are righteous, the rulers will be also." And so, Buffum proclaimed, "the time has come when the people of the United States are called upon to choose whom they will have" as leaders: men who would fight slavery and sin or those who would yield to these evils. Buffum did not support a party impulse — voting for a slate of abolitionist candidates. Rather, as he emphasized, he wanted to create a broader political consciousness that would swamp tainted political structures and restore integrity to institutions of governance. "Let every Christian unite in [this] holy cause of national reform," he urged, and henceforth righteousness would be a part of American political discourse. As a lecturing agent, Buffum carried this message to citizens throughout Massachusetts and New England, persuading "the people" to join antislavery societies, sign petitions demanding abolition in the District of Columbia, and becoming political activists.[35]

In deriving their reform energies from the people, and in pointing the masses toward political bodies, "modern" abolitionists spoke of their indebtedness to the Revolutionary era. Like the revolutionaries of 1776, Bay State reformers hoped to build a forceful collective movement that would ultimately compel political leaders and slaveholders to effect societal change. New Hampshire's James Farmer, an NEASS correspondent, noticed a "remarkable coincidence" between the "Spirit of '76" and the mass abolitionist movement of the 1830s. So did Philadelphians who moved from the Pennsylvanian Abolition Society to the New England and American Anti-Slavery Societies in the early 1830s. Referring to the grand Revolutionary tradition of civic mobilization, the Pennsylvania Anti-Slavery Society (allied with Garrison) asserted: "Such was the school of Liberty and human rights in which which we were educated and which we embrace in our association."[36]

The Revolutionary tradition resonated at the tactical as well as idealistic level. On the one hand, the Constitution itself provided an outlet for abolitionist ends: reformers could use the amending process to abolish slavery in the District of Columbia, to end northern rendition of fugitive slaves, and to destroy the domestic slave trade. On the other hand, the Constitution allowed abolitionists to mobilize northern citizens and agitate in the public sphere. "The Constitution is our shield," Amos Phelps announced in his lectures and writings, "not our opponents." According to Salem abolitionist Charles P. Grosvenor, reformers had essential constitutional rights to organize, publicly protest, and agitate political bodies. "Every government is based on some principles," Grosvenor argued in his 1835 treatise, "A Disquisition on the Constitution." In America, those principles revolved around "the people," who remained the "interpreters" of the Constitution and of the possibilities of democratic governance. None other than the founding generation, Grosvenor advised, had made this notion clear: If the people desired change, all they had to do was organize.[37]

Massachusetts abolitionists offered more elaborate constitutional justifications of their activities than anything ever produced by the PAS or the American Convention of Abolition Societies. Although these early movements took their essential petition and assembly rights for granted (perhaps as a function of being political and legal elites), they also did not take their activism far enough to need such constitutional rationalizations. The PAS would usually demur from pushing memorials on offended slaveholders or congressional leaders, and it never sought to alter the constitutional guarantee of slave property. Second-wave reformers, on the other hand, looked for every nuance in the American Constitution to bolster their mass agitation tactics.

Southerners' threats made this constitutional sanction all the more important. "There are ten thousand citizens of Massachusetts who would this day be lynched should they lisp their feelings or opinions south of the Mason-Dixon line," Samuel May commented, because "we speak for Liberty." But with a solid "constitutional shield" for their organizing tactics, as a Lowell reformer put it, Massachusetts reformers could encourage their fellow citizens to join "in the great abolition movement" without fear, to "burn up slavery" in a constitutional manner. "Nothing in the Constitution of the United States," Ellis Gray Loring of Boston declared in 1836, prohibited a citizen from joining an association with the avowed purpose of abolishing slavery. "There is a great deal of loose assertion on this point," Loring continued. "One man finds [immediate] abolitionism contrary to the letter, another to the spirit, of the Constitution." But, he concluded, "not one word" in that document prohibited northern antislavery agitation, for the Constitution might be altered to introduce abolitionist policies. "The Constitutional process," as Garrison himself referred to it in the 1830s, allowed reformers to seek an end to the slave trade, the rendition of fugitive slaves, or slavery itself in certain areas of the country — provided they could muster the popular support necessary to pass laws or amendments.[38]

Amos Phelps urged abolitionists to exploit Article V of the federal Constitution, by which "Congress, whenever two-thirds of both houses shall deem it necessary, or on the application of the legislatures of the several states [shall amend the Constitution]." In Phelps's eyes, this simple provision allowed northern citizens to mobilize for the eradication of southern slavery.[39]

Boston's David Lee Child echoed this strategy: modern abolitionists could agitate against slavery *because* the Constitution could be amended. Although both southern and northern politicians claimed that "we have nothing to do with the subject of slavery," abolitionists must insist that "we have a [constitutional] right to dispute this point." "Fellow citizens," Child asked an audience in South Reading, Massachusetts, in 1833, should "'We the People' choose to agitate the question of AMENDING the Federal Constitution with a view to extirpate from it this pestilent principle [of slavery], would it not be right and necessary to discuss the subject [first] in newspapers and in popular meetings?" Linking free speech to the amending process itself, Child (like Phelps) hoped to quash the long-held belief that southern slavery was inviolate. Indeed, those who would deny northern reformers' right to "interfere" with bondage would deny that Article V of the Constitution even existed. "To say that we have no right to discuss the subject of slavery is to say that the article of the Constitution which provides for amending the same Constitution is inapplicable."[40]

Modern abolitionists spoke of various amendments to the Constitution. Thomas Shipley and William Lloyd Garrison advocated one that would prohibit the return of southern fugitives by northern juries. "I agree with you," Garrison wrote Shipley in December 1835, "respecting the duty of procuring an amendment to our national Constitution . . . which [would nullify] the law which now requires the free states to send back into bondage those who escape from the lash and the whip."[41] Shipley also proposed an amendment outlawing the domestic slave trade. David Lee Child and Phelps favored amendments banning slavery in any federally controlled territory, particularly the District of Columbia.

Before they could alter laws and change constitutions, however, abolitionists had to capture the public's attention and organize antislavery societies. Here, too, the Constitution offered protection: if reformers could speak, preach, and write about slavery's evil, they could also organize, petition, and seek constitutional amendments. Indeed, if the people were not privy to the consciousness-raising tactics of abolitionist lecturers or writers, then the cause would dwindle in communities nationwide. "What should we do to fight slavery?" people would ask Amos Phelps. "Inform yourselves," he always responded, "inform others," join abolition societies and magnify abolition's influence. Unless abolitionists legitimated their activism via the Constitution and Bill of Rights, antiabolitionists would close off discussion on slavery in social as well as political arenas. "All we ask is inalienable rights," he wrote.[42]

The First Amendment, Bay State abolitionists argued, secured abolitionists' free speech, assembly, and petition rights. As Amos Phelps contended, the Bill of Rights was a living shrine to unpopular speech. To combat antiabolitionist activity in all sectors of society, from gag rules in state or federal government to the "silencing" of abolitionist speech in local churches, town meetings, and other public venues, Phelps crafted extended constitutional defenses of abolitionist agitation. One of the most frequent objections he encountered in small towns was that abolitionism in its new mass incarnation "will produce excitement" and utterly disrupt communities. Even those sympathetic to the cause, he wrote, would not let abolitionists "speak at a Temperance meeting" or in church. Moreover, people would tell others not to "talk" about slavery with their "children and family." Though clearly outside the realm of formal political institutions, Phelps feared that such prohibitions denied abolitionists "their rights."[43]

But how far could abolitionists take the Bill of Rights? "Are discussions" on the subject of slavery "unconstitutional?" asked Phelps on one occasion. Many people would say, "YES!" To such statements, he replied that "the Constitution guarantees free discussion" without any limitation whatsoever. Nor could free speech be monopolized by the wealthy, the politically powerful, or the worthy. Free speech, Phelps concluded, was "meant for all," particularly "the unpopular and the minority." "Why [else] was the [First] amendment put in?"[44]

In focusing on the Bill of Rights and the amendment process, Massachusetts abolitionists hoped to encourage citizens to become involved "in the great Abolition movement." Although depicted as "incendiary fanatics" who would stop at nothing to overthrow slavery if not the Union, abolitionists depicted themselves as patriotic citizens who merely used the Constitution to achieve their emancipatory goals.[45]

USING MASS ACTION principles, Massachusetts abolitionists revolutionized two longtime tactics: legal work and petitioning. Whereas early reformers had halted at political roadblocks or legal limitations, new-wave activists used the people to circumvent the obstacles to abolition. "The grand object of the Anti-Slavery Society," Garrison proclaimed, is "to alter the views of the people so that politicians, lawmakers and law executioners may be induced to rally en masse for the entire abolition of slavery."[46]

Courts of law must also feel the pressure of popular opinion, Massachusetts reformers argued. No longer a forum for lawyers and jurists alone, abolitionists now viewed trials as a stage for outraged citizens to influence the course of justice. Showing up en masse at fugitive slave trials in northern states, they might prevent the legal system from making a corrupt bargain with slavery or stop slaveholders from retrying alleged escapees. In August 1836, for example, a crowd of Massachusetts abolitionists ushered two black women out of a courthouse after they had been acquitted of being southern fugitives. Abolitionists acted when the slaveholders' attorney announced that he would have the women quickly retried. "A general rush was [then] made," Garrison wrote excitedly, "prisoners and crowd together — down the stairs of the court house, at the door of which . . . [they] entered a carriage and were driven away before anyone could prevent it."[47]

In Pennsylvania, too, modern abolitionist crowds tried to upset the cool course of the law. "Public sentiment has undergone a salutary change [on the topic of runaways]," a local "Garrisonian" reformer announced in July 1837, after a fugitive slave trial began in the southern part of the state. Reporting that huge crowds of "citizens" had packed the county courthouse — making an "audience" for the judge and lawyers to contend with — correspondent "W. H. J." emphasized the importance of "popular excitement" in all such cases. Although the judge ultimately released the fugitive on a technicality, W. H. J. underlined the crowd's power in determining justice. "There was in attendance a full representation of abolitionists in this county," he observed, "whose feelings had been enlisted in the cause." This throng established a wall of popular sentiment that "no slaveholder could penetrate!" Abolitionists thus learned "the importance of [mass] exertion" even in legal cases. "If more people took such action," the correspondent concluded, "few slaves would be returned south."[48]

According to mass action tacticians, the people could also purify courtrooms as jury members. The *Abolitionist* emphasized popular wisdom over judges' "arbitrary power." If fugitive slaves were guaranteed a jury trial in northern courts, Massachusetts activists maintained, then northern citizens could strike at southern slavery without leaving their own communities. If properly educated by abolitionists' speeches, sermons, and publications, juries would see that "such a being as a slave cannot exist" and refuse to return runaways to their masters.[49]

Modern reformers' mass action strategy revolutionized another abolitionist tactic, that "old medicine" of petitioning government. The petition became less a tool for elite strategists and more a sledgehammer of an exploding popular movement. "Everyone should engage in their constitutional privilege" of addressing state and federal governments, Philadelphia female activists proclaimed, "men, women, EVERYONE."[50] As the *Emancipator* observed in 1837, a flood of citizen memorials sent to the nation's capital would "awake [even] the slumbering Congress." Indeed, new-wave petition drives had come a long way from the two memorials sent to Congress by the PAS and Quaker reformers in 1790. The Pennsylvania Abolition Society had never accumulated more than a few hundred signatures during any petition drive. In the 1830s Massachusetts abolitionists routinely exceeded such numbers. According to a Lowell activist, local reformers garnered nearly three thousand signatures for one memorial "with almost no effort."[51] By 1837, according to the American Anti-Slavery Society, local and state abolition societies had accumulated over one million signatures over six or seven years.

Although modern petitions, like the early ones, cited biblical references, the Founding Fathers, and constitutional principles as sources to attack slavery, they all highlighted a common theme: the people would now compel Congress to confront the slavery issue. "Surely then as representatives of the people," one standard petition on the District of Columbia began, "you will bear with us when WE express our solemn apprehensions in the language of the patriot Jefferson that God is just." "We solemnly propose," it continued, "to press OUR national legislature with appeals until this Christian people abjure forever a traffic in the souls of men." "Let [memorials] be poured into the halls of the national legislature," the *National Enquirer* wrote in 1836 of a petition drive opposing Texas annexation, "until the members are literally overwhelmed with them and finally compelled to yield to the 'voice of the people'. They will understand the Roman maxim, *Vox Populi, Vox Dei.* . . . Let them hear it, and sooner or later they will obey it." "Let us," female abolitionists declared at a national convention, make our legislators "uncomfortable in their sinful negligence" of the slavery issue.[52]

The awesome quality of modern petition campaigns owed much to female tacticians, particularly in Massachusetts and Pennsylvania. According to a congressional study of 1836, women contributed over 40 percent of the 34,000 petition signatures between 1831 and 1835.[53] Garrison estimated that woman outpetitioned men by "three to one." By the mid-1830s female antislavery societies took the lead in planning and executing petition drives at local, state, and federal levels. "As women, as wives, as mothers, we are deeply responsible for the influence we have on the human race," a circular on petitioning by Boston's Maria Weston Chapman stated. Because petitioning was the "only right we ourselves enjoy," the circular encouraged female abolitionists in Massachusetts to elevate the tactic to new heights of power. "Let US," Boston's women proclaimed, "petition—petition—petition . . . until we cannot be denied. Let US know no rest till we have done the utmost to obtain the testimony of every woman, in every town, in every county of [Massachusetts]."[54]

To achieve its lofty goals, the Boston Female Anti-Slavery Society established "a systematic mode of operation" for petition drives in the 1830s. Working with female activists throughout the state, it dispatched canvassers "house to house, soliciting signatures to various petitions." These grassroots foot soldiers forwarded memorials to a local forewoman, who sent them on to Boston for presentation to the state legislature or Congress. Local reformers, the BFASS surmised, would have a better rapport with people in their own areas. They could persuade friends, neighbors, and community leaders to sign petitions and help canvass on behalf of the abolitionist cause. In addition, grassroots workers could help the BFASS pinpoint hot and cold areas of the state. This efficient precinct system, Boston women bragged near the end of the decade, reached "every true abolitionist in every town in the Commonwealth."[55]

The BFASS strategy became the foundation of a national "Circular" on petitioning issued by the first convention of female abolitionists. The circular advised activists to establish a clear line of command stretching from grassroots canvassers through state, regional, and national leaders. According to the plan, local abolitionists were to collect petition signatures in their own neighborhoods and towns and then report to county or city representatives; these representatives, in turn, would report to state committees, located in "principal towns or cities," which would report to a regional representative in Boston, New York, or Philadelphia; finally, the regional representatives would forward the regional results to the National Convention, which would send them to Congress. "Let each state be thoroughly furnished with petitions," New York's Juliana Tappan wrote of the plan, "and let New York cover New York, Pennsylvania cover Pennsylvania" until women had provided for the entire North. In collecting this mass of memorials, the circular warned, citizens signatures must be "COUNTED AND RE-CORDED" in each county or city (so that abolitionists could accurately tally national totals). "No petitions ought to be signed by individuals under sixteen," the circular continued, and canvassers should never attach duplicate lists of signatures to petitions, "lest they should lead to a suspicion that names were forged." Finally, female abolitionists must pay strict attention to deadlines: September for fall congressional sessions, November for winter ones.[56]

Gender politics helped inspire the female petition campaigns. After proving themselves as antislavery organizers and activists, many of these women forecast their own "emancipation."[57] "We have only to go steadily forward in the discharge of our duties in the overthrow of slavery," Anne Warren Weston of Boston wrote, "[and] we may also overthrow the injurious prejudices relative to the real duties and responsibilities of women."[58]

Both the Boston and Philadelphia Female Anti-Slavery Societies addressed petitions to "THEIR" congressional representatives. Although women could not vote, the BFASS asserted in one missive, women were "bound to urge" the nation's leaders to "regain, defend and preserve inviolate the rights of all." Women's petitions would prove just "how much" they could influence political institutions like Congress.[59] In Pennsylvania, female abolitionists pressed their congressmen to support memorials on abolition in the District of Columbia, Texas annexation, and overturning the gag rule.

In the gag rule's first year, Pennsylvania congressman Samuel McKean wrote twice from his seat in the "Senate Chamber" to Philadelphia's Mary Grew about the disturbing nature of women's political activism. "I have received your petition bearing signatures from 3300 women of Philadelphia," he replied, "and I will present it." "But," he quickly added, "you cannot be ignorant of the extreme sensibility of the subject" in Congress. With a congressional gag on the slavery issue, even referring to "abolitionist petitions" disrupted the national legislature. Women's memorials (signed by so many citizens whose husbands were voters) put northern representatives in trying positions. Though McKean presented the petition of the Philadelphia Female Anti-Slavery Society (according to the *National Enquirer*, he had presented six memorials in 1837), he asked if, in future, female abolitionists would "permit me to exercise due discretion" in bringing the subject of slavery forward.[60]

On the other hand, James Harper of Philadelphia County wrote from the Senate that women in his district should never "doubt my sincerity to present your memorials to Congress." In fact, Harper admitted that he was "happy" that the women had consistently forwarded petitions to him.

"Only when people compel their public servants to respect the public good," he wrote, would politicians transcend the boundaries of personal avarice or prejudice. Women's memorials reminded Congress that American citizens were *not* universally antiabolitionist. Harper presented the women's petitions two years in succession, but the gag rule provisions tabled them without discussion.[61]

When John Quincy Adams offered his elegant defense of petition rights in Congress in 1837, abolitionist women could not help but comment on their own heroism. "Thank you for the right to be heard in the hall of Congress," the BFASS wrote to Adams. Indeed, when Pennsylvania's state representatives began critiquing the gag rule and upholding the "inestimable rights" of Americans to be heard in Congress, Pennsylvania women commented on the irony that it was they (nonvoting members of the American republic!) who had forced the issue. Samuel McKean's letter to all abolitionists in 1837—asserting that "I will be happy at all times to present your petitions" because "the whole people appear to me in motion on this subject"—verified women's essential contribution to abolitionists' mass action strategies.[62]

THE MASS ACTION enthusiasm of modern abolitionists gave way to reality by the end of the 1830s. The people's movement could be stifled by political maneuvering, by alternate constitutional construction, or by the American people themselves. If Congress could pass and sustain a gag rule of citizens' abolitionist memorials, many activists asked, then how could reformers seriously consider amending the Constitution? Abolitionists learned that they could accumulate adherents by the hundreds of thousands and still not receive a full hearing.

Angered and even despairing, Massachusetts abolitionists split over how to revamp mass action strategies. Should reformers reemphasize nonpolitical persuasion, or should they focus more intensively on the ballot box to express the people's will? William Lloyd Garrison and his adherents argued the former position, Amos Phelps and his followers the latter. Abolitionism thus entered the 1840s as a house divided.

Although Massachusetts strategists failed to turn America into "one great anti-slavery society," they did succeed in remaking the slavery issue into one of "public sympathy." "There are now not less than twelve hundred anti-slavery societies in existence," Garrison informed an English abolitionist in 1837, whose "daily [and] unceasing efforts . . . to gain a complete mastery over public sentiment" had generated unprecedented popular attention on the slavery problem. Pastors, physicians, newspapers editors, and educators commented on slavery and abolitionism. Women organized massive petition drives throughout the North and helped assault southern communities with abolitionist propaganda. African Americans joined white reformers in public conventions denouncing southern masters. "The investigation [of slavery] has began where it ought," Amos Phelps asserted. "To my mind it is almost an axiom: the people of the North are better qualified to hit upon the true and best solution of slavery than the people of the South."[63]

Massachusetts abolitionists did more than bring the people into a nebulously defined debate over slavery's future. By articulating a plausible scenario of amending the Constitution (through an aggressive mass movement of outraged citizens), Bay State activists made clear that they saw slavery's position as contingent, not absolute. Northerners could use the nation's constitutional architecture to alter slavery — if they mobilized the masses. Mass abolition's original goal, as Garrison put it at the end of the 1830s, remained organizing "the people of the free states to remove slavery by all moral and political action, as prescribed by the Constitution."[64] Moral suasion would be a preferred route to emancipation, but abolitionists would not reject legislative and constitutional coercion, either. As female abolitionists proclaimed, reformers' "first and most important object is obtaining petitions for the abolition of slavery in the District of Columbia and the territories, all of which are generally conceded within the powers of Congress."[65]

Although John C. Calhoun remained sure that "abolitionist fanatics" would not literally overrun the Union, his motto became forewarned is forearmed. "Anticipating [mass abolitionism's] danger," Calhoun argued that no popular majority could ever assault slavery's smooth operation anywhere in America. For that would repudiate the Constitution's original bargain with southern masters and, in fact, provide southerners with a constitutional justification for physical "resistance." "I trust," he concluded in 1835, "that [the problem] may be arrested far short of such extremity."[66]

As Calhoun's constituents added, if abolitionists persisted in turning the federal government and the Constitution "into instruments for assaulting the vital rights of the southern states," then the southern "people" must "take matters into our own hands."[67] Most citizens of South Carolina, like Calhoun, did not now believe that they had to take extreme measures. Yet they realized that new abolitionists' mass action strategy had completely altered their predicament. Who could have imagined, Calhoun laughed, that southern masters would ever look fondly upon the nation's first abolition society, composed of those deferential and respectable Philadelphia gentlemen! Times had surely changed and Massachusetts rabble-rousers had upped their movement's ante.

CHAPTER SEVEN

A Whole Lot of Shoe Leather

Agents and the Impact of Grassroots Organizing in Massachusetts during the 1830s

> Without the organization of abolitionists into
> [local] societies the CAUSE WILL BE LOST.
> — William Lloyd Garrison, 1832

IN ONE OF THE epic journeys of the time, Benjamin Lundy undertook a massive tour of every American abolition society he could find in 1828. In less than a year, the veteran reformer traveled over 4,000 miles and visited an estimated 7,000 antislavery activists among 120 abolition groups in eight states (from New England to Tennessee), including a young man named William Lloyd Garrison. Although neither Lundy nor the Pennsylvania Abolition Society (PAS) developed this tactic further, a new generation of abolitionists in Massachusetts seized upon it, hiring agents to "visit every township, school district, and home" to mobilize the masses. Beginning with the New England Anti-Slavery Society (NEASS) in 1832 and spreading to New York, Ohio, and Michigan over the next decade, the agency system helped spawn an abolitionist revival throughout the North: the one hundred societies became a thousand, the seven thousand abolitionists a half million. Even antiabolitionists admitted that by utilizing "a host of lecturers . . . whose sole vocation is to diffuse their doctrine through every channel of society," modern reformers had made abolition a forceful public movement.[1]

The rise and success of the agency system in Massachusetts during the 1830s proved to be a transforming event for old and new abolitionists alike. Perhaps as much as the ideological imperative of immediatism itself, it signaled the advent of a new abolitionist identity in America, one based on a rural, grassroots commitment to activism and zeal, and one coalescing around race and gender. By hiring agents to roam New England, Bay State abolitionists devised a means of remaining in constant contact with the throngs of citizens they so urgently sought to mobilize. "Without the organization of abolitionists into [local] societies," William Lloyd Garrison declared in 1832, "the CAUSE WILL BE LOST."[2]

Still, local resistance, not mass conversion to abolitionism, remained the rule of the road for traveling agents. Indeed, Bay State reformers never organized more than a fraction of the state's overall population; perhaps only 2 or 3 percent of the citizenry joined abolition societies. Nevertheless, even those few percentage points boosted abolitionists' hopes in the 1830s. For agents *did* mobilize over ten thousand citizen-abolitionists in just a few years, including prominent local newspaper editors, clergymen, and philanthropists. In addition, agents' grassroots work shifted abolition's base of support from the PAS's urban milieu to the countryside. According to agent Samuel Joseph May, locals in Haverhill, Fall River, Groton, Stow, Lynn, Leicester, and myriad other towns in Massachusetts, Rhode Island, and Maine now "talked about" destroying southern slavery. So impressed was May with the rural response to abolitionism that he told Garrison, "I will avoid the large towns" in subsequent outings.[3] Finally, grassroots events brought together the kaleidoscope of Americans that new-style agitators hoped to energize — black and white, male and female, young and old. Despite the considerable obstacles, then, Massachusetts abolitionists vowed to build their new public movement in the grass roots.

THE ABOLITIONIST agency rested on a long American tradition of religious outreach. Indeed, the prior significance of religious missionaries cannot be ignored. Evangelicals had roamed the colonial countryside in search of converts since the First Great Awakening, and they remained an active part of religious life through the Revolutionary and early national periods. The Second Great Awakening intensified itinerant activities, as Bible societies and a new generation of traveling preachers — Lyman Beecher, Charles Grandison Finney, and eventually Theodore Dwight Weld — swayed the masses in western New York, southern Ohio, Kentucky, Indiana, and Michigan. According to these domestic missionaries, working among the people emphasized "moral action and spiritual awakening" better than anything else.[4]

The idea of reaching the people in small towns and communities also influenced a number of nonreligious groups in the 1820s and 1830s: political organizations used local ward agents to funnel masses of new voters into party organizations, reform groups assigned agents to disseminate pamphlet literature far and wide, and American businesses began utilizing traveling salesmen to bring product and people together. In the early 1830s, for instance, newspapers in Springfield, Massachusetts, began running advertisements for a "new line of mail coaches" between the western and eastern portions of the state. All that customers had to do was contact an "agent" for information.[5]

Massachusetts abolitionists used the agency to choreograph the reform movements of entire blocs of people. Nothing could be clearer: mobilize people in a republic and the republic would have to change its laws on slavery. At its founding in 1832, the NEASS announced that it would send agents throughout New England. Over the next several years, the society spent well over a third of its budget funding lecturers' travels. The agency became a cornerstone of abolitionist tactics.[6]

The New England Anti-Slavery Society inaugurated the agency system by appointing four agents in 1832 and 1833, including its vice president Arnold Buffum. Working for relatively short periods (usually three-month terms), these men spread the seeds of abolition everywhere they traveled. In 1834 and 1835 the NEASS combined forces with the American Anti-Slavery Society to dispatch agents on the lecture circuit for longer durations. Amos Phelps, Samuel J. May, and Charles Burleigh undertook year-long agencies in the middle of the decade. In addition, both the state and national societies deputized local agents to cover their hometowns. Boston minister George Washington Blagden and Salem preacher Cyrus P. Grosvenor became two of the lesser-known but still important local lecturers working in areas just outside of Boston. Finally, the NEASS assigned lecturers on an as-needed basis to bolster grassroots activity. For instance, both William Lloyd Garrison and David Lee Child worked the state's lecture circuit in the early 1830s (although neither held formal agency positions).

As Maps 1A–D in Appendix 2 illustrate, agents literally combed the countryside to rouse the citizenry. Garrison went far outside of Boston on his initial lecture tours in 1832 and 1833: beginning in Worcester, southwest of Boston, he traveled successively to Providence, Haverhill (on the Maine border), Portland (Maine), Boston, Providence again, and then through several Connecticut towns on the way to meetings in New York, New Jersey, and Pennsylvania. Buffum's first tours were even more grueling. Beginning in Salem in June 1832, he essentially made a big loop around the entire state of Massachusetts. In July he worked in Fall River, Attleboro, and Seekonk, on the Providence border. By August he made it to Springfield and Northampton in the western part of the Bay State. After brief stops in Vermont, Buffum hit northern Massachusetts (Andover, Haverhill, and Salem again) for lectures in October and November 1832. Agents and lecturers maintained busy road schedules no matter how small their "field." Charles Burleigh, appointed by the American Anti-Slavery Society to work central Massachusetts in 1835, covered nearly as much ground as did earlier agents traveling the entire state, even though his area covered only a fraction of the mileage. Between March and April he looped around several small towns about an hour's ride from Boston, including Groton, Sudbury, Townsend, and Marlborough. Though perhaps no more than sixty miles separated the beginning and end of his tour, Burleigh piled up mileage, visiting towns over and over again. Phelps and May, working similarly compact areas of southern and central Massachusetts for the New England Anti-Slavery Society, tallied impressive mileage too. Abolitionists could rightly brag of having traversed most of Massachusetts, including the smallest towns.

"Rambling about," as one activist put it, allowed Massachusetts abolitionists to gauge their weak and strong sites.[7] In 1834 a local female activist lamented that southern Massachusetts did not yet have the abolitionist energy of other areas. Over the next several years Phelps, George Thompson, Garrison, May, and others poured into the area around Plymouth and Bristol Counties. In addition, female societies networked to spread the message among Plymouth-area locals. Good results followed: several auxiliary antislavery societies formed by 1836, and the area subsequently became a mainstay of abolitionist support. Subscriptions to the *Liberator* rivaled those of more populous areas. Moreover, Plymouth County voters proudly returned John Quincy Adams (the North's most famous opponent of the gag rule) to office every year in the late 1830s.

Other towns surprised abolitionist agents. Worcester, the site of a lecture disbanded by Governor Levi Lincoln in the mid-1830s, offered a steady undercurrent of support to the cause. Leicester, just west of Worcester, impressed Samuel May so much that he settled there. Despite confrontational crowds, a small core of citizens in Haverhill and Lynn consistently opened their meetinghouses and provided sanctuary to weary reformers.

Trouble loomed in many other locales. Western Massachusetts remained hostile to traveling lecturers. According to Springfield papers, for example, locals should confront agents such as Arnold Buffum before he littered the area with his "disorganizing doctrines."[8] Citizens in many eastern towns (particularly near Boston) also hoped to keep agents at bay. The residents of Waltham were so indignant about Phelps's early visits that he discounted the site almost entirely.

Getting out into "the field" inspired abolitionist agents. On his first lecture tour, William Lloyd Garrison wrote not simply of his speeches and organizational matters but of how much he enjoyed meeting people outside the city. On one occasion, after jumping from his stagecoach and surveying the hinterland, Garrison declared that "moving about" in the fresh air would revolutionize American abolition.[9] The countryside invigorated Amos Phelps, Samuel May, and Charles Burleigh as well. Phelps, hailed as one of the strongest abolitionist orators of the 1830s, continually used his interaction with local people as grist for his written texts. He often copied questions, quotations, and ideas from circuit rides, turning them into polished essays months or even years later. Blunt challenges offered by skeptical citizens often inspired him. "What can you effect?" asked one local man who confronted him. "What you do will amount to nothing!" Not so, Phelps shot back, for ordinary citizens could organize themselves into powerful pressure groups and compel politicians to support abolition. Phelps worked this and similar rejoinders into set replies for other hostile audiences. When antiabolitionists shouted "I don't like fanaticism" or "What have I to do with southern slavery?" Phelps had his answers ready. "[Slavery] begat all inconsistencies in our national character," he wrote in his journal and told Plymouth audiences. Americans are known for their "courage, heroism, generosity and gratitude," not ignorance and apathy. Abolitionism purified the American character. Lecturing thus allowed Phelps to clarify his principles and broaden abolition's appeal to the citizenry.[10]

Arnold Buffum spent much of his time quieting northern fears about "amalgamation." "Does [your] anti-slavery society hold the same principles as Mr. Garrison?" a citizen asked in Greenfield, Massachusetts. "Do you hold that blacks and whites ought to intermarry?" "I replied," Buffum recalled, "that we hold that all men were created equal." If blacks and whites wanted to intermarry, that should be their right. At another lecture in Greenfield, Buffum spoke about the growing evils of southern slavery. "I gave them a strong one on slavery as it exists at the present time," he wrote Garrison, after which a colonizationist "came before the audience" to congratulate the speaker on his antislavery opinions but then went on to challenge his integrationist philosophy. "'Mr. Buffum, I like your principles on the subject of slavery,'" the man said. "'If you would only change your

A WHOLE LOT OF SHOE LEATHER

plan a little to unite with us [colonizationists],'" he continued, "'the two camps could kill America's [black] problem entirely?'" "I told him there were NO PRINCIPLES SUCH AS WE COULD UNITE IN OUR CAUSE," Buffum recounted, "so long as the people of color have been slandered by the Colonization Society." Buffum told the audience that reformers "must defend [blacks'] cause . . . in a straightforward, honest" way. Abolition lived up to America's noblest principles, whereas colonization mocked them.[11]

Buffum engaged other colonizationists in public debates throughout Massachusetts with varying degrees of success. In one highly publicized confrontation of 1833, he faced John Danforth, of the American Colonization Society (ACS), in Salem. At "25 cents" admission, one local paper reported, the lecture "hall was filled" for the showdown.[12] Buffum and Danforth sparred several other times in small towns unaccustomed to such fireworks. In Fall River, for example, they debated the legitimacy of slave violence. In Concord, New Hampshire, Buffum and another ACS representative argued about abolition's threats to the Union.[13] Whether or not he convinced everyone, Buffum felt that his public appearances won crucial converts to the cause.

Aside from lecturing, agents performed a variety of tasks to build a constituency in the countryside. During one typical stretch of time in 1834, for example, Charles Burleigh gave an antislavery lecture daily for two weeks straight in central Massachusetts, distributed petitions, drafted constitutions for auxiliary societies, met with newspapers editors, debated colonizationists, and networked with local female activists. On one occasion, he literally had to compose a local antislavery society's constitution on the spot: Burleigh had forgotten to replenish his supply from NEASS headquarters. As he later recalled, "lecturing has been one of the lesser items of my actual labors" on the road.[14]

Arnold Buffum remembered a similarly packed schedule. On his early lecture tours of eastern and western Massachusetts, he canvassed for petition signatures to Congress and distributed guidelines on forming auxiliary constitutions (which, he noted, would quickly disappear in abolition's hot spots). In southern Massachusetts, for example, near the Rhode Island border, Buffum asked Garrison to quickly forward "fifty printed constitutions for auxiliary societies . . . with petitions to Congress for emancipation in the District of Columbia" to a Providence abolitionist, which he would pick up and distribute after a lecture there.[15]

Even in the face of such grueling and often controversial work, few agents regretted their time on the road. As Garrison himself predicted, at least some of the people were coming alive on abolitionism. Agents could see it and feel it.

AGENTS' MOST IMPORTANT job remained the forming of local societies. "The friends of the abolition of slavery," the NEASS announced in 1834, "are now, undoubtedly, more numerous and powerful than they have ever been." The "strongest evidence of this fact," the group continued, "is the number of new anti-slavery societies that have been formed." There was certainly more hope than truth in such statements, for a majority of the state's citizens condemned abolitionist agents. Yet the activist ranks in Massachusetts did multiply at a steady pace in the 1830s: the twelve auxiliary societies in 1834 grew to over two hundred by the end of the decade, with an aggregate membership of over ten thousand citizens. The list of local organizations included young men's antislavery societies, female abolition groups, and "colored societies." As one newspaper commented, though abolitionists remained a minority, their growth in the countryside should alarm state and national officials.[16]

Agents often inspired local abolitionists to inaugurate auxiliary societies; their oratorical and administrative proficiency could make a critical difference. One Mansfield, Massachusetts, abolitionist discovered the power of agents' abilities when his own lectures failed to spark interest in the antislavery cause. "No one attended" his meetings, a local historian recalled. Several months later Charles Burleigh steamed into town for a series of lectures that, by the fall of 1836, spawned the Mansfield Anti-Slavery Society, which subsequently became one of the state's largest. With similar displays of verve and verbal prowess, Burleigh helped establish groups in Stow and Groton, Massachusetts. Samuel May's lectures south of Boston helped two local ministers start the South Scituate Anti-Slavery Society, which in 1835 attracted over seventy founding members. To the north of Boston, the work of May, Phelps, and Garrison around Salem prompted calls for a county antislavery society that would bring together hundreds of abolitionists in Salem, Danvers, Ipswich, Haverhill, and other tiny areas of Essex County.[17]

One of the best examples of agents' impact on locals comes from Plymouth County. When Amos Phelps and England's George Thompson began working there in December 1834, they received skeptical coverage from area papers. Although local reformers had asked Phelps and Thompson to help Plymouth increase sympathy for abolitionism, many locals seemed unsure about joining the cause. Who is Thompson? asked a newspaper correspondent, mimicking inquisitive residents. "He is named in your paper in a notice of an [upcoming] antislavery meeting." "What led him here"? Why bring in traveling agents and not "local men"? And, he concluded, "how will [his] oratory in New England break the chains of slavery at the South?"[18]

The correspondent answered that Thompson, like Phelps and all "friends of emancipation," had a fine reputation as a benevolent man. Abolitionists, he continued, hoped to "give a moral impulse to the cause of the oppressed" by pointing "the accumulated voice of public opinion" against southern slavery. Small towns like Plymouth formed potentially important constituencies in this strategy. Thompson would surely "give a soul-stirring address," the writer concluded, though skeptical persons should attend the Plymouth lectures and form their "own" opinions about antislavery agents. "I think I'LL be [there]," he finished, "and hear what Mr. Thompson and Mr. Phelps have to say."[19]

As subsequent newspaper reports indicated, Thompson and Phelps converted many locals to abolitionism. From pulpit sermons to town hall lectures, hundreds of Plymouth citizens joined agents in condemning bondage. For instance, while Thompson lectured a Baptist congregation on the evils of the domestic slave trade and the duty of "Christian ministers, mothers, and citizens . . . to cooperate" in antislavery efforts, two local ministers offered broader biblical condemnations of the institution of slavery.[20] The local antislavery ranks swelled after Phelps and Thompson departed.

Without traveling agents, then, local societies like the ones in Plymouth, Salem, and Mansfield might not have formed. As a Plymouth man wrote to his local paper, agents forced him to think about abolitionism in new ways. He hoped that a lecturer like Burleigh, Thompson, or Phelps would again "visit our town, when ALL [citizens] will have an opportunity of listening to him and forming an opinion . . . upon the subject" of slavery — a subject "which must be interesting to all" of the state's citizens.[21]

Although local societies contained between forty and one hundred members, several Bay State auxiliaries attracted three or four times as many residents. Mansfield's society drew almost three hundred people out of a town numbering just a few thousand; the Plymouth County society had over four hundred members out of a local population of approximately seven thousand. Considering the low population densities of many of these rural areas, abolitionist lecturers found these membership rates outstanding. In Plymouth County, for example, there were only seventy people per square mile, compared with Boston, which contained over five thousand persons per square mile. Even Salem, the "second city" of Massachusetts, had under one hundred persons per square mile; yet its several antislavery organizations attracted hundreds of members in the early 1830s.[22]

Auxiliary groups took constitutional vows of activism. The New England Anti-Slavery Society produced a set of guidelines for local societies, which most groups — in conjunction with agents — used as a start-up model. The South Scituate Anti-Slavery Society of Plymouth County exemplified the official standard that local organizations strove to meet. According to its constitution, "a number of people" in the area viewed abolition as a vital national concern; thus local abolitionists "proceeded" with the creation of an antislavery society "auxiliary" to state and national groups. Slavery, South Scituate officials wrote, "was a crime against God" and man and "ought to therefore be immediately abolished."[23]

Just as important, the South Scituate constitution emphasized the efficacy of northern agitation against southern slavery: "We believe that the citizens of the non-slaveholding states not only have the right to protest against slavery, but are under the highest obligation to seek its removal." Similarly, it pledged to fight racial discrimination in Massachusetts by using "all legal means" to secure for blacks "equal civil and political privileges with the white inhabitants of the land." Finally, it appointed an executive committee to schedule "regular meetings" of area abolitionists, communicate with state and national leaders, and plan local tactics such as petition campaigns and fund-raisers.[24]

With slight variation, most auxiliary societies followed this approach: they pledged to support the immediate abolition of slavery, fight racial discrimination in the North, and arouse local, state, and even federal officials (mostly via petitions and public lectures) on behalf of abolitionism. In Dorchester, local and state abolitionists used one Fourth of July holiday to place the slavery issue before the public. By singing antislavery hymns, reading the Declaration of Independence, and making speeches about citizens' duty to sign abolitionist petitions and form local societies, reformers converted dozens to their cause.[25] The Mansfield group sponsored antislavery speeches whenever possible. On one occasion in 1837, black activist Hosea Easton lectured Mansfield citizens on the need to help fund "colored schools" in the North.[26]

Other local groups provided a range of support to the cause. Lynn and Haverhill abolitionists produced thousands of petition signatures in the late 1830s. The Haverhill Anti-Slavery Society also made large monetary donations to the state abolition society for the distribution of pamphlets and petitions in northern Massachusetts. The Essex County Anti-Slavery Society (comprising Salem and other northern localities) pledged one of the largest sums of any group — eight hundred dollars — to sustain agents' lecturing and canvassing activities in northern Massachusetts.[27]

Massachusetts agents prized the activities of grassroots abolitionists, who often guided them through towns and offered first-hand confirmation of abolitionists' great hope: that local leaders would come to the fore once agents penetrated the countryside. In Fall River, for example, Samuel May encountered two ministers who had already formed a local abolition society. These men offered traveling lecturers a secure place to speak; May urged other agents to use their services. Essex County produced several important leaders in the 1830s: the celebrated poet John Greenleaf Whittier, the Reverend Samuel Sewall, and C. P. Grosvenor. So impressive was Grosvenor to Garrison and others traveling through Salem that the NEASS made him a state lecturing agent in 1835.[28]

In Plymouth, abolitionist agents connected with a number of town and county activists to build a sturdy local abolition society. After agents helped establish an auxiliary group, local ministers challenged their neighbors to face slavery head-on by joining the abolition movement. Mary Rogers and her husband Nathaniel P. Rogers, members of a prominent legal family in Plymouth, also became active in the society. Mary Rogers helped organize the town's first female antislavery society, corresponding with national abolitionist figures about what protest activities she and others should undertake.[29]

Newspaper publisher and editor Christopher A. Hack served as one of the most valued Plymouth area contacts. His journal *We, the People* offered positive press to the abolitionist movement in southeastern Massachusetts. But Hack did more: he became a critical organizing force in Plymouth and the surrounding countryside by helping to launch local societies, advertising abolitionist meetings, and defending abolitionist activities against state and national attacks. He even contacted one of the Bay State's premier political leaders, Edward Everett, on behalf of the cause. Discovering that Everett planned to run for governor in 1836, Hack asked him what he thought about slavery, abolitionism, and southern radicals who called for a crackdown on northern fanatics. Everett wrote back that he had nothing to apologize for as a statesman, and that although he was no friend of slavery he would not and could not publicly support northern abolitionism. Cognizant of Hack's pro-abolitionist paper and its influence in southern Massachusetts, however, Everett asked Hack to keep the letter "private."[30] Hack did, but he offered abolitionists abundant space to argue their cause.

Once again, these local success stories must be measured against many other towns' rigid opposition to abolitionist agents. Riots nearly broke out in Lynn, Haverhill, Worcester, and (although it contained a relatively strong antislavery society) Mansfield.[31] As a response to pro- and anti-abolitionist mob activity, the Massachusetts legislature passed "An Act More Effectually to Suppress Riots." Defining a riotous mob as either a group of "twelve" or more armed people, or a group of "forty" or more unarmed people, massed together against a public gathering, the law charged mayors, aldermen, and selectmen with the "duty" of dispersing mobs and, if necessary, using "armed force . . . to suppress rioters." Local officials invoked the law to deter would-be rioters. When a Mansfield mob tried to break up one abolitionist meeting in 1837, marching into the lecture with fife, drum, and bugle, reformers called in town constable Chandler Cobb. Cobb ordered the group "to disperse," citing "the riot act, chapter 129, page 735 of the Revised Statutes" of Massachusetts.[32] The mob grew more confrontational but finally dispersed after giving local abolitionists a real scare.

Such hair-raising tales notwithstanding, traveling agents found enough examples of local support and leadership to maintain the agency in the countryside. Raising funds, gathering petition signatures, filling lecture halls, and forming auxiliary societies—the NEASS's tactics depended on the work of grassroots activists as well as agents. Indeed, for optimistic itinerants like Samuel May, grassroots organizing illustrated that abolitionism still had the potential for growth in the Bay State, regardless of the opposition.[33]

AS PUBLICISTS and would-be shapers of popular opinion, Massachusetts abolitionists craved attention. Although lecturers spread the word, Bay State activists knew that another tactic could spread it farther and faster: newspapers. Agents joined auxiliaries in disseminating abolitionist papers such as the *Liberator* and the *Emancipator* throughout Massachusetts. As the *Liberator*'s "Account Books" reveal, citizens in the countryside provided the bulk of its in-state support (see Appendix 2, Map 2). Small-town subscribers exceeded their urban counterparts by a factor of two-to-one, with Abington, Fall River, and Newburyport outpacing Boston and other major urban centers in New England. Moreover, there was a correlation between agents' work and the *Liberator*'s subscription rates in the hinterland: wherever agents went, the rates usually increased.[34]

But agents' contact with nonabolitionist newspaper editors paid dividends too, as several local papers offered crucial space to abolitionist writers and speakers. As the New England Anti-Slavery Society proudly announced in 1834, a number of "newspapers and periodicals . . . advance the cause of abolition," although they are "chiefly occupied by other matter."[35] From the *Greenfield Freeman* in the western Massachusetts to the *New England Telegraph* in North Wrentham below Boston, abolitionists listed over twenty papers friendly to the cause. On his first sweep through the countryside in 1832 and 1833, Arnold Buffum made a point to meet with publishers in Salem and Springfield, Massachusetts, in Portland, Maine, and in Concord, New Hampshire. Charles Burleigh confronted local editors every chance he got. During one trip, Burleigh reported a private meeting with the editor of the *Concord Freeman*, a man sympathetic to abolition but more of "a colonizationist" at heart. Finding him "very friendly" nevertheless, Burleigh forthrightly asked the publisher to "open his columns to me to commune with the public through the press." Though Burleigh left without a formal agreement, the *Concord Freeman* proved to be one of abolition's best friends in the ensuing years, taking on not just local antiabolitionist editors, but the Boston press and "hot-headed" southern publishers as well.[36]

In fact, the *Concord Freeman* promoted abolitionism as a national cause. In October 1835 it splashed a story about a massive New York State convention of abolitionists across its front page. The paper also characterized the "American Anti-Slavery Almanack" as "coming from a respectable source," noting that it "treat[ed] issues of general importance" to all citizens concerned about southern slavery. The *Freeman* issued scathing editorials about the famous Boston antiabolition riot in 1835 and consistently allowed local writers to express their abolitionist sentiments.[37] One Concord essayist asked the state leaders not to close their eyes to abolition's "truth" and thereby "disgrace the heroes of Lexington, who fought under the banner 'All Men Are Created Equal.'" "Merciful heavens," he proclaimed at reading the call for Boston's antiabolitionist meeting, "has it arrived at this": a formal "Manifesto" denouncing a cause devoted to human freedom? "And in the CRADLE OF LIBERTY TOO! It is too much for a Son of Freedom to bear."[38]

By connecting with the local press and giving abolition a local edge, traveling abolitionists established what one agent called a vital popular link "to the cause."[39] When the *Lynn Record* or the *Essex Gazette* reprinted abolitionist articles or favorably covered agency work in local areas, abolitionist leaders could only smile. The *Haverhill Gazette*'s opposition to antislavery lectures ("the only aim of the Anti-Slavery Society is to AGITATE," it worried, "and this will do more EVIL than good") prompted the *Lynn Record* to reprint a *Liberator* article about "Immediatism": "We are sorry to see this respectable paper," it noted in a preface to the piece, "yielding to the popular slang" of antiabolitionism. The *Record*'s editor would much rather "espouse the rights of the much injured black man than the unjust claims of the WHITE."[40]

To be sure, many other papers rigidly opposed abolitionism. As early as 1833, the *Springfield Gazette* wrote that local newspapers must "raise a voice against" abolitionists' grassroots agitation. Though reformers had swept through "this section of the country," their "disorganizing doctrines have not yet taken FIRM root. . . . If you do not oppose them next time," the paper warned its readers, "the Buffums, Garrisons and Crandalls will" sway the people and abolition will grow like a weed. A Gloucester journal struck a keynote for many of the state's papers when it cheered antiabolitionist meetings in Boston that formally denounced "the insane attempts of abolitionist [agents]" to spread their cause via newspapers, town meetings, and petition campaigns.[41] Other local papers, finding agents guilty of "sedition," supported formal prohibitions of antislavery agitation.[42]

Struggling against such widespread opposition, agents forged allies among journalists in Salem, Essex, Haverhill, Lynn, and Plymouth, all of whom provided favorable coverage to the abolitionist cause. These papers spoke forcefully about the right of abolitionists to "publicly agitate" the slavery issue. Few activists could have replied more cogently to antiabolitionist rhetoric than a correspondent in a Plymouth paper, who railed against any attempt to stifle discussion about southern slavery. "Shutting up meeting houses, or the mouths of Anti-Slavery lecturers," he wrote, "would never accomplish [anything]." "The American nation must [face slavery] sooner or later," the correspondent continued, taking a cue from an agent's recent lecture. Yet the Bay State's civic, religious, and newspaper leaders had chosen the "cowardly course" of "suppression," which would ultimately do more harm than a frank and immediate national debate over slavery and abolition.[43]

Agent efforts north and south of Boston brought two influential papers into the pro-abolitionist camp: the *Salem Gazette* and the *Plymouth We, the People*. In the early 1830s both papers had worried about the growing influence of the "slave power," which, they asserted, had already encroached on white liberties in Congress. Yet such concern did not automatically translate into support for abolitionism itself. In fact, when northern as well as southern postmasters refused to forward abolitionist mail to the South, both papers wrote alarmist editorials focusing only on the violation of white rights, not on abolitionists' call to rise up in support of oppressed blacks. "We must be careful not to let our regard for our southern brethren," the *Gazette* warned, "carry us to the extreme of surrendering *our own rights.*" In a similar vein, *We, the People* fumed about the long train of southern bullying that had stifled white liberties, particularly freedom of petition and of the press. Southern calls to silence abolitionist agitation struck at "rights guaranteed by the Constitution." Northerners had to become more vigilant defenders of their liberties, for the slave power threatened white freemen as never before.[44]

Over the next several years, however, the two papers offered increasing public support for abolitionism. Indeed, extended contact with abolitionist agents (particularly Garrison, Phelps, and May) revolutionized the papers' coverage of the cause in the Bay State. For instance, the *Salem Gazette* began publishing encouraging announcements of abolitionist lectures and local antislavery meetings. After a round of agents' lectures in the spring of 1834, the paper reported on the formation of "An Anti-Slavery Society for Salem and Vicinity," and it subsequently reprinted highlights of the group's activities to "diffuse light" throughout northern Massachusetts.[45]

The *Gazette* also came to the defense of beleaguered abolitionists. The "intemperate wrath" of southern congressmen missed the mark, it observed in 1835, for Massachusetts abolitionists were "respectable" citizens, with legitimate humanitarian convictions; they were certainly not the "contemptible antagonists" dreamed up by antiabolitionists. Northern rioters and politicians, on the other hand, came under attack for their retrograde views. Mob activity in Haverhill, Lynn, and Worcester, not to mention Boston, brought short but pointed editorials from the *Gazette*. No matter how loudly southern and northern leaders called for shutting down abolitionists, the *Gazette* remained firm: the activists fought a worthy fight against southern bondage. Far from being "incendiaries," "they had the undoubted right to use and abuse the pulpit, press or public debate in the promotion of their cause."[46]

We, the People offered even more ardent support to abolitionists, especially those agents who were "diffusing valuable information" throughout the countryside. According to the paper's editor, abolitionism highlighted the great ideals of the American Revolution: equality and freedom for all people WITHIN the nation. Slavery was a sin, a political evil, and a monstrous perversion of essential liberties guaranteed to blacks. As the exemplar of "freedom" in the world, America had to start living up to its noble founding principles. Abolitionists, the paper's columns declared, could and should challenge their fellow citizens to become emancipationists.[47]

From the middle of the decade onward, *We, the People* supported abolitionist tactics locally and nationally. In 1834, for example, the paper reprinted three good-sized reports on abolitionist lectures to commemorate "Fore-Fathers Day" in Plymouth, each of which spoke to "the moral duty" of northern citizens to work against against southern slavery. The editor applauded the formation of a local abolitionist society, reprinting highlights of the founding meeting and the text of its constitution. Samuel May's public proclamation of NEASS nonviolent objectives, though not widely reprinted in the Bay State, found space in *We, the People* in 1835. In addition, *We, the People* covered meetings of the state antislavery society in Boston, republished lengthy pro-abolitionists essays from the *Liberator*, advertised for "a new and valuable work" on the history of the "People of Color," as well as editions of the "American Anti-Slavery Almanack," and offered editorial support of abolitionists' civil rights protests in northern states. The editor also took vigorous swipes at the "mob spirit" of antiabolitionists.[48] In sum, the Plymouth paper proved to be as faithful an abolitionist ally as a nonabolitionist journal could be in the 1830s. If several other papers passed them off as raving lunatics and un-American subversives, *We, the People*, defended abolitionists as "patriotic" and devoted citizens.[49]

This local press coverage was crucial. With the proliferation of newspapers in the 1830s, even remote areas of Massachusetts could be plugged into agents' movements and abolition's growth. The *Salem Gazette* penetrated several northern towns and villages, representing locales from the Maine border to the Atlantic coastline near Salem. Plymouth's *We, the People* had agents in "Middleboro, Bridgewater, Abbington, and Halifax," all small townships south of Boston. Gaining the support of local editors or newspapers, or even achieving some sort of truce (for example, getting editors to announce local antislavery activities without endorsing them), became part and parcel of abolitionist strategy to win over the people of Massachusetts.

Governor Edward Everett's personal collection of newspapers, now in the Massachusetts Historical Society, attests to abolition's impact on the state's highest official during the 1830s. Everett, congressman, presidential hopeful, and one of the best orators of the day, remained a lifelong opponent of abolitionism. A member of the American Colonization Society in the late 1820s, he feared abolition's divisive effects on state and national politics from the 1830s onward. The fiery new abolitionism portended political disintegration, community discord, and, in its worst tendencies, disunion. Antislavery convictions were one thing, he observed; agents' work in the countryside quite another.

Everett monitored abolitionists' movements in his home state via local newspapers. Pouring through papers from many small towns, he could see that these activists had stirred up the slavery issue and gained critical friends as well as a host of enemies among local editors. Everett must have paused the day he read James Gillespie Birney's speech to the American Anti-Slavery Society in conjunction with the *Essex County Gazette*'s support for it. Spread over six front-page columns, Birney's address proclaimed "that for the permanent safety of the union, it is indispensable that *the whole moral power of the free states* be concentrated and brought into action for the extermination of slavery." But the local editor really brought the message home, commenting that Birney's "powerful" and "eloquent speech" had "enriched the paper." "Let our learned and wise men," he observed, "let our shrewd and far-seeing politicians, who affect to detest the Christian and patriotic ardor of the Abolitionists read this speech." Indeed, "any reader" who doubted the cause should examine Birney's speech, "remembering that it is a RECENT SLAVEHOLDER WHO SPEAKS!" The editor had people like Everett and Daniel Webster in mind, "that part of the community," he concluded, who swear that "the North have nothing to do with [southern slavery]." Read Birney's speech, he challenged, for it "answers that objection."50

With newspapers in Lynn, Essex County, Plymouth, Concord, and, to the west, Northampton providing similar support for abolitionism, Everett wondered how far he could go in condemning it. Could he ban hotheaded abolitionist lecturers? On a copy of the *Boston Courier* for August 21, 1835, for example, Everett highlighted an important article that he labeled "A Legal Opinion on the Legality of State Laws to [prohibit] Interference with Slavery (*sic*)." Can a state legislature, a local correspondent asked, prohibit the publication of abolitionist articles "tending to promote insurrection?" The question involved grave constitutional matters, especially the relationship of northern states (and the federal government) to southern slavery. In both implicit as well as explicit ways, the writer concluded, the Constitution protected southern slavery from any outside interference. The Fourth and Tenth Amendments reserved certain power to the states alone, especially that over slavery; moreover, the very "compact" of Union shielded southern slavery. Slavery might be a moral evil, but the South alone must deal with it. "The DUTY of every northern man" is to uphold this concept — even to the point of passing legislation to prevent northern agitation against slavery.[51]

As Everett's newspaper collection illustrates, more than a few residents of Massachusetts supported abolitionism. That support was only part of Everett's worry. Censorship of whites might bring howls that the southern slave power controlled northern whites, too. Despite these concerns, Everett supported calls to curtail abolitionist activism in his state. By exploiting the local press, abolitionist agents had made a palpable impression on local citizens, as well as the governor himself.

HOSTILE LOCAL PAPERS especially condemned the impact of traveling agents on a town's gender and racial conventions. Sweeping in from outside of the area and championing a radical equality for all human beings, newspapers complained, agents caused needless "excitement." "Promiscuous" public meetings among black and white, male and female citizens offended residents' sensibilities. In Lynn, a correspondent complained that abolitionist agents attracted two "large meetings" in August 1835 — nearly prompting a riot — peopled "mostly by females, AS USUAL." Another riot almost occurred later that month at a meeting of "both sexes" in Haverhill. In Plymouth, Springfield, and Greenfield, citizens complained about abolitionists' "amalgamationist" meetings, at which blacks and whites "intermixed" without any "regard for caste."[52]

Black activists helped bolster the development of grassroots activism by selling *Liberator* subscriptions, rallying support for abolitionist speeches, and offering places of refuge for traveling agents. In the midst of his first lecture tour through Massachusetts, Maine, and Rhode Island, William Lloyd Garrison hailed local groups of African Americans as abolition's "best friend." Garrison stayed with black families in Haverhill, Massachusetts, and Portland, Maine, writing that such interaction with local black communities continually inspired him. In Haverhill, he proclaimed that after black New Englanders' support, "my obligations [to them] assume a mountainous height." When denied a chance to preach in local churches, Garrison often relied on blacks to supply a meetinghouse or public gathering place.[53]

Women served an even more prominent role at the grassroots level.[54] Indeed, circuit activity in Massachusetts towns proved that women could be key organizers and agitators, not simply maternal moralists.[55] On his first lecture tour outside of Boston in the summer of 1832, Garrison noted that local women "filled" meetinghouses, creating a palpable sense of enthusiasm: in Hallowell, Maine, women impressed Garrison with their vow to form a local "female antislavery society"; in Worcester, "the ladies" packed the town hall to overflowing; in Providence, there was "considerable interest" in abolitionism among the ladies.[56]

A private meeting with three women in Haverhill prompted Garrison to craft a mini-treatise on women's involvement in the abolition movement. Like Elizabeth Margaret Chandler, Garrison wrote about women's potential as grassroots activists. "The females of Britain" provided an important example of this potential, he noted, and the three Haverhill women's abolitionist efforts revealed "a talent, a spirit which if actively exerted, may be sufficient to save our country."[57]

Other traveling agents often reported that women did more than merely attend local meetings; rather, they proved to be energizing forces. Amos Phelps, who would later walk out of a meeting where Lynn reformer Abigail Kelley was appointed to work with him, wrote that wherever he went, women would ask, "What should WE do?" Phelps recalled "delightful meeting[s] with the ladies" on abolitionist tactics, as women helped fill lecture halls by bringing friends and distributing handbills. He cited "Mrs. Clarissa Tyson" of Wrentham, Massachusetts, as a stalwart supporter whom other abolitionists should contact when in town.[58]

Charles Burleigh, who worked for the American Anti-Slavery Society in the eastern half of Massachusetts during 1835, relied on local women to build a base of followers in small towns and communities. As Burleigh worked town after town — staying several nights, debating, organizing, lecturing — he remarked on the "interest of the ladies." In one striking instance in Marlborough, a small town outside Concord, he noted that women had literally outvoted men to form an auxiliary society. As Burleigh humorously put it, whereas the men at his lecture were opposed to the measure, "not a lady voted no, for they rose in favor, almost to a man."[59]

In Sudbury, Burleigh met a "choice woman," as he put it, one "who is AS zealous, well-informed, and intelligent" as any abolitionist. She was a "mountain to speak of," for she "has taken much pain" to advertise abolitionist speeches throughout the county, to convert skeptical friends, and to distribute antislavery literature. She and not he, Burleigh explained, had "produced all of the abolitionism that exists in this town" and "a good deal of the antislavery spirit in [several] other places." In Concord, two women interrupted his conversation with a local gentleman, forcing Burleigh to talk about abolition for nearly two hours. Burleigh was then invited home for dinner, where one of the women admitted that she was quite "prejudiced" against the abolition movement generally and William Lloyd Garrison in particular. After more discussion about the cause and Burleigh's explanation of "the facts" of abolition, she declared that "Garrison [and others] should be canonized." "She had written friends in Portland [Maine] to have nothing to do with" abolition, he reported, "but [she said] 'I must write them again and tell them better.'" The women's views had been "revolutionized," Burleigh concluded, and they would pay dividends for the movement.[60]

Local female antislavery societies exploded between 1833 and 1837. Women organized auxiliaries in Reading, Amesbury Mills, Lowell, Uxbridge, New Bedford, Weymouth, and Boxborough, Massachusetts, as well as in such places as Portland and Bangor, Maine; Providence, Rhode Island; and Concord, New Hampshire. In just four years, over thirty separate female groups existed outside of the flagship Boston Female Anti-Slavery Society (BFASS). "The rapid multiplication of [female] societies in this vicinity," the BFASS wrote, testified to the impressive growth of female activism.[61]

Although local women worked closely with traveling male agents, many of them viewed the BFASS as their guiding light. Cofounded by black and white Bostonians in 1833, it attracted people from a variety of religious and economic backgrounds. Quakers, Baptists, and Unitarians from middling and upper-crust segments of Boston society streamed into the organization. By the end of the decade, the BFASS had nearly four hundred members, including well-known literary activists like Lydia Maria Child, whose *An Appeal in Favor of the Colored Race* became an abolitionist best-seller, and Maria Weston Chapman, who edited the reports of the New England Anti-Slavery Society.[62]

Officers of the BFASS took it upon themselves to encourage female activism at the grass roots. In 1834 the group began an extensive correspondence campaign to "form plans of efficient cooperation" among the female abolition societies "rapidly" forming throughout New England. "Union is strength," Boston's women declared, sending letters to female abolitionists in Lowell, Reading, Amesbury Mills, Bangor, and Providence. "By combining" their efforts, women would "increase their strength and influence" in the abolitionist ranks and thereby enable the movement as a whole to "directly confront" the nation's lawmakers. The BFASS urged women to read and distribute antislavery newspapers in their communities (particularly the *Liberator*), to support agents' work in the countryside, and, most importantly, to communicate with one another about strategies.[63]

The BFASS offered most of the tactical directives to women in "the field." In the summer of 1835, for example, it announced plans to flood southern homes with abolitionist appeals. "We shall ardently beseech [southern women] to use the mighty influence now lying dormant in their hands," the BFASS wrote, "for the removal of this fearful crime [of slavery] from among them." It was hoped that "members of the female anti-slavery societies of New England" would get "in step" with this tactic. In the winter of 1838 Boston women emphasized the importance of female petitioning, especially the devising of "efficient" local methods of canvassing. "Would it not be well for local societies to supply ALL WOMEN [in the area] with petitions?" the group asked Bangor females. The BFASS advised local groups to follow its precinct plan by sending memorials and canvassing instructions to community leaders. Finally, it emphasized the significance of women's written work. Female antislavery societies, the BFASS admonished, should consult publications "peculiarly fitted to do good among an enquiring population": "Mrs. Child's Anti-Slavery Catechism," "Angelina Grimké's Letter to the Women of the South," and "Catherine Beecher in Answer to Her Late Work on Slavery," among others. "By purchasing these books and finding some method of circulating them," the Bostonians argued, "great good can be accomplished."[64]

Although few local female societies could match the BFASS in membership and prestige, most vowed to become indispensable supporters of the cause. As agents discovered, women in Amesbury Mills, Uxbridge, Reading, and other small towns pledged money, helped fill meetinghouses, generated subscriptions to antislavery papers, circulated petitions to Congress and the Massachusetts legislature, and distributed antislavery periodicals and literature.

Religion and reform became the dual entry points for many local female abolitionists. The Second Great Awakening challenged women as well as men to become exemplars of pious and benevolent behavior — shapers of a newly sanctified world. Local preachers tried to instill a radical religiosity in their parishioners. Women responded by forming a variety of reform organizations. Yet this approach often pitted conscience against conformity, for many local preachers did not want women to step beyond their roles as mothers, wives, and daughters. Abolitionist agents (and the BFASS) thus tapped a need among many evangelical women in New England who felt constrained in local religious groups. When asked to become coadjutors of the abolitionist cause, many local women eagerly jumped on board.

Abigail Kelley exemplifies women's role in spreading abolitionism through Massachusetts. Born in 1810, Kelley came from a farm family that had migrated to Lynn in the 1830s. Before embarking on a career as schoolteacher, lecturer, and reformer, she joined a local group of women who sought to protect "female industry" — shoe and garment workers exploited in industrial shops. After William Lloyd Garrison rolled into town for a series of public lectures on slavery in 1832, Kelley became an ardent abolitionist. A few years later she helped establish the Lynn Female Anti-Slavery Society and served as its corresponding secretary. In 1837 she engineered a fund drive that raised two hundred dollars for the NEASS — more than any single donation that year. In the same year she also steered petition drives that, according to one local minister, garnered 2,800 signatures (in a town of 20,000 citizens) with seemingly "little effort."[65]

Kelley's star continued to rise. She was a delegate to the National Convention of Anti-Slavery Women in 1837. The next year the state abolition society asked her to draft a clerical appeal challenging ministers throughout New England to roust pro-slavery apologists from their pulpits. And in 1839, the American Anti-Slavery Society assigned her an agency position of her own. "My mission has been among the people," she declared, "amid the little sources of public sentiment." The people often returned less flattering compliments. Several Connecticut towns denied her the right to speak. Even some abolitionists in Massachusetts frowned on her agency assignment. Nevertheless, women found her to be a continuing inspiration. "She had no equal," feminist Lucy Stone eulogized at her funeral in 1887.[66]

Because Abigail Kelley (like Lydia Maria Child and Angelina and Sarah Grimké) remains a recognizable figure, she illuminates the unheralded but critical efforts of myriad local women. Indeed, female abolitionists became a powerful constituency at the grass roots. Even before Kelley became an agent in 1839, local women pressed state and national leaders to hire female lecturers. William Lloyd Garrison received requests for Grimké lectures from the Smith sisters of Glastonbury, Connecticut. Lifelong abolitionists, they asked Garrison to have the "Grimkés stop in Connecticut" on their way from Boston to New York City to give a lecture in their small town. New Hampshire's James Farmer explained that Angelina Grimké was becoming increasingly popular in his area. Farmer had heard her speak to the New Hampshire legislature in 1837, and that lecture, he concluded, produced a real "spark" of reform in New Hampshire. Farmer's female assistant ("Miss Clark"), who had recently moved from Boston, wrote to Francis Jackson of the Massachusetts Anti-Slavery Society that she wanted news of Boston women's activities, particularly Lydia Maria Child's.[67]

Ironically, despite their grassroots support, women activists eventually divided the abolitionist leadership. Worried that women's rights issues would become part of the abolitionist agenda, Amos Phelps finally led an exodus of reformers from the Massachusetts Anti-Slavery Society in 1840. Yet other agents attuned to the energies of the field, like Garrison, May, and Burleigh, rarely objected to women's participation in the cause because their contact with female activists in the countryside had been critical from the beginning. Phelps was one of the few agents to take such a strong stand against working with female lecturers and committee members.

Liberator subscriptions provide another reason why many agents remained stalwart supporters of female activists. After 1830 women comprised just under 10 percent of the paper's almost three thousand subscribers in Massachusetts. Though a small percentage of the readership, female subscribers doubled the number of ministers, doctors, and lawyers *combined* who took the paper between 1830 and 1840. When linked to agents' stories about female activism on the circuit and to the interplay between agents and work done by female societies, the picture is one of an increasingly influential female constituency in Massachusetts's small towns and communities by the mid-1830s. As Samuel May would remark, unheralded local women such as "Cecilia Brooks" of South Scituate, Massachusetts, had been vital parts of abolitionist outreach tactics since virtually the beginning of "modern" abolitionism.[68]

BECAUSE OF African American and female efforts, grassroots activism connected abolitionist agents to a new constituency of activists. At the beginning of the 1830s, Massachusetts abolitionists wanted nothing more than to "revolutionize" public sentiment. That public sentiment could in turn revolutionize the movement, and that this public sentiment would be expressed by so many African American and rural females, shattered notions of just who might become an abolitionist. Only after agents spread out into the "field" did "modern" abolitionists see the true potential of organizing the American populace at large.

Although many citizens continually condemned abolitionist agents, Massachusetts reformers felt heat from a surprising source: esteemed abolitionists in Pennsylvania. Members of the PAS opposed all of the new tactics:

sending lecturers into small towns and communities, holding "promiscuous meetings" of men and women, blacks and whites, and focusing so intensely on organizing the people. Few Pennsylvania reformers embraced abolitionist agents who visited the Quaker State, refusing on some occasions to open meetinghouses to them. As one senior Pennsylvanian worried in 1833, the "fiery orators" of new-style abolitionism threatened the Union's well-being by arousing the people's passions. The new "abolition societies are numerous, powerful, enthusiastic and determined," he continued, but they might well instigate civil war.[69]

By the end of the 1830s, some "venerable" PASers even stopped referring to themselves as abolitionists. To them, the very term now connoted radicalism in its purest form. William Rawle declined an honorary membership in the New England Anti-Slavery Society in 1832. Jonathan Roberts, another influential member of the PAS, turned away from "the extreme school" of abolitionism, too. Both PAS president Joseph Parrish and crackerjack lawyer John Sergeant agreed that a strategy of "agitating [northern] communities" augured ill for the nation. Sergeant actually reached out to moderate southern politicians in Congress to quell sectional tensions. Even former PASer David Paul Brown, who served as head of the Garrisonian Philadelphia Anti-Slavery Society in the early 1830s, complained about agents' tactics. "The conduct and proceedings" of these new abolitionists, he wrote to his mentor William Rawle, "fail to meet with my entire approbation." Brown worried that agents' "zeal" would hurt the gains made by "conscientious emancipation."[70]

According to one nineteenth-century commentator who had been involved in the movement since the 1820s, Bay State abolitionists' "exertions to disseminate their doctrines" through every portion of society "by means of the press, public lectures, and discussion in public" marked a dividing line between old and new fighters of slavery. Whereas the "dignified" PAS worked diligently and deferentially among legal and political elites, the new abolitionists made the cause a noisy public affair among "thousands" and "thousands" of ordinary supporters. New abolitionists' reliance on black and female reformers, he concluded, offered yet another "striking" difference.[71]

Agents' grassroots work truly signaled a new era for abolitionism. On the one hand, Garrison's initial hopes for a coalition of young and old abolitionists in the 1830s were dashed by his group's grassroots activities.[72] On the other hand, the agency's impact in the countryside transformed abolition's constituency: new abolitionists realized that they did not need to rely on the old guard in an urban milieu. Of course, this split between old and new abolitionists over direction and style revealed a broader cultural shift that, to one degree or another, affected all segments of American society by the 1830s: the move from a rationalist, deferential, and republican world-view to a more democratic and emotional sensibility. For abolitionists, this meant the repudiation of prevailing notions of activism — those that had emphasized not just working within the American legal and political frame-work but having certain people do that work. Lawyers and politicians were prized in this pre–1830 phase because they could best manipulate the levers of law and government to attain abolitionist ends. Second-wave abolition-ists shattered this notion not by rejecting in toto political and legal activism but by focusing less on working strictly through formal institutional struc-tures and more on mobilizing the people (especially *new* groups of people) to fight slavery. It was, quite simply, the difference between working the courts and working the streets.[73]

Strategies and tactics — specifically, the agency system and grassroots ac-tivism — served as important indicators of this fault line. For it was on the circuit and in local communities that abolitionist agents saw the implica-tions of grassroots work, from the way people organized to which people organized and where. As Charles Payne explains in his wonderful book on the changing dynamics of civil rights activism in Mississippi of the 1960s, *I've Got the Light of Freedom* (1995), only through sustained work in local communities do leaders see the capacity for changing strategies and tac-tics.[74] Massachusetts abolitionists were perhaps the first social activists to realize the wisdom of this statement. In a short span of years, agents, with the help of local people, reoriented American abolitionism almost com-pletely. It would not be the last time that abolitionists divided over tactics, strategies, and personnel, but it was the first time that one could speak of American abolitionism in terms of a truly broad social movement.

The Struggle Continued

Who believes that slavery can long last?
—William Lloyd Garrison, 1864

IN DECEMBER 1864 the American Anti-Slavery Society (AASS) convened delegates to a national meeting in abolition's birthplace, Philadelphia. With Abraham Lincoln's Emancipation Proclamation now in effect and thousands of fugitive slaves leaving plantations each month, southern slavery seemed doomed. The Civil War, predicted by abolitionists in the 1850s and in no small part inspired by their activism, would demolish slavery in a few short years. William Lloyd Garrison therefore asked his fellow reformers to disband their organization. "Who now believes slavery is to continue ten years longer in our land?" Garrison asked. "We are very near Jubilee."[1]

Garrison's clarion call was also one for unity, for abolitionism had long been riven by factionalism over strategy and tactics. Within a decade of abolition's major upheaval in the 1830s (when the founding generation of activists gave way to "modern" reformers), the movement fragmented. Black and white abolitionists clashed over leadership roles in the American Anti-Slavery Society, male and female abolitionists clashed over the place of women's rights in a movement for racial reform, political reformers clashed with those opposed to forming an abolitionist political party, and the Massachusetts Anti-Slavery Society clashed with, and eventually split from, the American Anti-Slavery Society. An abolitionist movement persisted down to the Civil War, but it was deeply divided.

For a time in 1864, factionalism gave way to a united front. At the national meeting men and women who had not spoken or even written to one another in years exchanged warm embraces and fond memories. Garrison movingly read a letter from Arthur Tappan, the New York City abolitionist who had helped found the American Anti-Slavery Society before splitting with Garrison in the 1840s. "During the years that have intervened since we last met," Tappan's letter began, "I have often recalled the time when we were united in working for the slave. I regretted that any occurrence should have estranged us."[2]

Reality intruded before Garrison's motion to disband could be carried. Wary of his newfound optimism, two delegates (and like Tappan, onetime friends with whom Garrison had had a parting of the ways) urged AASS members *not* to disband. Frederick Douglass and Abigail Kelley adamantly argued that American racism was still too powerful to give up the fight. As Douglass professed, reformers' work would never be done until "the colored man was admitted a full member in good and regular standing in the American body politic."[3]

Abigail Kelley spoke in even harsher terms. According to her, American culture still frowned upon abolitionists' calls for full black equality. "I don't believe in the doctrine of instantaneous conversion," she tersely stated about Americans' commitment to racial injustice at the end of the Civil War. Kelley then lectured the delegates: "I want to remind you that we labored for 27 years previous [to the Civil War] . . . And now whence this sudden change? Because a great mass of people have come to believe" in abolition and civil rights? "Although there must have been an immense change in the public sentiment in consequence of the action of the Anti-Slavery Society," she warned that "we should not be too confident as to the character of [that] wonderful change since the war commenced."[4]

The words of Douglass and Kelley were a sobering reminder that second-wave abolitionists' most wildly optimistic goals would remain only that — wildly optimistic. Such optimism harkened back to the heady predictions of reformers at the start of the 1830s. Convinced that the first generation of abolitionists in Pennsylvania lacked the tactical key to ending bondage, second-wave reformers in Massachusetts burst onto the national scene in that decade predicting that their movement — racially integrated, media conscious, and grassroots oriented — would solve the vexing problem of slavery, avert racial rebellion, and establish the basis for a society of equals in short order. Yet second-wave abolitionism hit the wall in American political and social life. As Abigail Kelley put it nearly thirty years after she optimistically joined the movement to end slavery, "We have [Confederate president] Jeff Davis to thank" for making abolitionism a reality. And so many abolitionists would remain crusaders for racial justice into the Reconstruction period.[5] The American Anti-Slavery Society did not disband until 1870.

To be sure, abolitionism had traveled far in American culture by the

1860s. At the national level, many abolitionist principles were neatly integrated into government policy at the close of the Civil War. Thus a battle initially waged to defend the Union had been, almost by sleight of hand, turned into Abraham Lincoln's "new birth of freedom" for the American republic — a sleight of hand but for the very real abolitionist foundation supporting his mesmerizing words at Gettysburg, the Second Inaugural, and other memorable addresses. Slavery would finally be destroyed, Lincoln concluded, because it violated the basic premises of American ideology. Just as important, more than rhetoric would be needed to reform American race relations. Subsequent federal action by Lincoln's Republican Party — including a constitutional amendment ending slavery, another amendment theoretically protecting the rights of all citizens regardless of race, and a third securing black male voting rights — attempted to go even further on the road to racial reconciliation and justice. That effort, too, came up short with the rout of so-called Radical Republicanism in the 1870s. Nevertheless, the Civil War era did prove to be a Second American Revolution.[6] The yawning gap between American liberty and American slavery was now closed. Perhaps that is why even so famed an abolitionist as Wendell Phillips would call Lincoln's Republican Party "a milestone" in American political life. "It shows how far we have got," he said on one occasion.[7] Phillips, like other abolitionists, also realized that without the decades of struggle by thousands of activists (men and women of all ethnic groups and creeds, some well known, others unheralded), it is doubtful that the American nation would have come even that far. Abolitionists created a vast well of antislavery ideas, but they also continually pushed for action from the American people and government. That tradition of activism eventually influenced American political discourse during the age of Lincoln. It continued to inspire activists through the twentieth century, from W. E. B. Du Bois and the National Association for the Advancement of Colored People (NAACP) in the early 1900s to neo-abolitionist civil rights reformers of the 1950s and 1960s.

As the commanding presence of Frederick Douglass and Abigail Kelley at the 1864 antislavery convention also reminds us, abolitionism itself underwent a stunning change. Indeed, it exemplified the march of American democracy extolled by Lincoln. Begun during the American Revolutionary era and guided skillfully by a band of elite white activists through the backrooms of politics and the technicalities of law, abolitionism was many years later a pluralistic movement of outraged Americans demanding change. To see Douglass and Kelley stride onto the Philadelphia stage as leaders of a cause as old as the republic is to see why abolitionism became a force precisely when it did in the 1830s. Abolitionism did not die and then suddenly reappear at that moment — it was seized by new generations of activists at a time when American society felt the convulsions of myriad democratic movements.

African Americans and women formed the nucleus of the insurgent movement that transformed American abolitionism, and they remained at the center of national debates over slavery between the 1830s and the Civil War. African Americans were really the first agents of abolitionist change. For years after the American Revolution, black leaders had tried to enter and influence mainstream antislavery organizations and tactics. Viewed by early reformers as incompetent (they lacked political influence and legal standing), black activists were assigned segregated roles as teachers and community liaisons, if that.

Not content to remain quiet while white reformers did the work, however, black leaders established a parallel universe of abolitionist tactics during the post-Revolutionary era. Revolving around the public sphere — pamphleteering against slavery's immorality, producing personal memoirs of oppression, making stump speeches — these tactics utilized the only political space available to African Americans during the early republic. Black activists hoped to enlist the public's sympathy and emotion to destroy racial subjugation. To repeat James Forten's 1813 phrase, black activists hoped to issue "an appeal to the heart." If Americans would take seriously the stories of oppression and injustice, Forten and his black colleagues asserted, they too would act swiftly to end slavery and institute universal equality in deeds as well as words.

Despite an early and consistent push, literary tactics remained largely a part of African American life until a new generation of white reformers came to the fore in the 1820s and 1830s. Profoundly influenced not just by religious principles or economic and political changes but by black activism itself, white leaders like William Lloyd Garrison and Amos Phelps sought for the first time to integrate the movement to end slavery. Even where whites dominated positions of leadership during abolition's "modern" era, a black sensibility pervaded the movement. In new reformers' campaigns for complete racial vindication and a thoroughgoing investigation of white power, American society saw in abolition "blackness" projected before the public eye as never before.

The greatest indicator of this black influence was in print culture. That tactic — perhaps more than any other — defined abolitionism after 1830. It remains indelibly marked in our consciousness as the essence of abolition: Frederick Douglass's *Narrative of the Life of Frederick Douglass: An American Slave* (1845), Harriet Beecher Stowe's *Uncle Tom's Cabin*, with its appendix of true black narratives (1852), Garrison's fiery editorials telling Americans that abolitionists would be heard. These literary tactics flowed first from black abolitionism. Although they were magnified with white help, without a preceding black push, abolitionism would have looked and sounded both radically different and much less radical after 1830.

In a similar way, women helped produce both a new abolitionism and a new stage for projecting their political concerns. Previously excluded from formal roles in the movement, women became first-rank members of second-wave abolitionism. At one level, female reformers helped establish new strategies and tactics, particularly organizing at the grassroots level. Working in local communities throughout Massachusetts, women collected petition signatures, distributed books and pamphlets (especially those of female authors), organized antislavery meetings, funded abolitionist speakers, and often provided the critical votes for forming grassroots antislavery societies. Whether as protofeminists or concerned mothers, wives, and daughters, women changed the way abolitionists perceived the movement to end slavery. Their grassroots activities illustrated that every person in the republic had a role in ending bondage, not simply men in positions of political or legal power. In short, women gave practical meaning to second-wave abolitionists' grand strategy of turning the whole nation into one big antislavery society.

In engaging in political behavior as essentially nonvoting citizens, women also expanded notions of political activism. Significantly, the transformation of abolition took shape in an era when politics itself expanded in all directions. The debate over women's role in the republic was no ancillary concern — it was part of a broader reconsideration of political culture. For example, in petitioning individual senators or critiquing southern slavery in a public forum, female reformers collapsed distinctions between male and female, public and private — not completely, to be sure, but in a definite way. Throughout the North and in parts of the South, women broke out of explicitly female roles: they worked in northern factories, staffed reform organizations, and began their own movement for equal rights. Female abolitionism melded with these trends, making abolition itself appear much more than simply a movement to end slavery. Both northern and southern opponents of slavery spoke of abolition's disregard for notions of gender caste. Ultimately, then, female abolitionists created a reform world that could never be separated from the various events swirling around the republic, for it flowed from those larger changes.

The southern reply to Stowe's *Uncle Tom's Cabin* bluntly illustrates the point. In 1852 *Southern Literary Messenger* editor John Thompson vowed to "annihilate" Stowe in public, even though that smacked of impropriety. "I would have the review as hot as hell fire, blasting and searing the reputation of the vile wretch in petticoats who could write such a volume." Of course, Thompson was not simply attacking a northern woman who moved beyond her household station; he wanted to counteract her considerable public power. "I want [the review] to tell throughout the length and breadth of the land . . . that whenever *Uncle Tom's Cabin* is mentioned . . . men shall call up the *Messenger*'s annihilation of its author."[8]

Assigned the review, George Frederick Holmes warned readers that Stowe, like other abolitionist women, had used the narrative form not to "amuse . . . but to proselytize." "This is a fiction," he went on, one with corrosive affects on the master-slave relationship. According to Holmes, "a harsher intercourse" would now prevail on southern plantations to counteract the "tampering by incendiary missionaries" like Stowe. A harsher intercourse must now ensue between northern and southern politicians — especially between southern men and northern women on the battlefield of print. In short, southern masters could no longer dismiss female activists as "vile wretches in petticoats."[9] In just such a way, women were legitimized as political actors.

African American female activists surmounted even greater hurdles, but they too intensified their efforts through the Civil War. As Maria Stewart noted in the early 1830s, black women faced a double bind: both black and white men and women often questioned their public reform activities. As late as the 1860s, Harriet Jacobs would wrestle with such issues of legitimacy. Did she actually write *Incidents in the Life of a Slave Girl* (1861), that searing indictment of masters' sexual exploitation of female slaves? Jacobs fought back by claiming both her identity as author and her legitimacy as an activist in the then-still-evolving sectional clash between North and South. Who could better reply to the likes of George Holmes and John Thompson on the realities of the master-slave relationship than Jacobs?

Between Maria Stewart's rise to prominence in the 1830s and the publication of Jacobs stunning narrative at the start of the Civil War, countless northern free black women emerged as abolitionists, community organizers, and educational leaders. They ranged from virtual celebrities such as Sojourner Truth to the somewhat obscure emigration advocate Maryanne

Shadd Cary. More often than not, they worked without fanfare. Their often unheralded exertions are illuminated in pamphlets by unheralded writers such as Elizabeth Wicks and Eliza Dungy of Troy, New York, and Mary Still of Philadelphia. Separated by time and place, each of these activists wrote polemical essays celebrating black women's continuing contributions to the cause of racial reform. In 1834, for instance, Wicks marked the first anniversary of the African Female Benevolent Society of Troy by praising the work of local black women in communities everywhere. "Joyful tidings are spreading far and wide," she announced, and "the colored population are exerting themselves in every direction." Black women must continue to play a critical role as spiritual educators and grassroots leaders, she went on, for racial vindication to occur North as well as South, for black women as well as men. She also counseled her sisters to always "remember the two million slaves" still in bondage — and to aim their efforts toward ending that evil institution. Twenty years later Mary Still made an even-more-forceful call for black women to escalate their activism, particularly in the creation of an evangelical newspaper for the black church. Still issued a cautionary footnote: many black men continued to believe that African American females "have little to do with the business of the church" or with public reform more generally. Nevertheless, she maintained, black women "are the backbone" of the church and therefore significant players in African American communities throughout America. If they wanted to take a leadership role in the literary sphere, they need apologize to no one.[10]

By integrating black and female reformers so explicitly with the cause, second-wave abolitionists created a higher barrier for themselves by constantly posing larger questions to the American people. Should African Americans and women participate in American civic and political life? Who decided? No doubt the majority of Americans would have said no. But African American and female activism would not be stifled after 1830. In fact, one of the most striking aspects of abolitionism between 1830 and 1860 was the continued prominence of black and female voices. Black speakers and writers made headlines for their condemnation of bondage and for the impact of their tactics on white politics — from defending fugitive slaves in Cincinnati or Buffalo or Boston to publishing pamphlets, books, and newspapers denouncing white racist society.

This trend persisted into the Civil War with impressive effects. As Richard Blackett has shown, black American speakers such as John Sella Martin and Thomas Morris Chester helped shape transatlantic antislavery opinion. Blackett found nearly fifty black activists who traveled among British textile workers, many whose jobs in British manufacturing were affected by Union blockades of southern cotton exporters in the 1860s. These black activists helped convince many English working men and women to support the Union over the Confederacy. Similarly, as Wendy Venet has shown, female reformers kept pressure on Abraham Lincoln to end bondage by constitutional amendment. In Venet's estimation, women created the climate in which Lincoln ultimately drafted his Emancipation Proclamation — the first political blow on the road to national emancipation.[11]

Without a shift in the nature of American political culture during the 1830s, black and female activists might never have overleaped the boundaries of early abolitionism. That shift had much to do with broad economic and philosophical changes — the demise of indentured servitude in the North and a corresponding rise in a democratic sensibility. But American political culture was redefined, too, with important consequences for abolitionism. Images, print media, campaigning and organizing at the grassroots level — all of these factors came to define American politics after 1830. They also defined American abolitionism of that period. Second-wave reformers thus came of age when the essence of democratic governance was undergoing significant revision. Post–1830 reformers looked at their world in a fundamentally different way from Revolutionary-era reformers, believing that no man should be restricted from participating in politics but also that politics should not be limited to institutions — or white men. Political effects could be reached by publishing powerful stories, by organizing seemingly powerless people in petition drives, by telling ordinary citizens that they too could interpret the meaning of the Constitution.

After 1830 Americans had to take abolitionist activism seriously, for it framed the meaning of a series of related issues that, in some way, touched everyone in the republic: sectional identity, racial superiority, constitutional construction, gender roles, alternatives to political change, the meaning and uses of political culture. Few issues could simultaneously ignite so many overlapping debates in antebellum American political and social life. But it did not just magically happen. Men and women — black and white — had to devise strategies and tactics that addressed multiple issues in a changing economic, political, and religious landscape. That they did is the best reason to recall the transformation of abolitionism, despite its failure to end slavery before the Civil War. For abolition was less about naive idealism and more about everyday citizens agitating for real-world change.

Letters from Maryland Slaveholders to Judge William Tilghman, Chief Justice of the Pennsylvania Supreme Court, Regarding Fugitive Slaves

June 1790, Alexander Crabbin, Maryland
Writes that he is upset because his slave ran to an abolitionist in Delaware and "is to be set free [there]." Wants his "rightful property" returned.

August 1797, James Hallyday, Maryland
"I would spare no pains of expense to get the fellow again, as he keeps up a correspondence with my negroes, and is enticing them away from me."

July 1800, Samuel Wright, Maryland
Has been notified that his fugitive slave has been jailed in Philadelphia. Asks how he can prevent losing him in Pennsylvania courts.

December 1800, James Lloyd, Maryland
Wants ads put in "the best circulating papers of New Jersey and Delaware" for the return of his fugitive. Writes that he is concerned about "the rash of runaways" from his plantation: "This mischief is becoming intolerable."

January 1801, William Helmsley, Maryland
Wants help reclaiming his fugitive "Stephen," whom he thinks might set out for Pennsylvania.

September 1801, James Tilghman, Maryland
Describes three runaway slaves.

January 1804, William Helmsley, Maryland
Writes that six slaves have left his plantation in the last few years. "I expect the whole of THEM [his slaves] will go off if I can't recover those who are out."

November 1811, John Cummins, Maryland
His runaway will probably set out for Philadelphia.

November 1811, Benjamin Galloway, Maryland
Introduces a South Carolina slaveholder who is "in pursuit of a runaway in Philadelphia."

March 1814, John Cummins, Maryland
Writes that his fugitive slave has been seen in Philadelphia.

Maps

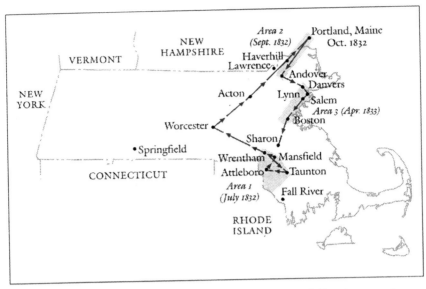

MAP 1A. Agent Travels in Massachusetts: William Lloyd Garrison's Travels, 1832–1833

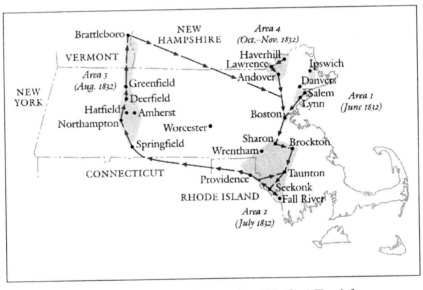

MAP 1B. Agent Travels in Massachusetts: Arnold Buffum's Travels for
the New England Anti-Slavery Society, 1832

APPENDIX 2

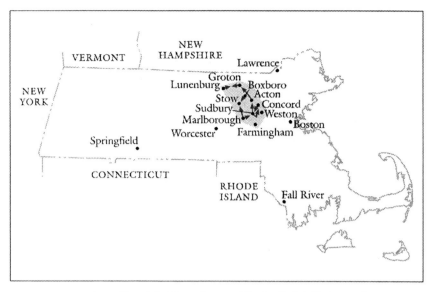

MAP 1C. Agent Travels in Massachusetts: Charles Burleigh's Agency in
Middlesex County, Massachusetts, March–April 1835

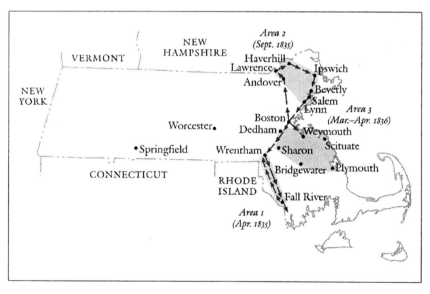

MAP 1D. Agent Travels in Massachusetts: Samuel May's Travels, 1835–1836

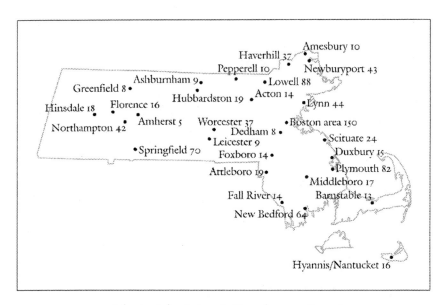

MAP 2. *Liberator* Subscriptions in Massachusetts, 1830–1840

Source: *Liberator* Account Books 1–4, 1831–1865, Anti-Slavery Collection, Boston Public Library.

Note: As the map shows, rural subscriptions played a critical role in the paper's early success.

Abbreviations

In addition to the abbreviations appearing in the text, the following abbreviations are used in the notes.

ACAS	American Convention of Abolition Societies
BPL	Boston Public Library, Boston
FASS	Female Anti-Slavery Society
Genius	*Genius of Universal Emancipation*
HSP	Historical Society of Pennsylvania, Philadelphia
Letters, BPL	"Anti-Slavery Letters to William Lloyd Garrison and Others," Anti-Slavery Collection, Boston Public Library
MHS	Massachusetts Historical Society, Boston
PAS Papers	Microfilm edition of the Pennsylvania Abolition Society Manuscripts originally housed at the Historical Society of Pennsylvania (32 vols.)
PFASS	Philadelphia Female Anti-Slavery Society

Introduction

1. Like other fields in American history, the study of abolitionism has been rejuvenated by work in women's history, African American history, and the development of American subcultures. One major theme in my tale of abolition's transformation is how women and African Americans (for so long defined outside the nexus of organized abolitionism) joined white reformers to explode a preexisting movement against slavery. To see this—how men and women remade abolitionism almost completely after 1830—we need to start our examination of the movement in the Revolutionary era and take it into the time of William Lloyd Garrison, Elizabeth Chandler, and Frederick Douglass.

The bibliography of works dealing with abolitionism continues to grow, particularly the subfields of African American reform and female activism. What follows is a general survey of works both old and new. One broadly conceived study that does analyze early antislavery activity (but not so much organized abolitionism itself) is James Brewer Stewart's still standard work, *Holy Warriors: The Abolitionists and American Slavery*, rev. ed. (New York: Hill and Wang, 1996). His revised edition notes that abolitionist scholarship has not diminished in recent years but rather has reached avalanche proportions; see especially his preface. In addiiton, see his pathbreaking recent work on race and abolitionism, which spans the entire early national period: James Brewer Stewart, "The Emergence of Racial Modernity and the Rise of the White North, 1790–1840," *Journal of the Early Republic* 18, no. 2 (Summer 1998): 181–217, and James Brewer Stewart with George Price, "*To Heal the Scourge of Prejudice*": *The Life and Writings of Hosea Easton* (Amherst: University of Massachusetts Press, 1999). Paul Goodman's stimulating but posthumously completed book on abolitionism pushed the boundaries back somewhat, arguing that African American reformers played an important role in the movement to abolish slavery, especially in the anticolonization movement of the 1820s; see *Of One Blood: Abolitionism and the Origins of Racial Equality* (Berkeley: University of California Press, 1998). On the early period, the best works include David Brion Davis, *The Problem of Slavery in the Age of Revolution* (Ithaca: Cornell University Press, 1975), which analyzes the philosophical underpinnings of abolitionism during the Revolutionary era; Gary B. Nash, *Race and Revolution* (Madison, Wis.: Madison House, 1990), which similarly situates early antislavery philosophies in the context of broader political debates of the era but, like Davis's volume, slights abolitionist tactics and strategies; Jean R. Soderlund, *Quakers and Slavery: A Divided Spirit* (Princeton: Princeton University Press, 1988), a monographic analysis of antislavery philosophies within Quakerism; and Merton L. Dillon, *Slavery Attacked: Southern Slaves and Their Allies, 1619–1865* (Baton Rouge: Louisiana State University Press, 1990), which highlights black resistance in the fight against slavery but almost totally ignores organized abolitionism until the 1820s. The one older work that sought to bridge the gaps between abolition's early and later phases also focused on antislavery philosophies to the exclusion of the organized movement; see Alice Dana Adams, *The Neglected Period of Anti-Slavery in America, 1808–1832* (1908; Gloucester, Mass.: Peter Smith, 1964). For general treatments of abolition in northern states, see Arthur Zilversmit, *The First Emancipation: The Abolition of Slavery in the North* (Chicago: University of Chicago Press, 1967); Gary B. Nash and Jean R. Soderlund, *Freedom by Degrees: Emancipation in Pennsylvania and Its Aftermath* (New York: Oxford University Press, 1991); and Shane White, *Somewhat More Independent: The End of Slavery in New York City, 1770–1810* (Athens: University of Georgia Press, 1991).

On the later period, the standard works are Dwight Lowell Dumond, *Antislavery: The Crusade for Freedom in America* (New York: Norton, 1961); Louis Filler, *The Crusade against Slavery, 1830–1860* (New York: Harper and Row, 1960); Stanley Harrold, *The Abolitionists and the South, 1831–1861* (Lexington: University of Kentucky Press, 1995); Aileen S. Kraditor, *Means and Ends in American Abolitionism: Garrison and His Critics on Strategy and Tactics* (New York: Random House, 1967); and Ronald G. Walters, *The Antislavery Appeal: American Abolitionism after 1830* (Baltimore: Johns Hopkins University Press, 1976) — all of which examine the movement after Garrison's rise to fame but ignore the continuity of American abolition from the 1780s through the 1830s. For two excellent examinations of religious awakenings and the antislavery movement, see Robert H. Abzug, *Cosmos*

Crumbling: American Reform and the Religious Imagination (New York: Oxford University Press, 1994), and Lewis Perry, *Radical Abolitionism: Anarchy and the Government of God in Antislavery Thought* (Ithaca: Cornell University Press, 1973).

The most recent influential studies of black and female abolitionists point out that groups formerly excluded from organized abolition became increasingly forceful activists after 1830. See, e.g., Julie Roy Jeffrey's very crucial reexamination of female activism, *The Great Silent Army of Abolitionism: Ordinary Women in the Antislavery Movement* (Chapel Hill: University of North Carolina Press, 1998). See also Mia Bay's recent book on African American reformers and the problem of race, *The White Image in the Black Mind: African-American Ideas about White People, 1830–1925* (New York: Oxford University Press, 2000); Jean Fagin Yellin, *Women and Sisters: The Antislavery Feminists in American Culture* (New Haven: Yale University Press, 1989); Donald M. Jacobs, ed., *Courage and Conscience: Black and White Abolitionists in Boston* (Bloomington: Indiana University Press, 1993); C. Peter Ripley et al., eds., *The Black Abolitionist Papers*, 5 vols. (Chapel Hill: University of North Carolina Press, 1985–92); and Jean Fagin Yellin and John C. Van Horne, eds., *The Abolitionist Sisterhood: Women's Political Culture in Antebellum America* (Ithaca: Cornell University Press, 1995). The classic treatment of black abolitionism is Benjamin Quarles, *Black Abolitionists* (New York: Oxford University Press, 1969). For a recent analysis of black pamphleteers, see Richard Newman, Patrick Rael, and Phillip Lapsansky, eds., *Pamphlets of Protest: An Anthology of Early African-American Protest Literature* (New York: Routledge, 2000).

2. William Smyth to Amos A. Phelps, ca. 1838, Phelps Papers, BPL; Henry E. Benson to George W. Benson, March 27, 1835, Letters, BPL; Letter from Bucks County, Pa., to *National Enquirer*, December 31, 1836; Westmoreland Anti-Slavery Society Constitution, reprinted in *National Enquirer*, September 14, 1837; *Address to the Citizens of Pennsylvania, from the Convention Held at Harrisburg, for the Formation of a State Anti-Slavery Society* (Philadelphia, 1837).

3. Lucretia Mott to Ann Warren Weston, June 7, 1838, Letters, BPL; James Freeman Clark, *Anti-Slavery Days: A Sketch of the Struggle Which Ended in the Abolition of Slavery* (Boston, 1883), 7, 15. Clark admitted that the PAS was the world's first abolition society, but he argued that it faded away well before William Lloyd Garrison came to the fore.

4. William Rawle on forming a national antislavery society, May 20, 1833, Rawle Family Papers, HSP.

5. Charles Follen, January 1836, quoted in *Fourth Annual Report of the Massachusetts Anti-Slavery Society* (Boston, 1836), 53.

6. Henry Louis Gates, ed., *Classic Slave Narratives* (New York: Mentor, 1987), 87 (Garrison). For the "Africaner's" comments on Garrison's inclusion of black protest voices in *Thoughts on African Colonization* (Boston, 1832), see *Portland Christian Mirror*, March 7, 1833.

7. Although many scholars attribute the rise of radical abolition after 1830 to changing religious motivations, others focus on economic events. With the growth of free-wage labor and a new class of northern capitalists, abolitionists saw more clearly than ever the anomaly of slavery in the modern world. See esp. John Ash-

worth, *Commerce and Compromise, 1820–1850*, vol. 1 of *Slavery, Capitalism, and Politics in the Antebellum Republic* (New York: Oxford University Press, 1995), 132–33. See also David Donald, "Toward a Reconsideration of Abolitionists," *Lincoln Reconsidered: Essays on the Civil War Era* (New York: Random House, 1961), 19–36.

8. David Brion Davis, *Slavery and Human Progress* (New York: Oxford University Press, 1984), 127–31.

9. Abzug, *Cosmos Crumbling*, 79, 127–33; Timothy L. Smith, *Revivalism and Social Reform: American Protestantism on the Eve of the Civil War* (New York: Oxford University Press, 1957), 7–10.

10. Gordon S. Wood, *The Radicalism of the American Revolution* (New York: Knopf, 1993), introduction.

11. Harry L. Watson, *Liberty and Power: The Politics of Jacksonian America* (New York: Hill and Wang, 1990), 12–13.

12. Article from the "Democratic Address," reprinted in *Concord Freeman*, October 3, 1835.

13. For changing political tactics of the Jacksonian era, one of the best sources remains Robert V. Remini, *The Revolutionary Age of Andrew Jackson* (New York: Harper and Row, 1976), esp. chaps. 1–4.

14. Lawrence Frederick Kohl, *The Politics of Individualism: Parties and the American Character in the Jacksonian Era* (New York: Oxford University Press, 1984), 209, 213–18.

15. Lewis Perry, *Intellectual Life in America: A History* (New York: Franklin Watts, 1984), 209, 213–18.

16. See Garrison to Andrew Jackson, July 27, 1824; to editor of *Newburyport Herald*, May 7, 1827; and to editor of *Boston Courier*, July 14, 1827—all in Walter M. Merrill and Lewis Ruchames, eds., *Letters of William Lloyd Garrison*, 6 vols. (Cambridge: Harvard University Press, 1971), 1:23–24, 41–43, 49–50, respectively. For a stimulating reevaluation of Garrison, see Henry Mayer, *All on Fire: William Lloyd Garrison and the Abolition of Slavery* (New York: St. Martin's Press, 1998).

17. Alexander Saxton, *The Rise and Fall of the White Republic: Class Politics and Mass Culture in Nineteenth-Century America* (New York: Verso, 1990); David Roediger, *The Wages of Whiteness* (New York: Verso, 1991); Noel Ignatiev, *How the Irish Became White* (New York: Routledge, 1995).

18. "Appeal to the Voters of the Commonwealth of Pennsylvania," in *Minutes of the State Convention of the Colored Citizens of Pennsylvania . . . 1848* (Philadelphia, 1849), 8–12.

19. For a convenient list of these groups, see Herbert Aptheker, ed., *A Documentary History of the Negro People in the United States*, rev. ed. (New York: The Citadel Press, 1968), 112–14.

20. *Freedom's Journal*, October 27, 1827.

21. Nancy A. Hewitt, "On Their Own Terms: A Historiographical Essay," in Yellin and Van Horne, *Abolitionist Sisterhood*, 23–30 (quotation, p. 25). See also Nancy Cott, *The Bonds of Womanhood: "Woman's Sphere" in New England, 1780–1835* (New Haven: Yale University Press, 1977), and Suzanne Lebsock, *The Free Women of Petersburg: Status and Culture in a Southern Town, 1784–1860* (New York: Norton,

1984); also Acting Committee Minutes, September 30, 1830, PAS Papers, reel 2, and Acting Committee Report, September 1826, North Carolina Manumission Society Minutes, 1816–34, in *James C. Sprunt Historical Studies*, edited by H. M. Wagstaff (reprint ed., Chapel Hill: University of North Carolina Press, 1934), 136.

22. David Walker before the Boston GCA, reprinted in *Freedom's Journal*, December 19, 1828; Elizabeth Margaret Chandler in *Genius*, October 30, 1829.

23. Charles Follen, January 1836, quoted in *Fourth Annual Report of the Massachusetts Anti-Slavery Society* (Boston, 1836), 53.

24. On the rise of literacy, see most recently Joyce Appleby, *Inheriting the Revolution: The First Generation of Americans* (Cambridge: Harvard University Press, 2000); Newman, *Pamphlets of Protest*; and John W. Quist, *Restless Visionaries: The Social Roots of Antebellum Reform in Alabama and Michigan* (Baton Rouge: Louisiana State University Press, 1998).

25. For a perceptive analysis of African American literary politics, see David Waldstreicher, *In the Midst of Perpetual Fetes: The Making of American Nationalism, 1776–1820* (Chapel Hill: University of North Carolina Press, 1997), esp. chap. 6, "Mixed Feelings: Race and Nation."

26. *Freedom's Journal*, March 16, 1827. For a reprint of Forten's essay, see issues from February and March 1827. See also Newman, *Pamphlets of Protest*, 66–73.

27. The literature on social movements has grown steadily in recent years. My understanding of how movements begin and how they evolve over time owes most to Flora Davis, *Moving the Mountain: The Women's Movement in America since 1960* (New York: Simon and Schuster, 1991), which traces the women's movement during its "second-wave" of the sixties and seventies; Lawrence Goodwyn, *The Populist Moment: A Short History of the Agrarian Revolt in America* (New York: Oxford University Press, 1978), a classic analysis of populism that uses "movement culture" (the web of ideas and tactics that defines protest era) as the key trope; Charles M. Payne, *I've Got the Light of Freedom: The Organizing Tradition and the Mississippi Freedom Struggle* (Berkeley: University of California Press, 1995), a study of the grassroots organizing tradition in the civil rights era, especially the significance of local activists in rejuvenating social reform causes; Clayborne Carson, *In Struggle: SNCC and the Black Awakening of the 1960s* (Cambridge: Harvard University Press, 1981), which is not only the classic account of that organization but also a superb analysis of how movements constantly seek to replenish their idealism via new protest tactics; Bruce Laurie, *Artisans into Workers: Labor in Nineteenth-Century America* (New York: Hill and Wang, 1989), which examines the development of a movement culture among labor activists in mid-antebellum America; Jack Greenberg, *Crusaders in the Courts* (New York: Basic Books, 1994), and Stephen V. Wasby, *Race Relations Litigation in an Age of Complexity* (Charlottesville: University of Virginia Press, 1996), both of which analyze the relevance of legal tactics to social reform movements in general and the Civil Rights movement in particular; William Chafe, *Never Stop Running: Allard Lowenstein and the Struggle to Save American Liberalism* (New York: Oxford University Press, 1993), a biography of student organizer and political activist Lowenstein's several decades' fight to reform American society by utilizing (and upholding) American values and American governing

structures; Todd Gitlin, *The Sixties: Years of Hope, Days of Rage* (New York: Bantam Books, 1987), and Terry Anderson, *The Movement and the Sixties* (New York: Oxford University Press, 1995), both of which trace student movements amid the cultural and political transformations of the 1960s; Tara Hunter, *To 'Joy My Freedom: Southern Black Women's Lives and Labors after the Civil War* (Cambridge: Harvard University Press, 1997), part of a new wave of studies focusing on black female workers-reformers in the Reconstruction South, which illustrates the ways in which race and gender were fluid concepts in times of great social/political upheaval; and Eric Marcus, *Making History: The Struggle for Gay and Lesbian Equal Rights* (New York: HarperCollins, 1992), and Randy Shilts, *The Mayor of Castro Street: The Life and Times of Harvey Milk* (New York: St. Martin's Press, 1982), which trace the development of gay and lesbian protest from different angles — Marcus examining the radicalization of the movement among grassroots participants, Shilts using Milk's story to portray a movement determinedly American.

Chapter One

1. Here I take my cues from Gordon S. Wood, *The Radicalism of the American Revolution* (New York: Knopf, 1992), and Robert A. Ferguson, *Law and Letters in American Culture* (Cambridge: Harvard University Press , 1984). For a helpful review article on "Legal Elites," see Alfred Konefsky, "Law and Culture in Antebellum Boston," *Stanford Law Review* (April 1988): 1119–59. My use of the term "elite" in this chapter signifies a tactical style and outlook, not the aristocratic pretensions of PAS members. Currents of democratic rhetoric notwithstanding, early national society remained one of a "governing" or "power elite"; in addition, the rise of legal professions and merchant classes added new layers to American political leadership. It is useful to compare the tactical styles of early national radical groups (such as artisans and laborers) with those of the PAS, for the PAS did not approve of mob action, strikes, or similar tactics. On artisan and worker protest tactics, see esp. Paul A. Gilje, *The Road to Mobocracy: Popular Disorder in New York City, 1763–1834* (Chapel Hill: University of North Carolina Press, 1987); Howard B. Rock, *Artisans of the New Republic: The Tradesmen of New York City in the Age of Jefferson* (New York: New York University Press, 1979); and Sean Wilentz, *Chants Democratic: New York City and the Rise of the American Working Class, 1788–1850* (New York: Oxford University Press, 1984). For a close-up view of elite sensibilities, see esp. Tamara P. Thornton, *Cultivating Gentlemen: The Meaning of Country Life among the Boston Elite, 1785–1860* (New Haven: Yale University Press, 1989).

2. John Langdon to Benjamin Franklin of PAS, May 6, 1788, Loose Correspondence, PAS Papers, reel 11.

3. See David Brion Davis, *The Problem of Slavery in the Age of Revolution* (Ithaca: Cornell University Press, 1975), 213, and Jean R. Soderlund, *Quakers and Slavery: A Divided Spirit* (Princeton: Princeton University Press, 1985), 184–87. See also Wayne J. Eberly, "The Pennsylvania Abolition Society" (Ph.D. diss., Pennsylvania State University, 1973), esp. chap. 1.

4. Graham Russell Hodges, *Slavery and Freedom in the Rural North* (Madison, Wis.: Madison House, 1997), 91.

5. Minutes of Monthly Committee Meeting on Free Blacks in Philadelphia, PAS Papers, reel 25.

6. David Brion Davis, *Slavery in the Age of Revolution*, 196; Soderlund, *Quakers and Slavery*, 43–45.

7. Soderlund, *Quakers and Slavery*, 184.

8. David Brion Davis, *Slavery in the Age of Revolution*, 255.

9. See Graham Hodges recent work on slavery and African Americans in New York, *Root and Branch: African Americans in New York and East Jersey, 1613–1863* (Chapel Hill: University of North Carolina Press, 1999).

10. David Brion Davis, *Slavery in the Age of Revolution*, 250–55.

11. John Langdon to Benjamin Franklin of PAS, May 6, 1788, Loose Correspondence, PAS Papers, reel 11; editorial, *Genius*, July 1834.

12. The PAS also derived important sources of funding from wealthy benefactors. See Eberly, "Pennsylvania Abolition Society," 30–36.

13. Benjamin Rush to Jeremy Belknap, January 1, 1788, Belknap Papers, MHS.

14. "Extract of a Letter from . . . Rhode Island," August 23, 1788, PAS Papers, reel 11.

15. PAS to Governor Livingston of New Jersey, January 19, 1789, PAS Papers, reel 12.

16. *Respublica v. Richards*, 2 Dallas 224 (April 1795), summary found in Helen Tunnicliff Catterall, ed., *Judicial Cases Concerning American Slavery and the Negro*, 5 vols. (New York: Octagon Books, 1968), 4:260.

17. See Shane White, *Somewhat More Independent: The End of Slavery in New York City, 1770–1810* (Athens: University of Georgia Press, 1991), and Gary B.

Nash and Jean R. Soderlund, *Freedom by Degrees: Emancipation and Its Aftermath in Pennsylvania* (New York: Oxford University Press, 1991).

18. The classic treatment of emancipation schemes in northern locales is Arthur Zilversmit, *The First Emancipation: The Abolition of Slavery in the North* (Chicago: University of Chicago Press, 1967).

19. Thomas Arnold of Providence, R.I., to PAS, May 12, 1789, Loose Correspondence, PAS Papers, reel 11.

20. PAS to ACAS, April 2, 1804, PAS Papers, reel 2.

21. The PAS's 1790 petition appears in John P. Kaminski, *A Necessary Evil?: Slavery and the Debate over the Constitution* (Madison, Wis.: Madison House, 1995), 212.

22. Benjamin Rush to Jeremy Belknap, January 1, 1788, Belknap Papers, MHS.

23. Rush to Belknap, May 6, 1788, ibid.

24. Thomas Arnold of Providence to PAS, May 12, 1789.

25. On the petitions to the first federal Congress, see Howard Ohline, "Slavery, Economics, and Congressional Politics, 1790," *Journal of Southern History* 46 (August 1980): 335–59; William C. diGiacomantonio, "For the Gratification of a Volunteering Society: Antislavery and Pressure Group Politics in the First Federal Congress," *Journal of the Early Republic* 15, no. 2 (Summer 1995): 169–97; and Richard S. Newman, "Prelude to the Gag Rule: Southern Reaction to Antislavery

Petitions in the First Federal Congress," *Journal of the Early Republic* 16, no. 4 (Winter 1996): 571–600.

26. Stanley Elkins long ago criticized second-wave abolitionists for their "anti-institutionalism" but failed to consider early abolitionists' rigid reliance on them. See Elkins, *Slavery: A Problem in American Institutional and Intellectual Life* (New York: Grosset and Dunlap, 1959).

27. David Paul Brown, ca. 1833, Miscellaneous Papers, HSP.

28. Proposal of Samuel Garrigues, Acting Committee Minutes, September 25, 1828, PAS Papers, reel 2; Acting Committee Minutes, July 2, 1792, PAS Papers, reel 1.

29. *An Inquiry into the Causes of the Insurrection of the Negroes in the Island of St. Domingue* (London ed., 1792).

30. Ibid.

31. Thomas Collins of Delaware Abolition Society to PAS, April 16, 1788, Loose Correspondence, PAS Papers, reel 11.

32. Again, I wish to emphasize the elite-style tactics of PAS leaders. David Brion Davis (*Slavery in the Age of Revolution*, 215–16) argues that men of "affluence" generally dominated early abolitionist activity. I maintain that PAS lawyers exerted the most influence over tactics and strategies. Davis elaborates on this theme in a more recent exchange with John Ashworth and Thomas Haskell, conveniently reprinted from the original *American Historical Review* debates. See Davis, "Reflections on Abolitionism and Ideological Hegemony," in Thomas Bender, ed., *The Antislavery Debate: Capitalism and Abolitionism as a Problem in Historical Interpretation* (Berkeley: University of California Press, 1992), 161–79. Nash and Soderlund (*Freedom by Degrees*, 116–19) contend that PAS members were not all that affluent and not all that elite and that artisans joined the society as well.

33. See esp. Morton J. Horwitz, *The Transformation of American Law, 1780–1860* (Cambridge: Harvard University Press, 1977), and Gerald W. Gawalt, *The Promise of Power: The Emergence of the Legal Profession in Massachusetts, 1760–1840* (Westport, Conn.: Greenwood, 1979).

34. See esp. Paul Finkelman, ed., *The Law of Freedom and Bondage: A Casebook* (New York: Oceana Publications, Inc., 1986); Thomas D. Morris, *Southern Slavery and the Law, 1619–1860* (Chapel Hill: University of North Carolina Press, 1996); and Philip Schwarz, *Twice Condemned: Slaves and the Criminal Laws of Virginia, 1705–1865* (Baton Rouge: Louisiana State University Press, 1989).

35. William Rawle, "Opinion on the Constitutionality of Slavery in Pennsylvania," Rawle Family Papers, p. 154, HSP.

36. "Testimonial" of Robert Purvis, February 1841, in "Orations" of David Paul Brown, Miscellaneous Papers, HSP.

37. For descriptions of the PAS legal elite, I have relied on Horace Binney, *Leaders of the Old Philadelphia Bar* (Philadelphia, 1859).

38. See Isaac Parrish, *Brief Memoirs of Thomas Shipley and Edwin P. Atlee, Read before the Pennsylvania Society for Promoting the Abolition of Slavery* (Philadelphia, 1838), 15–20.

39. For a synthesis of the culture of reform in the post-Revolutionary period, see

Robert H. Abzug, *Cosmos Crumbling: American Reform and the Religious Imagination* (New York: Oxford University Press, 1994). Recent scholars of early national legal culture argue that organized benevolence had a dark side: "weighty" reformers' notions of propriety, morality, and order derived from a desire to control an increasingly fractious society. Thus even before market relations and industrialism took full shape, late-eighteenth-century reform had a coercive aspect. For a perceptive review of this recent literature, see Konefsky, "Law and Culture in Antebellum Boston," as well as Joel Bernard, "Between Religion and Reform: American Moral Societies, 1811–1821," *Proceedings of the Massachusetts Historical Society* 105 (1994): 1–38.

40. James Jackson of Georgia, January 12, 1790, *Annals of the Congress of the United States, 1789–1824*, 42 vols., edited by Gales and Seaton (Washington, D.C., 1834–56), 1st Cong., 2d sess., 1241.

41. Jeremy Belknap to Ebenezer Hazard, May 7, 1790, Belknap Papers, MHS.

42. John Adams to Jeremy Belknap, October 22, 1795, Tucker-Belknap Correspondence, *Collections of the Massachusetts Historical Society* (hereafter cited as *MHS Collections*), 5th ser., 416.

43. Ralph Lerner, *The Thinking Revolutionary: Principle and Practice in the New Republic* (Ithaca: Cornell University Press, 1987), 66–69; Edmund Randolph to Benjamin Franklin, August 2, 1788, Loose Correspondence, PAS Papers, reel 11.

44. Robert Pleasants to PAS, May 12, 1788, PAS Papers, reel 11.

45. Robert Pleasants to PAS, December 12, 1794, ibid.

46. Archibald McLean to PAS, February 15, June 6, 1796, ibid.

47. Robert Pleasants to PAS, April 2, 1795, ibid. See also Douglas R. Egerton, *Gabriel's Rebellion: The Virginia Slave Conspiracies of 1800 and 1802* (Chapel Hill: University of North Carolina Press, 1993), esp. introduction.

48. Archibald McLean to PAS, June 6, 1796, Loose Correspondence, PAS Papers, reel 11.

49. Notation from February 19, 1790, meeting of the Providence Abolition Society, Minutebook, 1789–1827, *Quaker Collection*, Rhode Island Historical Society.

50. See, e.g., Benjamin Rush to Jeremy Belknap, January 1, February 28, April 6, May 1788, and June 21, 1792, all in *MHS Collections*, 6th ser.

51. Isaac Backus to Massachusetts Ratifying Convention, February 4, 1788, in William G. McLoughlin, ed., *The Diary of Isaac Backus*, 3 vols. (Providence, R.I.: Brown University Press, 1979), 3:1220; Harrison Gray Otis in House of Representatives debate over "The Petition of Free Blacks," January 2–3, 1800, *Annals of Congress*, 6th Cong., 1st sess., 229–45 (Otis quotation, 231).

52. St. George Tucker to Jeremy Belknap, January 24, 1795, Tucker-Belknap Correspondence, *MHS Collections*, 5th ser., pp. 375–437.

53. Dr. E. A. Holyoke to Jeremy Belknap and Nathanial Appleton to Belknap, ca. 1797, Tucker-Belknap Correspondence, ibid.

54. James Winthrop to Jeremy Belknap and James Sullivan to Belknap, ca. 1797, ibid.

55. Thomas Arnold to James Pemberton of PAS, May 12, 1789, PAS Papers, reel 63.

56. "Extract of a Letter from Rhode Island," August 23, 1788, Loose Correspondence, PAS Papers, reel 11.

57. See reports of PAS to ACAS, 1801–9, PAS Papers, reel 2. Pennsylvania abolitionists could not explain Bay State apathy, nor have recent historians. For fuller treatment of this theme, see Gary B. Nash, *Race and Revolution* (Madison, Wis.: Madison House, 1990). The group that supplanted the PAS drew supporters from decidedly nonelite ranks in Massachusetts — and therefore mobilized around the likes of Daniel Webster and Harrison Gray Otis.

58. Acting Committee draft report, October 3, 1825, Acting Committee Minutes, PAS Papers, reel 2.

59. By 1809 the PAS would increase its educational efforts in the state, but it also maintained its legal aid system for Pennsylvania and other blacks in need of counsel. In addition, the PAS tried to encourage the creation of other state and local abolition societies. In 1825 it announced that though there was "little of a local nature [that] remains [for abolitionists] . . . there is much to do nationally." Acting Committee Reports, April 1825, PAS Papers, reel 2.

60. Arnold Buffum to Joseph Sturge of England, April 9, 1839, Letters, BPL.

Chapter Two

1. For the most recent exposition of petitioning in the Revolutionary age, see Pauline Maier, *American Scripture: Making the Declaration of Independence* (New York: Knopf, 1997), esp. 50–51, 225–34.

2. PAS to Kentucky Abolition Society, October 30, 1809, Loose Correspondence, PAS Papers, reel 11.

3. Thomas R. R. Cobb, quoted in William W. Freehling and Craig M. Simpson, *Secession Debated: Georgia's Showdown in 1860* (New York: Oxford University Press, 1992), 16.

4. Acting Committee Minutes, January 15, 1818, PAS Papers, reel 2.

5. Grenville Sharpe to PAS, ca. 1790, Loose Correspondence, PAS Papers, reel 11.

6. PAS to Washington, Pa., Abolition Society, ca. February 1790, ibid.

7. Draft petitions to Congress on the "District of Columbia" and the "Florida Territory," written in the ACAS, October 1827, PAS Papers, reel 12. PAS members usually served prominent roles on American Convention committees: on these two occasions, Edwin Atlee, William Rawle, and Thomas Earle were on the petition committees.

8. PAS to Washington, Pa., Abolition Society, ca. February 1790, and PAS to Grenville Sharpe, London, May 3, 1790, Loose Correspondence, PAS Papers, reel 11.

9. The petition was actually delivered to Congress on January 2, 1792. See Acting Committee Minutes, January 2, 1792, PAS Papers, reel 1.

10. PAS to Washington, Pa., Abolition Society, ca. February 1790, and "Address to the People of the United States," 1804, Loose Correspondence, PAS Papers, reel 11.

11. PAS draft petition to Congress on the overseas slave trade, February 28, 1790, Acting Committee Minutes, PAS Papers, reel 1.

12. PAS to Grenville Sharpe, February 28, 1790, Loose Correspondence, PAS Papers, reel 11.

13. PAS to Grenville Sharpe, May 3, 1790, ibid.

14. For allusions to the character of PAS signatories, see PAS to Gov. Collins, January 19, 1789, and PAS to London Society for Abolishing the Slave Trade, May 3, 1790, Loose Correspondence, PAS Papers, reel 11.

15. *Genius*, January 1829; Benjamin Lundy to Isaac Barton of ACAS, January 21, 1828, PAS Papers, reel 12.

16. Benjamin Lundy to Isaac Barton, March 20, 1828, ibid.

17. John Parrish to James Madison, May 28, 1790, and Madison to Parrish, June 6, 1790, Cox-Parrish-Wharton Collection, HSP.

18. Acting Committee Special Meeting, February 2, 1813, PAS Papers, reel 1.

19. See Timothy Pickering to Joseph Bloomfield, June 1, 1798, and Oliver Wolcott to ACAS, June 1, 1798, Incoming Correspondence, PAS Papers reel 29.

20. William W. Freehling, *Secessionists at Bay, 1776–1854*, vol. 1 of *The Road to Disunion* (New York: Oxford University Press, 1990), 144. For more on this theme, see Michael A. Morrison, *Slavery and the American West: The Eclipse of Manifest Destiny and the Coming of the Civil War* (Chapel Hill: University of North Carolina Press, 1997), esp. chap. 2.

21. Acting Committee Minutes, January 1819, PAS Papers, reel 2.

22. Thomas Shipley to William Rawle, ca. 1814, Rawle Family Papers, HSP.

23. See Rawle's abstract of the "Proposed Fugitive Slave Bill," Legal Files, PAS Papers, reel 27.

24. John Sergeant to Roberts Vaux, January 16, 1822, Vaux Papers, HSP.

25. Emler letter, January 1823, ibid.

26. Ibid.

27. PAS to Washington, Pa., Abolition Society, February 7, 1789, Loose Correspondence, PAS Papers, reel 11.

28. William Meredith to Roberts Vaux, February 11, 1825, Vaux Papers, HSP; Edwin Atlee to Convention of Abolitionists in Philadelphia, December 1833, PAS Papers, reel 29.

29. Acting Committee Minutes, 1790, PAS Papers, reel 1.

30. Ibid.

31. Acting Committee Minutes, 1793, PAS Papers, reel 1; "Laws of Maryland in Regard to Slaves, 1715–1797," PAS Papers, reel 24.

32. Acting Committee Minutes, February 28, 1791, PAS Papers, reel 1.

33. Acting Committee Minutes, November 19, 1818, PAS Papers, reel 2.

34. Acting Committee Minutes, January 4, 1821, ibid.

35. Acting Committee Minutes, December 3, 1818, ibid.

36. Mason to Constitutional Convention, August 22, 1787, in John P. Kaminski, ed., *A Necessary Evil?: Slavery and Debate over the Constitution* (Madison, Wis.: Madison House, 1995), 59.

37. Ibid., 42.

38. Ibid., 61.

39. Paul Finkelman, "Slavery and the Constitutional Convention: Making a Covenant with Death," in Richard Beeman, Stephen Botein, and Edward C. Carter II, eds., *Beyond Confederation: Origins of the Constitution and American National Identity* (Chapel Hill: University of North Carolina Press, 1987), 188–225.

40. PAS to London Society for Abolishing the Slave Trade, ca. 1789, Loose Correspondence, PAS Papers, reel 11.

41. "An Act to Prohibit the Carrying on the Slave Trade from US to Any Foreign Place or Country," announced in Acting Committee Minutes, April 7, 1794. The PAS had appointed a committee of seven to keep tabs on the congressional memorials, February 10, 1994. See Acting Committee Minutes, PAS Papers, reel 1.

42. For a compilation of slave-trading convictions by the PAS, see "Summarys [*sic*] of Acting in District Court," PAS Papers, reel 24

43. *Annals of the Congress of the United States, 1789–1824*, edited by Gales and Seaton, 42 vols. (Washington, D.C., 1834–56), February 12, 1790, 1st Cong., 2d sess., 1228–29, 1242–43.

44. PAS petition to Congress, 1790, in Kaminski, *Necessary Evil*, 212.

45. Ibid.

46. PAS to Providence Abolition Society, March 15, 1791, and Acting Committee Minutes, October 3, 1791, PAS Papers, reel 1.

47. "Circular Letter to the Abolition Societies of the United States," October 25, 1790, Acting Committee Minutes, PAS Papers, reel 1.

48. Acting Committee Minutes, January 25, 1817, PAS Papers, reel 2.

49. Rawle to ——, March 23, 1825, Rawle Family Papers, p. 173, HSP.

50. Acting Committee Minutes, December 25, 1817, and Report of Committee, January 5, 18, 1818, PAS Papers, reel 1. The special committee included PASers Jonas Preston, Benjamin Tucker, Joseph Paul, Abraham Pennock, and R. C. Wood.

51. Quarterly Meeting, November 19, 1819, PAS Papers, reel 1.

52. Richard S. Newman, "Prelude to the Gag Rule: Southern Reaction to Antislavery Petitions in the First Federal Congress," *Journal of the Early Republic* 16, no. 4 (Winter 1996): 571–600 (quotations, 582–83).

53. *Proceedings of the American Convention for Promoting the Abolition of Slavery . . . 1826* (Philadelphia, 1826), 5–10.

54. Charles Miner, "Slavery and the Slave Trade in the District of Columbia," reproduced in *Abolitionist*, October 1833.

55. Ibid.

56. Ibid.

57. "Our Excellent Citizen, Miner," January 1829, in *Genius*.

58. *Proceedings of the American Convention for Promoting the Abolition of Slavery . . . 1821* (Philadelphia, 1821), 7; *Proceedings of the American Convention for Promoting the Abolition of Slavery . . . 1826* (Philadelphia, 1826), 8.

59. *Proceedings of the American Convention . . . 1826*, 9.

60. *Proceedings of the American Convention for Promoting the Abolition of Slavery . . . 1829* (Philadelphia, 1829), 10–11, 26–28.

61. Ibid., 53–55.

62. William Rawle on the proposal to form a National Antislavery Society, May 20, 1833, Rawle Family Papers, HSP.

63. See Acting Committee Minutes, ca. 1822 and 1828, PAS Papers, reel 2.

64. Benjamin Lundy to Isaac Barton, January 21, 1828, Loose Correspondence, PAS Papers, reel 11.

65. *Freedom's Journal*, February 21, 1829; *Genius*, January 8, 1830.

66. Newman, "Prelude to the Gag Rule, 575–76.

67. Representative Weems of Maryland, *Annals of Congress*, 20th Cong., 2d sess., 167, 181–87.

68. The petition of the four former slaves as well as southern replies is found in ibid., 4th Cong., 2d sess., 2015–26.

69. John Rutledge of South Carolina, ibid., 6th Cong., 1st sess., 230.

70. See Newman, "Prelude to the Gag Rule," 592, 598.

71. Ibid., 578–79.

72. William Rawle on the proposed AASS, May 20, 1833, Rawle Family Papers, p. 183, HSP.

73. PAS to London Society for Abolishing the Slave Trade, April 2, 1790, PAS Papers, reel 12; William Rawle on the proposed AASS, May 20, 1833, Rawle Family Papers, p. 183, HSP; R. J. Leech to Jonathan Roberts, July 2, 1836 (alluding to Roberts's opposition to "modern" abolitionist petitioning tactics), Roberts Papers, box 5, HSP.

Chapter Three

1. Case of Elizabeth, August 31, 1836, in which judge Archibald Randall of the Court of Common Pleas declared Elizabeth free. See "Cases in Which Slaves Were Awarded Freedom in Court, 1773–1833," Legal Files, PAS Papers, reel 24.

2. "Another 'Slave Case,'" an article appearing in the *Philadelphia National Enquirer*, November 5, 1836, detailed the case of fugitive slave "John Powell, alias Samuel White," who fled from Worcester County, Md., to Philadelphia. In the same issue, the *Enquirer* reported the case of Severn Martin, "a very respectable colored man" from New Jersey who had been kidnapped back into slavery in August 1836. After Martin's friends in the black community discovered the crime, Pennsylvania and other abolitionists worked to retrace his capture and sale and then return him to freedom.

3. Thomas Jeffery, Harford County, Md., to Reah Frazier, Attorney at Law, Lancaster, Pa., Dreer Collection, HSP.

4. PAS to Washington, Pa., Abolition Society, April 20, 1790, Acting Committee Minutes, PAS Papers, reel 1.

5. See G. S. Rowe, *Embattled Bench: The Pennsylvania Supreme Court and the Forging of a Democratic Society, 1684–1809* (Newark: University of Delaware Press, 1994).

6. Legal measures such as the Quaker State's abolition decree would bolster the PAS's legislative tactics. "We conceive it our duty to extend a portion of [our]

freedom to others," the Pennsylvania Abolition Act proclaimed in 1780, as it outlined the specific legal steps that would eventually eradicate slavery. According to the
law, slaves born after a certain period would be freed at a certain age. *An Act for the
Gradual Abolition of Slavery . . . March 1, 1780*, reprinted in Paul Finkelman, ed., *The
Law of Freedom and Bondage: A Casebook* (New York: Oceana Publications, Inc.,
1986), 42–48. On gradual abolition plans in northern states, see Arthur Zilversmit,
The First Emancipation: The Abolition of Slavery in the North (Chicago: University of
Chicago Press, 1967). For an interesting revisionist treatment of New York's aboli-
tion act, see Shane White, *Somewhat More Independent: The End of Slavery in New
York City, 1770–1810* (Athens: University of Georgia Press, 1991).

7. Joseph Parrish, "Eulogy" for Thomas Shipley before the PAS, November 1836.
See Parrish, *Brief Memoirs of Thomas Shipley and Edwin P. Atlee. . . .* (Philadelphia,
1838), 15–20.

8. Carol Wilson, *Freedom at Risk: The Kidnapping of Free Blacks in America,
1776-1865* (Lexington: University of Kentucky Press, 1994), 42; Acting Committee,
ca. 1817, PAS Papers, reel 1; Parrish, *Brief Memoirs*, 10–20.

9. Carol Wilson, *Freedom at Risk*, 42. Although every last detail of PAS legal work
is unavailable, the broader contours of the group's caseload can still be recon-
structed. The society kept thorough records of its most important cases, including
copies of official documents, depositions of black and white litigants, transcriptions
of trial testimony and judges' opinions, and notes made by abolitionist lawyers. In
addition, the group organized a series of more specific files that shed light on certain
aspects of PAS legal work. For instance, one folder details nearly fifty "Cases in
Which Slaves Were Awarded Freedom in Court"; another file is a compilation of
notes on and prosecutions of overseas slave traders in federal courts, from Pennsylvania down through South Carolina; still other folders contain "Legal Opinions of
the Society's Counsellors," "Laws Relating to Slavery" in several states, and "Binding Agreements" between black persons and white owners, for which the PAS
served as agent. The society's Correspondence and Acting Committees also tracked
legal cases, the files of which offer more clues on the nature and extent of PAS work.
Finally, modern-day collections of early legal work (esp.

Helen Tunnicliff Catterall, ed., *Judicial Cases Concerning American Slavery and the
Negro*, 5 vols. [New York: Octagon Books, 1968], and the complete list of *Pennsylvania Reports*), as well as original newspaper accounts of various trials and personal
letters from Pennsylvania judges and other lawyers, make it possible to know not
just what the PAS did and when, but the kinds of cases it took on, how the caseload
changed over time, how slaveholders and blacks felt about individual cases, and how
judges viewed abolitionist legal activities.

10. Thomas Jeffery, Harford County, Md., to Reah Frazier, Attorney at Law,
Lancaster, Pa., Dreer Collection, HSP.

11. See, e.g., *National Enquirer*, October 15, 1836. The service took place in
Philadelphia's First Presbyterian Church on September 19, 1836.

12. "Testimonial of Gratitude," February 1841, in David Paul Brown, "Orations,"
Miscellaneous Papers, HSP.

13. "Memoranda of Laws in Relation to Slavery in the United States," Legal Files, PAS Papers, reel 24.

14. Transcription of John Taylor, *Elements of the Civil Law* (London and Cambridge: Charles Bathurst, 1755), ibid. In addition to other citations in the "Memoranda of Laws," see handwritten copies of laws and statutes relating to slavery from various southern states, including Louisiana's "Civil Codes" and "Act of Assembly, June 7, 1806"; South Carolina's definition in "2 Brew. Dig: 229" that "slaves shall be adjudged in the law to be chattels personal"; "The Laws of Maryland in Regard to Slaves, 1715–1789," "The Laws of Maryland in Regard to Slaves, 1715–1797," and "An Act Concerning [Black] Petitions for Freedom [in Maryland]," 1791 — all in ibid.

15. See, e.g., copies of a 1796 Maryland law stating that "no petitions for freedom shall arise in the General Court [of Maryland] but in the county" where the person originally resided, ibid.

16. Rawle to PAS, February 1, 1793, regarding "the bill under consideration in Congress relative to fugitive slaves," ibid.

17. Rawle on the constitutionality of slavery in Pennsylvania, March 26, 1794, and on the formation of a new national antislavery society, May 20, 1833, Rawle Family Papers, pp. 153 and 183, respectively, HSP.

18. Acting Committee Minutes, November 1804, PAS Papers, reel 1.

19. Parrish, *Brief Memoirs*, 10–15.

20. "Narrative of Samuel Johnston," Legal Files, PAS Papers, reel 24.

21. The PAS collected official depositions of Peter Umfries and Nero Amessen, free people of color in New Jersey; Jonathan Leaming, Coachman's former master; Nathaniel Holmes, a "vendue" (shopkeeper) who testified that he had heard Coachman's current master refer to the black man's freedom; Violett Bradford, Deborah Hewit, and Amos Tommas, who had been neighbors of Coachman; the Cape May County "tax assessor"; and Elijah Godfrey, Coachman's first master. All of these depositions and legal documents are collated under the heading, "William Coachman v. G. Hand," Cape May County, N.J., 1802–4, Legal Files, PAS Papers, reel 24.

22. "Thomas Robinson Cases," September 1788, Legal Files, ibid.

23. The PAS worked for the freedom of "Robert," "Ann or Nanny," "A negro man of Philadelphia," and "Isaac." See "Thomas Robinson Cases," Legal Files, ibid.

24. See depositions, writs, and other legal information used by the PAS in these freedom suits: "*In re* Negro Silas," Trenton, N.J., 1790, in "Slaves Awarded Freedom in Court"; 1798 cases; and trial notes in *Abraham v. Eleanor Talbott, Winchester, Virginia* (ca. 1802), all in Legal Files, ibid.

25. *Respublica v. Aberilla Blackmore*, 2 Yeates 234 (1797), and "Respublica v. Chittier" (unreported) [1815], Legal Files, ibid. *Blackmore* is also reprinted in Finkelman, *Law of Freedom and Bondage*, 54–56.

26. Deposition of Mary Francis Argine, a Native of Port-au-Prince, November 8, 1825, in "the city of Philadelphia," and PAS to Mayor of Norfolk and Dr. Senac [*sic*], Main St., Norfolk, November 9, 1825, Legal Files, PAS Papers, reel 24.

27. Chief of Havannah tribe to PAS, ca. 1819, ibid.

28. Alexander McLean to William Silas Densmore, June 1804, in "Cases in Which Slaves Were Awarded Freedom in Court" and "List of Free Colored Persons Detained by John Henderson of Rocky Springs, Mississippi, Circa 1821," ibid.

29. See PAS petition to Congress, December 25, 1817, in Acting Committee Minutes for same date, PAS Papers, reel 1.

30. Billy G. Smith, *Blacks Who Stole Themselves: Advertisements for Runaways in the Pennsylvania Gazette, 1728–1790* (Philadelphia: University of Pennsylvania Press, 1994); Stephen G. Whitman, *The Price of Freedom: Slavery and Manumission in Baltimore and Early National Maryland* (Lexington: University of Kentucky Press, 1997).

31. "Case of Pricilla [*sic*]" (undated) [ca. 1820s], including a "Deed of Manumission," which was not validated by the court; a deposition of "Recorder Bowers," the official who released Pricilla from custody when she was apprehended by her master; and trial notes of "Judge King," who vowed to postpone a "final opinion" on Pricilla's ultimate freedom. See "Cases in Which Slaves Were Awarded Freedom in Court," Legal Files, PAS Papers, reel 24.

32. The following cases resulted in indenture agreements between masters and runaway slaves: "Harry," October 1791; "Azor," June 1794; *George Stiles v. Daniel Richardson*, March 1799; *Negro Aqua v. Oliver Pollack, Esq.*, August 1791 — all in "Slaves Awarded Freedom in Court," Legal Files, PAS Papers, reel 24.

33. "The Acting Committee to Bulah Barker," regarding the freedom claims of two black persons in "Landon County, Virginia, 1810," ibid.; Case of "Rudolph Boice," November 28, 1792, ibid.; John Needles, Baltimore, to Isaac Barton, Philadelphia, September 10, 1829, and Master "Robins" of Maryland to Isaac Barton, 1832, Incoming Correspondence of ACAS, PAS Papers, reel 29.

34. See William Rawle's guidelines on indenture contracts, Legal Files, PAS Papers, reel 24.

35. "Petition of John Bassa of Philadelphia County," and "Writ of Habeus Corpus" for Bassa by Isaac Hopper of the PAS, ibid.

36. *Butler v. Hopper*, 4F. Cas. 904 (1806), reprinted in Finkelman, *Law of Freedom and Bondage*, 61–64.

37. Philip J. Schwarz, *Slave Laws in Virginia* (Athens: University of Georgia Press, 1996), 1–12.

38. James Huston focuses on abolition's connections to bondage only for the later period — i.e., after the 1830s. See James L. Huston, "The Experiential Basis of the Northern Antislavery Impulse," *Journal of Southern History* 56 (November 1990): 609–40.

39. *An Act for the Gradual Abolition of Slavery*, reprinted in Legal Files, PAS Papers, reel 24. The act exempted national political figures serving in Congress (temporarily located in Philadelphia) during the 1790s.

40. Case of "Stephen Carpenter, a yeoman" from Oxford Township in Philadelphia County, who "did not register his slaves or servants properly agreeable to directions of 1780," in "Slaves Awarded Freedom in Court," PAS Legal Files, Micro-

film Reel 24; *Commonwealth, ex rel. Jesse (a Black Man), v. Craig*, 1 S. and R. 23 (September 1814), reprinted summarily in Catterall, *Judicial Cases*, 4:273; *Respublica v. Negro Betsey et al.*, 1 Dallas 469 (September 1789). See also the brief of Miers Fisher and E. Tilgham, PAS legal advisers in the "Case of a Female Slave and Her Children Not Being Registered under Provision of the Gradual Abolition Act," January 1789, "Legal Opinions" File, PAS Papers, reel 24; see also *Commonwealth v. Negress Hester*, 1 Brown 369 (1811). For summaries, see Catterall, *Judicial Cases*, 4:256 and note about "Hester's Case," 4:270.

41. *Respublica v. Findlay*, 3 Yeates 261 (October 1801), in Catterall, *Judicial Cases*, 4:264; *Wilson v. Belinda*, 3 S. and R. 396 (September 1817), ibid., 4:276.

42. *John (a Negro Man) v. Dawson*, 2 Yeates 449 (1799), ibid., 4:263; *Lucy (a Negro woman) v. Pumfrey*, Addison 380 (February 1799), ibid., 4:262.

43. See deposition of John Johnson of Boston to PAS, ca. 1805; a "Writ to Take Notice to [Mrs.] Robins" of a legal inquiry into her husband's slave trading with foreign merchants and the "affirmation" by Matthew Lawler, Mayor, that the PAS had delivered the writ to Mrs. Robins and that she failed to appear in "Judge Wolbert's Chambers, March 28, 1805," for an official deposition. All documents in "Isaac Sherman v. Captain Robins," "Summaries of Acting in District Court," Legal Files, PAS Papers, reel 24.

44. "Isaac Sherman v. the Brig ARCTIC," November 1806, ibid. See, e.g., "Memoranda of Vessels Which Have Sailed for the Coast of Africa in the Year 1795," ibid. In 1795 alone the PAS tracked eight separate cases. By July 1799 it had compiled a list of twenty-six more cases, including captains' names, ship destinations, and numbers of slaves.

45. "*In re* Negro Silas," in "Slaves Awarded Freedom in Court"; "Writ of Habeus Corpus" sworn out by Isaac Hopper; and "Petition of John Bassa of Philadelphia County" — all in Legal Files, PAS Papers, reel 24.

46. *Wright Alias Hall v. Deacon*, S. and R. 62 (January 1819). See also Catterall, *Judicial Cases*, 4:277.

47. *Respublica v. Blackmore*, 2 Yeates 234 (May 1797). Documentation on this case can be found under the heading "Pennsylvania v. Aberilla Blackmore," in "Slaves Awarded Freedom in Court," Legal Files, PAS Papers, reel 24. See also a thoughtful reprint of the main part of the decision in Finkelman, *Law of Freedom and Bondage*, 54–56.

48. Thus, despite the fact that Pennsylvania offered slaveholders in the two new counties extra time to register their slaves — until November 1782 — the Blackmore family asserted that it had no reason to comply with the statute. See the transcription of court arguments by Blackmore's attorneys in "Pennsylvania v. Aberilla Blackmore" (hereafter cited as Transcription, Blackmore). See also "An Act to Redress Certain Grievances within the Counties Westmoreland and Washington," April 1782, Legal Files, PAS Papers, reel 24.

49. Transcription, Blackmore (Ross's argument).

50. David Redack to Washington, Pa., Society for the Abolition of Slavery, March 15, 1798, Loose Correspondence, 1788–1809, PAS Papers, reel 11.

51. Transcription, Blackmore (Blackmore's counterargument).

52. David Redack to Washington, Pa., Society for the Abolition of Slavery, March 15, 1798.

53. Case of "Kitty," the "slave of Betty Chittier" of Virginia, Legal Files, PAS Papers, reel 24.

54. See abstracts for the case of "Kitty" prepared by the six legal advisers assigned to the case: Peter Du Ponceau, William Rawle, William Meredith, John Hallowell, William Lewis, and John Reed (in reply to PAS queries), ibid.

55. Ibid.

56. Ibid.

57. See Acting Committee note on the case for November 1815 meeting, PAS Papers, reel 1.

58. Case of "Marshall Green and Susan Johnson," December 10, 1825, in "Slaves Awarded Freedom in Court," Legal Files, PAS Papers, reel 24 (transcription of David Paul Brown's arguments).

59. Ibid. For the previous court case, see *Ex Parte Simmons*, 22 Fed. Cas. 151 (4 Wash. C.C. 396) (October 1823), in Catterall, *Judicial Cases* 4:279–80.

60. Case of "Marshall Green and Susan Johnson," December 10, 1825.

61. Alexander Addison, Washington County, Pa., Abolition Society, to PAS, January 1, 1792, Loose Correspondence, PAS Papers, reel 11.

62.
Richard S. Newman, "Prelude to the Gag Rule: Southern Reaction to Antislavery Petitions in the First Federal Congress," *Journal of the Early Republic* 16, no. 4 (Winter 1996): 582.

63. The PAS received an early copy of the Maryland petition. See Acting Committee Minutes, September 1822, PAS Papers, reel 2; see also Minutes, February 20, 1823.

64. Horace Binney, "Eulogy" for William Tilghman, ca. 1822, Tilghman Papers, HSP.

65. Samuel Wright to William Tilghman, July 29, 1800, and James Lloyd to Tilghman, December 25, 1800, Tilghman Papers, HSP.

66. William Hemsley to William Tilghman, January 13, 1804, and James Hollyday to Tilghman, August 15, 1797, ibid.

67. Tilghman quoted in Catterall, *Judicial Cases*, 4:276.

68. *Commonwealth, Ex. Rel. Negro Lewis v. Holloway*, 6 Binney 213 (January 1814), ibid., 4:272.

69. *Butler v. Delaplaine*, 7 S. and R. 378 (October 1821), ibid., 4:278–79. Judge Duncan cited the success of two vacation "Springs" in Pennsylvania. Because these spas were "frequented so principally, and in great numbers, by families from Maryland and Virginia, attended by slaves," abolitionists' expansive claims for the Abolition Act could not be sustained.

70. *Johnson v. Tompkins et al.*, 13 Fed. Cas. 540 (Baldwin 571), April 1833, ibid., 4:287.

71. *Hill v. Low*, 12 Fed. Cas. 172 (4 Wash. C.C. 327), October 1822, ibid., 4:279.

72. James Forten, *A Series of Letters by a Man of Color* (Philadelphia, 1813), reprinted in Herbert Aptheker, ed., *A Documentary History of the Negro People in the United States*, rev. ed. (New York: The Citadel Press, 1968), 59–66.

73. Supply source of Garrison's quote.

74. Amos A. Phelps, *Lectures on Slavery and Its Remedy*, and William Lloyd Garrison, "Declaration of Sentiments," written for the AASS, both in William H. Pease and Jane H. Pease, eds., *The Antislavery Argument* (Indianapolis: Bobbs-Merrill, 1965), 65–85.

75. Lewis Gunn, speech before the Philadelphia Young Man's Anti-Slavery Society, quoted in *National Enquirer*, November 12, 1836.

76. Ibid.

77. William Meredith to Roberts Vaux, February 12, 1825, Roberts Vaux Papers, HSP.

78. Ibid.

Chapter Four

1. Charles Gardner, speaking at the Fourth Annual Meeting of the AASS, June 1837, in C. Peter Ripley et al., eds., *The Black Abolitionist Papers*, 5 vols. (Chapel Hill: University of North Carolina Press, 1985–92), 3:206–15.

2. Forten to Garrison, December 31, 1830, ibid., 85-86. Many modern abolitionist scholars have skimmed over black influences on white reformers. For example, in his much-praised book, *The Abolitionists and the South, 1831–1861* (Lexington: , 1995), 16–17, Stanley Harrold claims that blacks were the first abolitionists but then delves little into the workings and impact of black activism between the Revolution and the Civil War. Ronald Walters's work on antebellum abolitionism, *The Antislavery Appeal: American Abolitionism after 1830* (Baltimore: Johns Hopkins University Press, 1976), ignores black reformers altogether because, as he observes, their tactics shed little light on white perceptions about the movement after 1830. Even scholars of black abolitionism give short shrift to the influence of African American tacticians during the early national period. On the other hand, see James Brewer Stewart's revised edition of *Holy Warriors: The Abolitionists and American Slavery* (New York: Hill and Wang, 1996) for a fine synthesis of new studies on race and their impact on abolitionism, as well as Donald Jacobs's work on an integrated Boston abolitionism in his collection of essays, *Courage and Conscience: Black and White Abolitionists in Boston* (Bloomington: Indiana University Press, 1993).

3. Ripley's *Black Abolitionist Papers*, hailed as one of the most significant compilations of antebellum documents in recent decades, begins its definitive collection of black writings in 1830. The introduction focuses briefly on the early period and then skips to black activity in the 1820s and 1830s. Similarly, John Bracey, August Meier, and Elliot Rudwick's important collection of essays, *Blacks in the Abolitionist Movement* (Belmont, Calif.: Wadsworth Publishing Co., 1971), including work by William Cheek, Larry Gara, Leon Litwack, and Jane and William Pease, devotes almost

no space to pre–1830 black activism. See also Patrick Rael, "The Lion's Painting: African American Protest after 1830" (Ph.D. diss., University of California at Berkeley, 1994), for an excellent discussion of this trend. Finally, Richard Blackett and Benjamin Quarles, two of the most prominent scholars of black activism whose work spans over forty years, briefly discuss the early national period in their respective volumes on black protest but, again, concentrate on the post–1830 period. See R. J. M. Blackett, *Building an Anti-Slavery Wall: Black Americans in the Atlantic Abolitionist Movement, 1830–1860* (Ithaca: Cornell University Press, 1983), and Benjamin Quarles, *Black Abolitionists* (New York: Oxford University Press, 1969).

4. When examining antebellum black protest, it is well to recall Ira Berlin's admonition about studying North American slavery: variations in time and space are critical. Berlin, *Slaves without Masters: The Free Negro in the Antebellum South.* New York: Random House, 1974. African American reform constantly evolved, and African American reformers often clashed over strategy and tactics. The split between Frederick Douglass and Henry Highland Garnet over whether or not to explicitly call for black rebellion in the South remains one of the most notable examples. In that 1843 debate (at a convention of black activists in Buffalo), Douglass prevailed and Garnet's fiery "address to the slaves" was not printed in the convention's official minutes. This theme of an evolving black protest style and agenda is dealt with more extensively in Richard Newman, Patrick Rael, and Phillip Lapsansky, eds., *Pamphlets of Protest: An Anthology of Early African-American Protest Literature* (New York: Routledge, 2000), introduction.

5. For black resistance to enslavement during the seventeenth and eighteenth centuries, see, e.g., Eugene D. Genovese, *From Rebellion to Revolution: Afro-American Slave Revolts in the Making of the Modern World* (Baton Rouge: Louisiana State University Press, 1979), 4–5; Cedric J. Robinson, *Black Social Movements in America* (New York: Routledge, 1997), 1–20; James Walvin, *Questioning Slavery* (New York: Routledge, 1997), 1–10; and Peter H. Wood, *Black Majority: Negroes in Colonial South Carolina from 1670 through the Stono Rebellion* (New York: Knopf, 1974), 285–330.

6. The PAS recognized the significance of black community building. In a series of community studies between the 1790s and the 1830s, for instance, it commended Philadelphia's free blacks for their industriousness. One report observed that they were probably more pious and well mannered than many white citizens. See, e.g., PAS, *The Present State and Condition of the Free People of Color of the City of Philadelphia* (Philadelphia, 1838). See also Billy G. Smith, *The Lower Sort: Philadelphia's Laboring People, 1750–1800* (Ithaca: Cornell University Press, 1990), 195.

7. See Shane White, "We Dwell in Safety and Pursue Our Honest Callings: Free Blacks in New York City, 1783–1810," *Journal of American History* 75, no. 2 (1988): 448–51, and *Somewhat More Independent: The End of Slavery in New York City, 1770–1810* (Athens: University of Georgia Press, 1991). See also James Oliver Horton and Lois Horton, *Black Bostonians: Family Life and Community Struggle in the Antebellum North* (New York: Holmes and Meier, 1979); Roy E. Finkenbine, "Boston's Black Churches: Institutional Centers of the Antislavery Movement," in Jacobs, *Courage*

and Conscience. The most recent treatment of northern black culture and activism is James Oliver Horton and Lois Horton, *In Hope of Liberty: Culture, Community and Protest among Northern Free Blacks, 1700–1860* (New York: Oxford University Press, 1997).

8. See Gary B. Nash, *Forging Freedom: The Formation of Philadelphia's Black Community* (Cambridge: Harvard University Press, 1988), and Julie Winch, *Philadelphia's Black Elite: Activism, Accommodation, and the Struggle for Autonomy, 1787–1848* (Philadelphia: Temple University Press, 1993).

9. *Laws of the African Society, Instituted at Boston . . . 1796* (reprinted for the Society, Boston, 1802); Philadelphia "Society" constitution, in Herbert Aptheker, ed., *A Documentary History of the Negro People in the United States*, rev. ed. (New York: , 1968), 18–19.

10. Douglas R. Egerton, *Gabriel's Rebellion: The Virginia Slave Conspiracies of 1800 and 1802* (Chapel Hill: University of North Carolina Press, 1993), introduction.

11. Shane White, "It Was a Proud Day: African Americans, Festivals and Parades in the North, 1741–1834," *Journal of American History* 81 (June 1994): 13–50; Schwarz, *Slave Laws in Virginia*, chaps. 2–3.

12. In 1789 two Boston women asked the Massachusetts General Assembly to return blacks to Africa, where they might receive equal treatment. PAS Acting Committee Report, ca. 1790, PAS Papers, reel 1.

13. See Sidney Kaplan, *The Black Presence in the Era of the American Revolution, 1770–1800* (Greenwich, Conn: New York Graphic Society, 1973).

14. *Annals of the Congress of the United States, 1789–1824*, 42 vols., edited by Gales and Seaton (Washington, D.C., 1834–56), 6th Cong., 1st sess., 229 (Harrison Gray Otis of Massachusetts, 231; James Jones of Georgia, 235).

15. William Whipper, *An Address Delivered in Wesley Church . . . before the Colored Reading Society of Philadelphia* (Philadelphia, 1828), 107.

16. "Yambo, an African, in South Carolina" asked for an end to routine whippings by masters. But slaveholders saw an insidious critique in his words: that they were not paternalistic! See *Columbian Herald*, August 12, 14, 1790.

17. J. O. Gales to North Carolina Manumission Society, September 6, 1816, North Carolina Manumission Society Minutes, 1816–34, in *James C. Sprunt Historical Studies*, edited by H. M. Wagstaff (reprint ed., Chapel Hill: University of North Carolina Press, 1934).

18. See Emmanuel Eze, *Race and Enlightenment* (New York: Blackwell, 1997).

19. "Petition of Jacob Nicholson, Jupiter Nicholson, Job Albert, and Thomas Pritchet," all manumitted blacks from North Carolina who were threatened with reenslavement before moving to Philadelphia in the 1790s. See *Annals of Congress*, 4th Cong., 2d sess. (1796–97), 2015–18.

20. Allen's eulogy, originally presented to his congregation in December 1799, was rewritten for the January 1800 issue of the *New York Spectator*. In a foreword to the piece, the editor of the paper wrote: "He [Allen] has been prevailed upon to admit the following sketch of his discourse to be published. It will show that the African Race participate in the common events of our country—that they can re-

joice in our prosperity, mourn our adversity, and feel with other citizens, the propriety and necessity of wise and good rulers, of an effective government, and of submission to the laws of our land."

21. James Forten to the Hon. George Thatcher, January 1800, Cox-Parrish-Wharton Collection, HSP. As yet, there is no collection of black petitions, although a work, entitled "The Black Petitions Project," is under way at the University of South Carolina. In addition, James Horton is engaged in the ongoing "Afro-American Communities Project," which will provide a wider context for examining black life in the early republic. See, e.g., James Horton, *Free People of Color: Inside the African American Community* (Washington, D.C.: Smithsonian Institution Press, 1993). My reference to the "Black Elite" refers to Julie Winch's book, *Philadelphia's Black Elite*.

22. African Americans did not speak in a single, unitary voice during the early republic—within black communities there was disagreement over a variety of issues, from how to fight racial injustice to what goals blacks should strive for. Though these divisions became more apparent in the later antebellum years, they existed in the early republic as well.

23. Jones, *A Sermon . . . on the Abolition of the Slave Trade* (Philadelphia, 1808). Hamilton's pamphlet, originally printed in 1809, appears in Aptheker, *Documentary History*, 52–53.

24. Thomas Jefferson, *Notes on the State of Virginia* (1787), reprinted with notes in William Peden, ed., *Thomas Jefferson: Notes on the State of Virginia* (Chapel Hill: Published for the Institute of Early American History and Culture, Williamsburg, Va., by the University of North Carolina Press, 1955), 140, 280 n. 9.

25. Both Africanus and Rusticus wrote in the March and April 1790 editions of the *United States Gazette*, then located in New York City.

26. Ibid.

27. "Complaint or Reflection of One of the African Race, 'LundonDerry,'" Miscellaneous extract in Cox-Parrish-Wharton Collection, vol. 14, 37–38, HSP.

28. James Forten to Moses Thatcher, January 1800, Cox-Parrish-Wharton Collection, HSP; Richard Allen and Absalom Jones, *A Narrative of the Proceedings of the Black People, during the Late Awful Calamity in Philadelphia, in the Year 1793, and a Refutation"* (Philadelphia 1794), 21–28.

29. Russell Parrott, *An Oration on the Abolition of the Slave Trade* (Philadelphia, 1812), 3–10, and *An Address on the Abolition of the Slave Trade* (Philadelphia, 1816), 3–12.

30. Russell Parrott, *An Oration on the Abolition of the Slave Trade* (Philadelphia, 1812), 3–10, and *An Address on the Abolition of the Slave Trade* (Philadelphia, 1816), 3–12.

31. George Lawrence, *An Oration on the Abolition of the Slave Trade* (New York, 1813), and Rev. Peter Williams, *An Oration on the Abolition of the Slave Trade* (New York, 1808), both reprinted in Aptheker, *Documentary History*, 51–59.

32. *The Sons of Africa: An Essay on Freedom: With Observations on the Origins of Slavery: By a Member of the African Society in Boston*, printed for the African Society (Boston, 1808), reprinted in ibid., 52.

33. *An Essay on Freedom with Observations on the Origins of Slavery* (Boston, 1809), partially reprinted in ibid., 51–52.

34. Lemuel Haynes, *The Nature and Importance of True Republicanism* (1801), reprinted partially in Kaplan, *Black Presence in the Era of the American Revolution*, 105–7.

35 Allen and Jones, *Proceedings of the Black People*, 21–28.

36. James

Forten, *A Series of Letters by a Man of Color* (Philadelphia, 1813), reprinted in Aptheker, *Documentary History*, 59–66.

37. Ibid.

38. *The First Annual Report of the American Society for Colonizing the Free People of Colour of the United States* (Washington, D.C., 1818), 1.

39. The PAS briefly opposed the ACS in 1827, but only after a decade of silence. See Acting Committee Minutes, September 27, 1827, PAS Papers, reel 2.

40. Robert Alexander Young, *The Ethiopian Manifesto* (New York, 1829), reprinted in Aptheker, *Documentary History*, 92.

41. *Freedom's Journal*, August 17, 1827.

42. Prince Saunders, *Memoir Presented to the American Convention for Promoting the Abolition of Slavery* (Philadelphia, 1818), 3–19.

43. Ibid.

44. *Meeting of the People of Color at Bethel Church*, January 1817, pamphlet, reprinted in Aptheker, *Documentary History*, 71–72.

45. "Letter from Bishop Allen," in *Freedom's Journal*, November 2, 1827.

46. *Philadelphia Report*, reprinted in *Freedom's Journal*, July 18, 1828.

47. See Peter P. Hinks, *To Awaken My Afflicted Brethren: David Walker and the Problem of Antebellum Slave Resistance* (University Park: Pennsylvania State University Press, 1997), 64–115.

48. "Address Delivered before the General Colored Association at Boston, by David Walker," *Freedom's Journal*, December 19, 1828.

49. Ibid.

50. Ibid. To be sure, Walker pointed out in a speech before the GCA, a small portion of "our white brethren are making mighty efforts" to fight racial oppression, slavery, and colonization, and he "gratefully acknowledged" their work. Indeed, blacks should "co-operate with them as far as we are able." *Freedom's Journal*, August 17, 1827.

51. "Address Delivered before the General Colored Association at Boston, by David Walker."

52. Quoted in Garrison, *Thoughts on African Colonization*.

53. Ibid.

54. Maria W. Stewart, "Lecture Delivered at the Franklin Hall," September 21, 1832, in Sue E. Hochins, ed., *Spiritual Narratives* (New York: Oxford University Press, 1988), 51. See also Marilyn Richardson, "'What If I Am a Woman?': Maria W. Stewart's Defense of Black Women's Political Activism," in Donald M. Jacobs, ed., *Courage and Conscience: Black and White Abolitionists in Boston* (Bloomington: Indiana University Press, 1993), 191–206.

55. Maria W. Stewart, "An Address Delivered at the African Masonic Hall," February 27, 1833, in Hochins, *Spiritual Narratives*, 63–65, 67.

56. Ibid.

57. For a reprint of the convention record, see Aptheker, *Documentary History*, 102–3.

58. *Freedom's Journal*, September 7, 1827.

59. In an important article on black reform, Donald Yacovone argues that African American activists entered the 1830s as less-than-equal partners with the new generation of white reformers who formed America's first formal "immediatist" organizations. Still seeking white "patronage," free blacks accepted "white strategies of resistance and protest"; only later did blacks create their own movement. See Yacovone, "The Transformation of the Black Temperance Movement, 1827–1854: An Interpretation," *Journal of the Early Republic* 8, no. 3 (Fall 1988): 282–97. On immediatism, see Donald Jacobs, "Malcolm X, David Walker, and William Lloyd Garrison: Gaining Freedom 'By Any Mans Necessary,'" in Felton Best, *Black Resistance Movements in the United States and Africa, 1800–1993* (Buffalo, N.Y.: Edwin Mellon Press, 1996).

60. *First Annual Report of the Board of Managers of the New England Anti-Slavery Society*, January 9, 1833 (Boston, 1833), 13–43.

61. Garrison to "Mssrs. J Telemachus Hilton, Robert Wood, and J. H. How" of Boston, August 13, 1831, in Walter M. Merrill and Lewis Ruchames, eds., *Letters of William Lloyd Garrison*, 6 vols. (Cambridge: Harvard University Press, 1971), 1:126.

62. Lydia Maria Child, *Authentic Anecdotes of American Slavery* (Boston, 1835, 1838), 1; *National Enquirer*, November 11, 1836.

63. Charles C. Burleigh, July 1830, *National Enquirer*, November 11, 1836.

64. Comments of "Africaner" in *Portland Christian Mirror*, March 7, 1833. "I must confess," he wrote after reading Garrison's "Thoughts On African Colonization," "that [the black complaints] . . . have had more effect on my mind than all the rest" of the pamphlet. Garrison thus appeared to submerge his own identity in blackness.

65. *Liberator*, January 8, 1831.

66. "Abolition and Anti-Slavery," *Pennsylvania Freeman*, September 10, 1840; Unknown member of the PAS, "Thoughts on the Emancipation of the Black People," ca. 1819, Cox-Parrish-Wharton Collection, HSP.

67. See esp. C. Peter Ripley et al., eds. *Witness for Freedom: African American Voices on Race, Slavery, and Emancipation* (Chapel Hill: University of North Carolina Press, 1993), 11–13, and Leon Litwack, "The Emancipation of the Negro Abolitionist," in Bracey, Meier, and Rudwick, *Blacks in the Abolition Movement.*

Chapter Five

1. Of the over seventy signers, more than twenty were African Americans.

2. *First Annual Report of the New England Anti-Slavery Society* (Boston, 1833), 18–43.

3. American racial ideologies have become the focus of many nineteenth-century studies, in particular immediate abolitionists' sometimes paternalistic attitudes. Among the most illuminating works are

James Brewer Stewart with George Price, *"To Heal the Scourge of Prejudice": The Life and Writings of Hosea Easton* (Amherst: University of Massachusetts Press, 1998) and Stewart's important article, "The Emergence of Racial Modernity and the Rise of the White North, 1790–1840," *Journal of the Early Republic* 18, no. 2 (Summer 1998): 181–217, and responses to it from Jean Soderlund, James Horton, and Ronald Walters; Mia Bay, *The White Image in the Black Mind: African-American Ideas about White People, 1830–1925* (New York: Oxford University Press, 2000); and George M. Fredrickson, *The Black Image in the White Mind: The Debate on Afro-American Character and Destiny, 1817–1914* (New York: Harper and Row, 1972). For the best and most recent treatments of the coming of immediatism and the nature of antebellum religion, see

Robert Abzug, *Cosmos Crumbling: American Reform and the Religious Imagination* (New York: Oxford University Press, 1994); James Brewer Stewart, *Holy Warriors: The Abolitionists and American Slavery*, rev. ed. (New York: Hill and Wang, 1996), and "Boston, Abolition, and the Atlantic World, 1820–1861," in

Dona ld M. Jacobs, ed., *Courage and Conscience: Black and White Abolitionists in Boston* (Bloomington: Indiana University Press, 1993), 101–26; and Daniel Walker Howe, "The Evangelical Movement and Political Culture in the North during the Second Party System," *Journal of American History* 77 (March 1991): 1216–39.

4. For a recent analysis of colonization's strategic implications, see Douglas R. Egerton, "Averting a Crisis: The Pro-Slavery Critique of the American Colonization Society," *Civil War History* 43 (June 1997): 142–56.

5. "Report of the Committee Appointed at Boston to Consult about the Expediency of Affording Aid to the Colonization Society," *Sixth Annual Report of the American Society for Colonizing the Free People of Color* (Washington, D.C., 1823), 48–52;

6. *First Annual Report of the New England Anti-Slavery Society*, 18–43.

7. Jeremy Belknap to Ebenezer Hazard, May 7, 1790, Belknap Papers, MHS.

8. Unidentified writer to the *Massachusetts Centinel*, June 14, 1788, reprinted in John P. Kaminski, ed., *A Necessary Evil?: Slavery and the Debate over the Constitution* (Madison, Wis.: , 1995), 112–13; Rev. Isaac Backus in the Massachusetts Ratifying Convention, February 4, 1788, ibid., 91–92; Rev. John Kenrick, *The Horrors of Slavery* (Newton, Mass., 1818).

9. Unidentified Maine colonizationist, quoted in Early Lee Fox, *The American Colonization Society, 1817–1840* (Baltimore: Johns Hopkins Press, 1919), 13.

10. Extract of a sermon sent to Rev. T. M. Harris, Harris Papers, MHS; Mrs. S. P. Hale to Edward Everett, March 28, 1826, Everett Papers, MHS; Unidentified Maine clergyman to ACS, quoted in ACS newspaper, *The African Repository*, 1:146.

11. Daniel Webster to John Bolton, May 17, 1833, in Charles Wiltse, ed., *The Papers of Daniel Webster: Series I, Correspondence*, 7 vols. (Hanover, N.H.: University Press of New England, 1974–89), 3:252–53. Joseph Story and Daniel Webster formed a local anti-slave-trading society, approaching such noted figures as clergy-

men William Ellery Channing and Elisha Bates. The group met for a few years, prosecuted only a few cases in New England, and eventually disbanded.

12. Isaac Knapp in the *Tenth Annual Report of the American Colonization Society* (Washington, D.C., 1827), 5–12; Caleb Cushing, *An Oration . . . at Boston before the Colonization Society of Massachusetts on the Anniversary of American Independence, July 4, 1833* (Boston, 1833), 2–10.

13. *Boston Courier*, August 21, 1835 (Unidentified correspondent [with Edward Everett's notation of approval], Everett); *Portland Christian Mirror*, February 28, 1833 (Africaner); *Springfield Gazette*, August 25, 1835, October 23, 1833. Some Bay State colonizationists pushed for federal aid to the ACS. If money was a problem in implementing colonization, some leaders thought, a national tax would not be objectionable; if no single state was competent to undertake such a plan, then the federal government should sponser the entire program. "The patronage of the general government," Rev. C. Colton of Massachusetts argued in one meeting, would make colonization work on a national basis. Many, if not most, southern colonizationists argued the opposite: the ACS had no "other object than the removal of our free colored population," as one Virginian asserted in an ACS meeting of 1827, and it should not get entangled with the federal government. The Georgia legislature, perceiving a dangerous tendency in northern support for colonization, formally opposed government involvement in the ACS.

14. "Report of the Committee Appointed at Boston to Consult about the Expediency of Affording Aid to the Colonization Society," in the *Sixth Annual Report of the American Society for Colonizing the Free People of Color*, 48–52; *Seventh Annual Report of the American Society for Colonizing the Free People of Color* (Washington, 1824), 29 (Society of Inquiry); *Fifteenth Annual Report of the American Colonization Society* (Washington, D.C., 1932), 57 (Hampden Colonization Society).

15. Garrison, "To the Editor of the Boston Courier," July 9, 1829, in Walter M. Merrill and Lewis Ruchames, eds., *Letters of William Lloyd Garrison*, 6 vols. (Cambridge, Mass.: , 1971), 1:84–86; "Report of the Colonization Committee of the Society of Inquiry," ca. 1829, Phelps Papers, BPL.

16. Report of Massachusetts legislature, cited in Fox, *American Colonization Society*, 80.

17. *Eleventh Annual Report of the American Colonization Society* (Washington, 1828), 31.

18. Cushing, *An Oration . . . at Boston*, 4–8; Editor of the *Vermont Chronicle*, quoted in Fox, *American Colonization Society*, 81.

19. Everett quoted in *Fifteenth Annual Report of the American Colonization Society*, xii.

20. According to the 1830 census, Massachusetts had just over 7,000 free blacks out of a total population of nearly 610,000 persons. In the 1780s, by contrast (when slavery was declared unconstitutional in the state), there were less than 1,000 blacks. See *Genius*, March 1831, for a reprint of the 1830 census. See also James Horton, *Free People of Color: Inside the African American Community* (Washington, D.C.: Smithsonian Institution Press, 1993), 25–27.

21. "No Amalgamationist," an essay appearing in *Plymouth, We the People*, September 25, 1835; John Holmes to Ebenezor Warren of Massachusetts, December 17, 1820, in Vaughan Family Papers, MHS.

22. Cushing, *An Oration . . . at Boston*, 4–8, 20.

23. Garrison to Henry E. Benson, July 30, 1831, in Merrill and Ruchames, *Letters of . . . Garrison*, 1:123–25; "Report of the Colonization Committee of the Society of Inquiry," 1829, Phelps Papers, BPL.

24. See the entire reprint of Garrison's *Thoughts on African Colonization* (Boston, 1832) for its documentary use of black sources; see also the *First Annual Report of the New England Anti-Slavery Society* for a similar black documentary foundation to immediatist doctrine.

25. In the February 5, 1830, issue of *Genius*, Garrison made special note of *The Rights of All*, a newspaper edited by New York black activist Samuel Cornish; in the March 5, 1830, issue, he made note of Walker's *Appeal* in a short notice entitled "More of the Pamphlet," which he liked for its destruction of southerners' paternalist "affectations."

26. *Genius*, February 5, 1830.

27. *Genius*, January 8, February 5, 1830.

28. See, e.g.,, Garrison to Simeon S. Jocelyn, May 30, 1831, in Merrill and Ruchames, *Letters of . . . Garrison*, 1:119–20.

29. Garrison to Mssrs. J Telemachus Hilton, Robert Wood and J. H. How of Boston, August 13, 1831, in Merrill and Ruchames, *Letters of . . . Garrison*, 1:126.

30. Oliver Johnson, *William Lloyd Garrison and His Times*, rev. ed. (New York, 1881), 73; Amos A. Phelps to Charlotte Phelps, May 6, 19, 1834, Phelps Papers, BPL.

31. Phelps, *Lectures on Slavery and Its Remedy* (Boston, 1834); Oliver Johnson, *Garrison and His Times*, 74.

32. Donald Yacovone, *Samuel Joseph May and the Dilemmas of the Liberal Persuasion, 1797–1871* (Philadelphia: Temple University Press, 1991), 36–38.

33. Other prominent colonizationists-turned-immediatists included, e.g., Rev. John Pierpont of Boston, New Haven minister Leonard Bacon, and Providence lawyer and jurist Tristam Burgess.

34. Charles Burleigh to Samuel J. May, April 9, 1835, Letters, BPL.

35. *Pennsylvanian*, December 5, 8, 11, 1833.

36. *Pennsylvanian*, December 12, 1833.

37. J. R. Tyson, *Discourse before the Young Man's Colonization Society of Philadelphia*, October 24, 1834 (Philadelphia, 1834), 8–11.

38. *Pennsylvanian*, December 11, 1833 (Bedell); *Poulson's Daily Advertiser*, July 4, 8, October 17, 1833.

39. PAS, *The Present State and Condition of the Free People of Color of the City of Philadelphia*, January 5, 1838 (Philadephia, 1838), 17–20.

40. William Rawle on the plan to form a "National Anti-Slavery Society," May 20, 1933, Rawle Family Papers, HSP.

41. R. J. Leech to Jonathan Roberts, July 2, 1836, Roberts Papers, box 5, HSP.

42. On the beliefs of colonizationists, see, e.g., Joseph Parrish to John Sergeant (Congressman from Pennsylvania), January 1840, Cox-Parrish-Wharton Collection, HSP.

43. Unidentified Pennsylvania reformer, ca. 1819, Cox-Parrish-Wharton Collection, HSP; Lindley Coates to Joseph Parrish, June 25, July 29, 1837, ibid. Both Parrish and Coates were members of the Pennsylvania Anti-Slavery Society as well as the PAS; however, both men began their careers in the PAS and retained a measure of its benign racism.

44. Arnold Buffum to Joseph Sturge of England, April 9, 1839, Letters, BPL.

45. Thomas Shipley, "Slavery in the United States," ca. 1835, ibid.

46. Thomas Earle, "Negro Slavery, No. II: Slavery in the United States," a letter to the London Abolition Society, June 16, 1824, in Library Company of Philadelphia, Afro-Americana Collection.

47. See Shipley's disbursement of funds for Garrison's lecture in Acting Committee Minutes, September 1830, PAS Papers, reel 2.

48. Shipley, ibid., and "Resolution," *First Annual Report of the Board of Managers of the Philadelphia Anti-Slavery Society* (Philadelphia, 1835), 5–6; *First Annual Report of the New England Anti-Slavery Society*, 49–50. Arnold Buffum became the NEASS's first vice president and paid lecturer; Thomas Shipley and Edwin Atlee, both signers of the AASS's "Declaration of Sentiments" in 1833, introduced Garrison to black and female activists in Philadelphia; and Thomas Earle, eventual Liberty Party candidate for U.S. vice president in 1840, became a leading political abolitionist in the 1830s and 1840s. Other lesser-known Pennsylvanians migrated into Garrison's immediatist movement in the early 1830s, including James and Lucretia Mott (veterans of "Free Produce" groups in the mid-1820s), lawyer and editor Evan Lewis, and Lewis Gunn and Charles Burleigh, members of the American Convention prior to the 1830s.

49. *Abolitionist*, April 1833 (Snelling).

50. Scituate Anti-Slavery Society Constitution, in *Plymouth We, the People*, January 9, 1835.

51. *First Annual Report of the New England Anti-Slavery Society*, 23–42.

52. Joseph R. Dailey to Robert Purvis, August 15, 1833, Letters, BPL.

53. BFASS to Portage, Ohio, FASS, June 6, 1837, BFASS Letterbook, MHS. See also Debra Gold Hanson, "The Boston Female Anti-Slavery Society and the Limits of Gender Politics," in Jean Fagin Yellin and John C. Van Horne, eds., *The Abolitionist Sisterhood: Women's Political Culture in Antebellum America* (Ithaca: Cornell University Press, 1995), 45–65.

54. *National Enquirer*, July 8, 1837.

55. Amherst Anti-Slavery Society Records, July 19, 1833, Novemb er 24, 1834, Anti-Slavery Collection, BPL.

56. *Plymouth We, the People*, September 25, 1835.

57. See William Lloyd Garrison, "To the Liberator," September 13, 1832 (Providence), September 24, 1832 (Portland), and Garrison to Ebenezer Dole, June 29, 1832 (Boston and Philadelphia), all reprinted in Merrill and Ruchames, *Letters of . . . Garrison*, 1:166–72, 172–77, 154–56.

58. William Lloyd Garrison to Simeon S. Jocelyn, May 1, 1833, ibid., 225; Jennie F. Copeland, "Mansfield In Other Days," in *Mansfield News*, March 27, April 3, 1931.

59. Amos A. Phelps to Charlotte Phelps, October 17, 1834, Letters, BPL.

60. *First Annual Report of the New England Anti-Slavery Society*, 9–22. Some scholars have portrayed post–1830 abolitionists' commitment to southern slaves as a mere rhetorical ploy. Far from getting more involved with the experience of bondage (by reaching out to the enslaved or confronting slaveholders in the southern states), Bay State abolitionists evinced increasing concern with ephemeral principles such as moral perfectionism, pacifism, and sabbatarianism. On the other hand, scholars such as Stanley Harrold have argued that northern immediatists battled southern slavery "on its own ground" in the late 1840s and 1850s, establishing free labor colonies in the Border South (to quicken the pace of southern emancipation) and undertaking antislavery missions among slaves (under the guise of spreading the gospel). Yet even Harrold argues that Massachusetts abolitionists were the least important group to challenge southern slavery via these confrontational tactics. See Stanley Harrold's *The Abolitionists and the South, 1831–1861* (Lexington: , 1995), and James Brewer Stewart's "Young Turks and Old Turkeys: Abolitionist Historians and the Aging Process, 1830–1879," a perceptive review of recent scholarship that downplays abolitionists' confrontation with slavery in *Reviews in American History* 11 (June 1983): 226–32.

61. *First Annual Report of the New England Anti-Slavery Society*, 8–22.

62. AASS, "Declaration of Sentiments," 1833, quoted in William H. Pease and Jane H. Pease, eds., *The Anti-Slavery Argument* (Indianapolis: Bobbs-Merrill, 1965), 65–71.

63. See William Rawle note on forming the AASS, May 20, 1833, Rawle Family Paper, HSP.

64. Phelps, *Lectures on Slavery and Its Remedy*, reprinted in Pease and Pease, *Anti-Slavery Argument*, 72–75, 78–81.

65. As with their views on northern racism, white abolitionists could conceive of both their mission to and relationship with southern blacks in racialist language: slaves were helpless victims, beaten down and oppressed to such a point that only white abolitoinists could speak for them. Ironically, this argument gained increasing support for the northern cause among middle-class households. See George M. Fredrickson, *The Arrogance of Race: Historical Perspectives on Slavery, Racism, and Social Inequality* (Middleton, Conn.: Wesleyan University Press, 1988).

66. Phelps, "Notes on Slavery and Emancipation," Phelps Papers, BPL.

67. Garrison to Joseph Gales and William W. Seaton, September 23, 1831, in Merrill and Ruchames, *Letters of . . . Garrison*, 1:135.

68. *National Enquirer*, August 6, 1837.

69. James R. Bradley to Lydia Maria Child, June 3, 1834, in C. Peter Ripley et al., eds., *The Black Abolitionists Papers*, 5 vols. (Chapel Hill: University of North Carolina Press, 1985–92), 3:136–41. For an excerpt of Bradley's letter, see *Anti-Slavery Almanac* (New York, 1839 ed.).

70. For an advertisement for Equiano's narrative and Burleigh's comments, see *National Enquirer*, July 30, 1837.

71. David Lee Child, *The Despotism of Freedom* (Boston, 1833), app., 71.

72. Ibid., 21, 27, 36.

73. Ibid., 63.

74. *Abolitionist*, January 1, 1833.

75. Ellis Grey Loring to William Ellery Chaning, December 17, 1837, Channing Papers, MHS; *Plymouth We, the People*, October 18, 1834.

76. Arnold Buffum to William Lloyd Garrison, July 16, 1832, Letters, BPL.

77. Garrison in *Liberator*, September 3, October 15, 1831.

78. Ibid.

79. Ibid.

80. Item 17, Phelps Papers, BPL.

81. Viewing slaves as oppressed countrymen, some white abolitionists in Massachusetts began advocating physical confrontation with southern slaveholders seeking to reclaim southern fugitives in northern territory. On more confrontational attitudes and actions among northern abolitionists in the 1840s, see Harrold, *Abolitionists and the South*, esp. chap. 4, "John Brown's Forerunners."

82. In a book on the rise of sectionalism and the coming of the Civil War, John Ashworth argues that national political disputes over slavery were very much the product of politicized black resistance. "Indeed," he writes, "it is not too much to say that behind every event in the sectional controversy over slavery lurked black resistance to slavery." Ashworth, *Commerce and Compromise, 1820–1850*, vol. 1 of *Slavery, Capitalism, and Politics in the Antebellum Republic* (New York: Cambridge University Press, 1995), 8–9.

83. Thomas Shipley resolution, Acting Committee Minutes, ca. 1835, PAS Papers, reel 2.

84. Lucretia Mott to Ann Warren Weston, June 7, 1838, Letters, BPL.

Chapter Six

1. Henry Stanton, "Proceedings of the Massachusetts Anti-Slavery Society . . . at Its Fifth Annual Meeting," in *Fifth Annual Report of the Massachusetts Anti-Slavery Society* (Boston, 1837) (hereafter cited as *Fifth Annual Report, MASS*), xiii, xxxxii–xxxix.

2. "The Reverend Mr. Scott of Lowell," ibid., vii.

3. David Lee Child, *The Despotism of Freedom* (Boston, 1833), 53.

4. Samuel Joseph May, *Recollections of the Anti-Slavery Conflict* (Boston, 1869).

5. *Genius*, November 6, 1829.

6. William Lloyd Garrison, editorial notes in *Genius*, November 6, December 25, 1829, January 8, February 5, 1830.

7. Ibid., January 8, February 5, 1830.

8. Benjamin Lundy, "Sugar Culture in Hayti" (editorial), *Genius*, February 5, 1830.

9. Garrison, note on "twelve petitions" (in virtual reply to Lundy's moderation), ibid.; Garrison to Ebenezer Dole, July 14, 1830, in Walter M. Merrill and Lewis

Ruchames, eds., *Letters of William Lloyd Garrison*, 6 vols. (Cambridge, Mass.: , 1971), 1:104–6. See also Garrison's words in James Gillespie Birney, "A Letter on the Political Obligations of the Abolitionists, with a Reply by William Lloyd Garrison" (Boston, 1839).

10. See esp. Maria Weston Chapman, *Right and Wrong in Massachusetts* (Boston, 1839), 6–7.

11. BFASS circular letter, August 15, 1836, in *National Enquirer*, August 24, 1836.

12. *Liberator*, November 29, 1834.

13. "Elizabeth Margaret Chandler," in *National Enquirer*, October 29, 1836. See also Mary P. Ryan, *Womanhood in America from Colonial Times to the Present* (New York: New Viewpoints, 1975), 181.

14. Benjmain Lundy, ed., *The Poetical Works of Elizabeth Margaret Chandler* (Philadelphia, 1834), introduction. The differences between Lundy's "women's page" in the *Genius* before 1828 and Chandler's after 1828 are striking. Lundy continually urged women to serve as archetypal republican mothers in the antislavery cause—instilling sympathetic attitudes about race and slavery in the nation's sons and daughters. Chandler, however, consistently emphasized explicit female activism, like petitioning. See Lundy's reprints of Chandler's essays from the *Genius* in various forms.

15. *Genius*, September 2, 1829.

16. *Genius*, September 16, 25, 1829.

17. *Genius*, May, June 1831. By June 1831 the paper had become a monthly publication.

18. For a classic treatment of the emergence of women's activism in New England, see Nancy Cott, *The Bonds of Womanhood: "Woman's Sphere" in New England, 1780–1835* (New Haven: Yale University Press, 1977).

19. Amos A. Phelps, *Lectures on Slavery and Its Remedy* (Boston, 1834); Oliver Johnson, *Garrison and His Times*, 74, 73; Phelps, "Notes on Slavery and Emancipation," Phelps Papers, BPL.

20. Phelps, "Notes on Slavery and Emancipation."

21. Ibid., section entitled "Doctrine of Reform."

22. Ibid., sections entitled "What Would You Have Us Do?" and "What Can We Do?"

23. Ibid.

24. *First Annual Report of the New England Anti-Slavery Society* (Boston, 1833), 9–21.

25. *Fifth Annual Report, MASS*, 4–17. The NEASS was renamed the MASS in 1836.

26. Chapman, *Right and Wrong in Massachusetts*, 6–7, 51; *First Annual Report of the New England Anti-Slavery Society* (Amasa Walker at NEASS founding meeting, January 20, 1832).

27. *Fourth Annual Report of the Massachusetts Anti-Slavery Society* (Boston, 1836), 53 (Charles Follen); Arnold Buffum to William Lloyd Garrison, January 19, 1834, Letters, BPL; Phelps, Item 5, "The Coloured Population," Phelps Papers, BPL.

28. James B. Stewart with George Price, *"To Heal the Scourge of Prejudice": The Life and Writings of Hosea Easton* (Amherst: University of Massachusetts Press, 1998), p. 67.

29. Garrison to Harriott Plummer, March 4, 1833, ibid., 206–11; *Fourth Annual Report of the Massachusetts Anti-Slavery Society*, 29–30.

30. *Circular to the Societies of Anti-Slavery Women in the United States* (issued by the First Annual Convention of Anti-Slavery Women), reprinted in *National Enquirer*, July 8, 1837.

31. Joshua Coffin to Samuel Sewall, ca. 1837, Letters, BPL.

32. William Lloyd Garrison to George W. Benson, October 2, 1835, in Merrill and Ruchames, *Letters of . . . Garrison*, 1:538.

33. Amherst Anti-Slavery Society Records, Anti-Slavery Collection, BPL.

34. *Liberator*, October 6, 1832, January 21, 1832.

35. Arnold Buffum to WIlliam Lloyd Garrison, January 28, 1835, Letters, BPL.

36. James Farmer to Francis Jackson, February 15, 1836, May 3, 1837, Anti-Slavery Collection, BPL; *First Annual Report of the . . . Pennsylvania Anti-Slavery Society* (July 4, 1835).

37. Phelps, "Notes on Slavery and Emancipation," esp. section entitled "Free Discussion," Phelps Papers, BPL; Charles P. Grosvenor, "Disquisition on the Constitution," ca. 1836, in *Fourth Annual Report of the Massachusetts Anti-Slavery Society* (Boston, 1836).

38. *Fifth Annual Report, MASS*, v, vi–viii ("The Reverend Mr. Scott of Lowell"), xiii–xiv (Loring); William Lloyd Garrison to Thomas Shipley, December 17, 1835, in Merrill and Ruchames, *Letters of . . . Garrison*, 1:582–85.

39. Phelps, "Notes on Slavery and Emancipation," Phelps Papers, BPL.

40. David Lee Child, *Despotism of Freedom*, 53.

41. WIlliam Lloyd Garrison to Thomas Shipley, December 17, 1835, in Merrill and Ruchames, *Letters of . . . Garrison*, 1:582–84.

42. Phelps, "Notes on Slavery and Emancipation," section entitled "Free Discussion," Phelps Papers, BPL.

43. Phelps, "Notes on Slavery and Emancipation," "Free Discussion," and "Slavery, Vol. II: Hints, Subjects, Plans," ibid.

44. Phelps, "Slavery, Vol. II: Hints, Subjects, Plans," ibid. In a separate treatise designed to help other abolitionists combat prejudice and opposition, Philadelphia lawyer Lewis Gunn echoed Phelps's thoughts on the First Amendment. In 1837 he proposed to publish a "Textbook on Slavery," which, in "four to five hundred octavo pages," would collate relevant constitutional as well as religious writings on abolitionism. For citizens, this would have the virtue of condensing "a dozen or two pamphlets" into one book; converting people to the cause, after all, meant not "burdening" them with too much material.

For activists, however, it would bring together the "peculiar excellencies" of various abolitionist tracts into "one volume" that could be quick-referenced. Topics would range from the nature of slavery and its "remedy" to essays treating abolitionists' "right to discuss the subject" in public and so forth. "The author has long been of the opinion that a work of this nature would be of essential service to the cause of emancipation," Gunn wrote in one advertisement for the work. He was specifically interested in how his textbook might bolster mass action against slavery. Writing such a volume, he explained, occurred to him "when I was traveling as a lecturer," for he "found it absolutely necessary to prepare a book for his own use," one that might "take up any subject" or question and provide abolitionists with a brief but articulate constitutional defense of their cause. See ads for Gunn's "Textbook on Slavery" starting with the *National Enquirer*, August 17, 1837.

45. For abolitionists' constitutional scruples and the broader political world they inhabited, see Russell B. Nye, *Fettered Freedom: Civil Liberties and the Slavery Controversy, 1830–1860* (East Lansing: Michigan State University Press, 1963); William M. Wiecek, *The Sources of Antislavery Constitutionalism in America, 1760–1848* (Ithaca: Cornell University Press, 1977); and Donald Yacovone, *Samuel Joseph May and the Dilemmas of the Liberal Persuasion, 1797–1871*. Philadelphia: Temple University Press, 1991.

46. William Lloyd Garrison to editor of *Emancipator*, May 31, 1839, in Merrill and Ruchames, *Letters of . . . Garrison*, 2:475.

47. William Lloyd Garrison to Henry E. Benson, August 4, 1836, ibid., 2:152.

48. "W. H. J." to *National Enquirer*, October 8, 1836.

49. Editorial, *Abolitionist*, August 1833.

50. PFASS, "Address to the Women of the Free States," October 8, 1836. On female petitioning, see esp. Deborah Bingham Van Broekhoven, "'Let Your Names Be Enrolled': Method and Ideology in Women's Antislavery Petitioning," in Jean Fagin Yellin and John C. Van Horne, eds., *The Abolitionist Sisterhood: Women's Political Culture in Antebellum America* (Ithaca: Cornell University Press, 1995), 179–200.

51. "The Reverend Mr. Scott of Lowell," *Fifth Annual Report, MASS*, v–viii.

52. William Lee Miller, *Arguing about Slavery: The Great Battle in the United States Congress* (New York: Knopf, 1996), 110–12.

53. See *Fifth Annual Report, MASS*, 17.

54. BFASS, "To the Women of New England," in *National Enquirer*, August 24, 1836.

55. BFASS to Providence FASS, June 6, 1837, and to Portage, Ohio, FASS, August 29, 1836, BFASS Letterbook, MHS.

56. Quoted in *National Enquirer*, July 8, 1837.

57. See esp. Yellin and Van Horne, *Abolitionist Sisterhood*, introduction.

58. Quoted in *National Enquirer*, July 8, 1837. See also Carolyn Williams, "The Female Anti-Slavery Movement: Fighting against Racial Prejudice and Promoting Women's Rights in Antebellum America," ibid., 159–78.

59. Quoted in *National Enquirer*, July 8, 1837.

60. Samuel McKean to Mary Grew, February 20, 1837, Philadelphia FASS Letterbook, PAS Papers, reel 26.

61. James Harper to Mary Grew, January 28, 30, 1837, ibid.

62. Samuel McKean to Mary Grew, September 28, 1837, ibid.

63. William Lloyd Garrison to Elizabeth Pease, November 6, 1837, in Merrill and Ruchames, *Letters of . . . Garrison*, 2:325; Phelps, "Notes on Slavery and Emancipation," Phelps Papers, BPL.

64. Garrison to editor of *Emancipator*, May 31, 1839, in Merrill and Ruchames, *Letters of . . . Garrison*, 2:467, 469.

65. *National Enquirer*, July 8, 1837.

66. John C. Calhoun to Duff Green, U.S. Telegraph, August 30, 1835, in Clyde Wilson, ed., *The Papers of John C. Calhoun*, 23 vols. (Columbia: University of South Carolina Press, 1959–   ), 12:547–48.

67. "Report and Resolutions of a Public Meeting at Pendleton [S.C.]," ibid., 12:548–51.

Chapter Seven

1. Benjamin Lundy to Isaac Barton, Acting Committee, ACAS, January 21, 1829, PAS Papers, reel 29; First Annual Meeting of the New York Anti-Slavery Society, quoted with approval in Lundy's *National Enquirer*, December 17, 1836 (first quotation); "Prospectus of the Anti-Abolitionist," Pottstown, Pa., quoted in *National Enquirer*, June 10, 1837 (second quotation).

2. John Myers, "The Agency System of the American Anti-Slavery Society" (Ph.D. diss., University of Michigan, 1961); William Lloyd Garrison to *Liberator*, September 7, 1832, in Walter M. Merrill and Lewis Ruchames, eds., *Letters of William Lloyd Garrison*, 6 vols. (Cambridge, Mass.: , 1971), 1:162–63.

3. Samuel Joseph May to William Lloyd Garrison, September 2, 1835, Letters, BPL.

4. Hugh Davis, *Joshua Leavitt: Evangelical Abolitionist* (Baton Rouge: Louisiana State University Press, 1992), 62. For updated treatments of the American Baptist Home Missionary Society and the American Home Missionary Society, see John Quist, *Restless Visionaries: The Social Roots of Antebellum Reform in Alabama and Michigan*. Baton Rouge: Louisiana State University Press, 1998, esp. 103–54.

5. "Democratic Address," *Concord Freeman*, October 3, 1835; *Springfield Hampden Journal and Advertiser*, April 2, 9, 1834.

6. "Committee on Agencies" Minutes from September 1834, in "American Anti-Slavery Meetings One through Six," BPL. For early Massachusetts agency work, see Arnold Buffum to William Lloyd Garrison, July 16, August 31, 1832, Letters, BPL.

7. Charles C. Burleigh to William Lloyd Garrison, September 29, 1835, Letters, BPL.

8. *Springfield Gazette*, October 23, 1833; *Springfield Republican Journal*, August 29, 1835.

9. *Liberator*, October 13, 1832.

10. Amos A. Phelps, "Journals," Phelps Papers, BPL. This paragraph collates material from volumes 1 and 2 of the journals, particularly items with the headings "Objections to Emancipation," "Hints, Subjects, Plans," and "What Would You Have Us Do?"

11. Arnold Buffum to William Lloyd Garrison, August 31, 1832, Letters, BPL.

12. *Portland Christian Mirror*, March 7, 1833.

13. Arnold Buffum to William Lloyd Garrison, July 16, 1832, Letters, BPL.

14. Charles Burleigh to Samuel J. May, April 9, 1835, ibid.

15. Arnold Buffum to William Lloyd Garrison, July 16, 1832, ibid.

16. "The Reverend Mr. Scott of Lowell," *Fifth Annual Report of the Massachusetts Anti-Slavery Society*, January 1837 (Boston, 1837), vi–vii; *Salem Gazette*, August 4, 1835.

17. Jennie F. Copeland, "Mansfield in Other Days," in *Mansfield News*, March 1937, April 3, 1931; *Plymouth We, the People*, January 9, 1835; *Salem Gazette*, June 13, July 4, 1834.

18. *Plymouth We, the People*, December 19, 1834.

19. Ibid.

20. "Qui" to *Plymouth We, the People*, December 26, 1834.

21. Ibid.

22. See Stanly B. Parsons et al., *United States Congressional Districts, 1788–1841*, 2 vols. (Westport, Conn.: Greenwood, 1978), 2:17.

23. *Plymouth We, the People*, December 15, 1834.

24. "South Scituate Anti-Slavery Society," ibid.

25. For a sample schedule of public "exercises" by local abolitionist societies, see "Dorchester Anti-Slavery Society's Celebration, July 4, 1835," Broadside Collection, MHS.

26. Copeland, "Mansfield in Other Days," in *Mansfield News*, March 27, April 3, 1931. For an excellent treatment of Easton, see James Brewer Stewart with George Price, *"To Heal the Scourge of Prejudice": The Life and Writings of Hosea Easton* (Amherst: University of Massachusetts Press, 1998).

27. Cyrus Pitt Grosvenor to MASS, February 10, 1836, Letters, BPL.

28. Samuel J. May to Benjamin Bacon, April 13, 1835, and William Lloyd Garrison's "Report" to MASS, May 27, 1836, ibid.

29. Mary Rogers, Plymouth FASS, to Margarette Forten, Philadelphia, August 22, 1834, PFASS Correspondence, PAS Papers, reel 26.

30. Edward Everett to Christopher A. Hack, "Editor of We, the People," Plymouth, Mass., May 28, 1835, Everett Papers, microfilm, reel 25, MHS.

31. Leonard Richards portrays antiabolitionism as essentially an urban phenomenon, but Massachusetts reformers encountered mobs in rural as well as urban areas. See Richards's fine book, *"Gentlemen of Property and Standing": Anti-Abolition Mobs in Jacksonian America* (New York: Oxford University Press, 1970).

32. *Springfield Republican Journal*, August 29, 1835 (Massachusetts law); Copeland, "Mansfield in Other Days," in *Mansfield News*, March 27, April 3, 1931.

33. May to Henry Grafton Chapman, February 10, 1836; to William Lloyd Garrison, September 2, 1835; to Amos A. Phelps, September 7, 1835, January 1, 1836—all in Letters, BPL.

34. No exhaustive research exists on *Liberator* subscriptions. I have compiled figures in this essay by working with the newspaper's Account Books 1–4, 1831–65 (Anti-Slavery Collection, BPL), checking these findings against reports from traveling agents in Massachusetts.

35. *Second Annual Report of the New England Anti-Slavery Society*, January 15, 1834 (Boston, 1834), 16–17.

36. Charles Burleigh to William Lloyd Garrison on travels and meetings in and around Concord, Mass., April 9, 1835, Letters, BPL.

37. *Concord Freeman*, August 8, 1835 ("American Anti-Slavery Almanack"), October 24, 1835 (Boston riot), October 31, 1835 (New York State convention of over one thousand local abolitionists "from every county"), all in Everett Papers, MHS.

38. Essay by "Shades of Warren," *Concord Freeman*, August 5, 1835.

39. Burleigh to Garrison, April 9, 1835.

40. Quoted in *Lynn Record*, October 9, 1835.

41. "Temperance, Colonization, Anti-Crandallism," in *Springfield Gazette*, October 23, 1833; *Gloucester Telegraph*, October 24, 1835.

42. See, e.g., *Boston Courier*, August 24, 1835, and *Concord Yeoman's Gazette and Middlesex Whig*, ca. August 1835, in Everett Papers, MHS.

43. "Middleborough" on "Antislavery" activity both locally and nationally, in *Plymouth We, the People*, March 6, 1835.

44. *Salem Gazette*, August 11, 1835; *Plymouth We, the People*, August 28, 1835.

45. *Salem Gazette*, June 7, 13, July 4, 1834, December 29, 1837.

46. *Salem Gazette*, August 4, 1835.

47. *Plymouth We, the People*, August 7, 1835.

48. *Plymouth We, the People*, December 26, 1834, January 9, August 28, 1835. See also the following issues for abolitionist coverage: August 28, 1835 (MASS meeting), September 11, 1835 (Amos Kendall's letter to New York Postmaster), October 2, 1835 (Grimké letter from *Liberator*), and October 9, 1835 ("mob spirit"). And see advertisements for "American Anti-Slavery Almanack," beginning August 7, 1835, and "History of the People of Color," beginning September 27, 1834, and running through the next year.

49. *Plymouth We, the People*, October 9, 1835.

50. "Mr. Birney's Speech" (editorial), *Essex County Gazette*, Haverhill, Mass., June 6, 1836.

51. "A Legal Opinion," *Boston Courier*, August 21, 1835, Everett Papers, MHS.

52. *Lynn Record*, reprinted in *Salem Gazette*, August 11, 1835; *Briggs Bulletin*, reprinted in *Salem Gazette*, September 4, 1835; *Plymouth We, the People*, September 22, 1835; *Springfield Gazette*, October 23, 1833.

53. William Lloyd Garrison to Harriet Minot, April 9, 1833, in Merrill and Ruchames, *Letters of . . . Garrison*, 1:218–19.

54. See Julie Roy Jeffrey's excellent work on female antislavery activists, *The Great Silent Army of Abolitionism: Ordinary Women in the Antislavery Movement* (Chapel Hill: University of North Carolina Press, 1998).

55. Aileen S. Kraditor's *Means and Ends in American Abolitionism: Garrison and His Critics on Strategy and Tactics* (New York: Random House, 1967) focuses on the late 1830s, when debates over women's formal place in the American Anti-Slavery Society exploded. Other scholars address the "woman question" by looking at the growth of female antislavery societies in the mid-1830s. Still others — including Jean Fagan Yellin, Blanche Glassman Hersh, and Nancy Hewitt — have looked at the way women helped shaped antislavery and reform discourse in the 1820s and 1830s. For a recent treatment of Abby Kelley, see Dorothy Sterling, *Ahead of Her*

Time: Abby Kelley and the Politics of Anti-Slavery (New York: Oxford University Press, 1991).

56. William Lloyd Garrison to *Liberator*, September 7, 28, 1832, in Merrill and Ruchames, *Letters of . . . Garrison*, 1:164, 179–80.

57. William Lloyd Garrison to Harriott Plummer, March 4, 1833, ibid., 1:206–10.

58. Amos A. Phelps, "Journals," Item 8, p. 12, and Phelps to Charlotte Phelps, May 19, 1834," Phelps Papers, BPL, in which he discusses a "delightful meeting with the ladies" of Philadelphia in the early 1830s; "Committee on Agencies" Minutes, July 12, 1836, "American Anti-Slavery Society Meetings . . . ," Anti-Slavery Collection, BPL.

59. Burleigh to Samuel J. May, April 8, 9, 1835, Letters, BPL. Burleigh's recollections of several weeks of lecturing appear in long letters to various people. For information on female activism, see ibid.

60. Ibid.

61. BFASS to Amesbury Mills FASS, May 17, 1834, BFASS Letterbook, MHS.

62. On the BFASS, see Debra Gold Hansen, "The Boston Female Anti-Slavery Society and the Limits of Gender Politics," in Jean Fagin

Yellin and John C. Van Horne, eds. *The Abolitionist Sisterhood: Women's Political Culture in Antebellum America* (Ithaca: Cornell University Press, 1995), 46–49.

63. BFASS to Amersbury Mills FASS, April 17, May 17, 1834; to NYFASS, July 21, 1835; and to Bangor, Maine, FASS, January 7, 1838—all in BFASS Letterbook, MHS.

64. Ibid.

65. Keith Melder, "Abby Kelley and the Process of Liberation," in Yellin and Van Horne, *Abolitionist Sisterhood*, 231–34, 246, 248.

66. Ibid., 240, 248.

67. Abby and Julia Smith to William Lloyd Garrison, April 15, 1837; James Farmer to Francis Jackson, March 24, 1838; and Miss —— Clark to Francis Jackson, January 19, 1837—all in Letters, BPL. The first letter is interesting, for the two women ask Garrison to change their mother's *Liberator* subscription to reflect that it was hers, not her deceased husband's: "The Liberator was directed to our father," the sisters wrote, but the subscription should be in the name of "Mrs. Smith, our mother." In that letter they also ask Garrison to tell the Grimkés to "stop in Connect-icut on their way to New York."

68. *Liberator* Account Books 1–4, 1831–65, Anti-Slavery Collection, BPL; Samuel J. May to Sarah T. Benson, January 15, 1837, Letters, BPL.

69. Sidney George Fisher, February 15, 1837, in M. Wainwright, ed., *A Phila-delphia Perspective: The Diary of Sidney George Fisher* (Philadelphia: Historical Society of Pennsylvania, 1967).

70. David Paul Brown to William Rawle, March 27, July 7, 1834, Rawle Family Papers, HSP.

71. "E. N.," *Pennsylvania Freeman*, September 9, 1840.

72. William Lloyd Garrison to George Shepard, September 13, 1830, in Merrill and Ruchames, *Letters of . . . Garrison*, 1:107–9.

73. Cleveland Sellers, *River of No Return* (Jackson: University of Mississippi Press, 1991 reprint ed.), 19, uses the same image to illustrate how the National Association for the Advancement of Colored People and the Student Nonviolent Coordinating Committee divided over civil rights strategies and tactics in 1960.

74. Charles M. Payne, *I've Got the Light of Freedom: The Organizing Tradition and the Mississippi Freedom Struggle* (Berkeley: University of California Press, 1995), esp. 242–56.

Epilogue

1. *Proceedings of the American Anti-Slavery Society, at Its Third Decade. . . .* (New York: Arno Press, 1969), 1–65. For developments on southern plantations during the Civil War, see William Freehling, *The South vs. the South* (New York: Oxford University Press, 2001), and Donald Yacovone, *A Voice of Thunder: A Black Soldier's Civil War* (Urbana: University of Illinois Press, 1997).

2. *Proceedings of the American Anti-Slavery Society, at Its Third Decade.*

3. Ibid.

4. Ibid.

5. Ibid.

6. James McPherson, *Abraham Lincoln and the Second American Revolution* (New York: Oxford University Press, 1991), remains the foremost exponent of this thesis.

7. Phillips quoted in James Brewer Stewart, *Holy Warriors: The Abolitionists and American Slavery*, rev. ed. (New York: Hill and Wang, 1996), 178.

8. Thompson quoted in Eric L. McKitrick, *Slavery Defended* (New York: Prentice-Hall, 1963), 99–110.

9. For Holmes's review, see ibid.

10. Cary, Wicks, and Still quoted in Richard Newman, Patrick Rael, and Phillip Lapsansky, eds., *Pamphlets of Protest: An Anthology of Early African-American Protest Literature* (New York: Routledge, 2000), 198–213, 114–21, 254–61.

11. See Richard Blackett, *Thomas Morris Chester, Black Civil War Correspondent* (Baton Rouge: Louisiana State University Press, 1989), and Wendy Hamand Venet, *Neither Ballots nor Bullets: Women Abolitionists and the Civil War* (Charlottesville: University of Virginia Press, 1991).

Primary Sources

Printed Collections

Annual Reports of the American Society for Colonizing the Free People of Color of the United States, 1818–1836. Vols. 1–20. Negro University Press Reprint: New York, 1969.

Annual Reports of the Board of Managers of the New-England/Massachusetts Anti-Slavery Society, 1833–1842. 2 vols. Reprint, Negro University Press: Westport, Conn., 1970.

Catterall, Helen Tunnicliff, ed. *Judicial Cases Concerning American Slavery and the Negro.* 5 vols. New York: Octagon Books, 1968.

Merrill, Walter M., and Lewis Ruchames, eds. *The Letters of William Lloyd Garrison.* 6 vols. Cambridge: Harvard University Press, 1971.

Ripley, C. Peter, et al., eds. *The Black Abolitionist Papers.*

Newspapers

Antislavery Newspapers
  Abolitionist
  Anti-Slavery Almanac
  Emancipator
  Freedom's Journal
  Genius of Universal Emancipation
  Liberator
  National Enquirer
  Pennsylvania Freeman
Maine
  Portland Christian Mirror
Massachusetts
  Boston Courier
  Concord Freeman
  Concord Yeoman
  Gloucester Telegraph
  Haverhill Gazette
  Lynn Record
  Mansfield News
  Plymouth We, the People

Salem Gazette
Springfield Gazette
Springfield Republican Journal
Pennsylvania
  Pennsylvanian
  Philadelphia Independent Gazetteer
  Poulson's Daily Advertiser
South Carolina
  Columbian Herald

Manuscript Collections

Boston, Massachusetts
  Boston Public Library
    Anti-Slavery Collection
    Amos A. Phelps Papers
  Massachusetts Historical Society
    Jeremy Belknap Papers
    Boston Female Anti-Slavery Society Letterbook
    William Ellery Channing Papers
    Broadside Collection
    Edward Everett Papers
    T. M. Harris Papers
    Vaughan Family Papers
Philadelphia, Pennsylvania
  Historical Society of Pennsylvania
    Cox-Parrish-Wharton Collection
    Miscellaneous Papers
    Rawle Family Papers
    Jonathan Roberts Papers
    William Tilghman Papers
    Roberts Vaux Papers
  Pennsylvania Abolition Society Papers
    Philadelphia Female Anti-Slavery Society Records

Pamphlets

Allen, Richard. *A Narrative of the Proceedings of the Black People, during the Late Awful Calamity in Philadelphia, in the Year 1794*. Philadelphia, 1794.

Child, David Lee. *The Despotism of Freedom*. Boston, 1833.

Child, Lydia Maria. *Anti-Slavery Catechism*. Boston, 1837 ed.

——. *An Appeal in Favor of the Colored Race*. Boston, 1833 ed.

——. *Authentic Anecdotes of American Slavery*. Boston, 1837.

Cushing, Caleb. *An Oration . . . at Boston before the Colonization Society of Massachusetts on the Anniversary of American Independence, July 4, 1833*. Boston, 1833.

Forten, James. *A Series of Letters by a Man of Color*. Philadelphia, 1813.

Garrison, William Lloyd. *Thoughts on African Colonization*. Boston, 1832.

Hamilton, William. *An Address to the New-York African Society, for Mutual Relief*. New York, 1809.

Haynes, Lemuel. *The Nature and Importance of True Republicanism*. Boston, 1801.

Jones, Absalom. *A Sermon . . . on the Abolition of the Slave Trade*. Philadelphia, 1808.

Parrott, Russell. *An Address on the Abolition of the Slave Trade*. Philadelphia, 1816.

——. *An Oration on the Abolition of the Slave Trade*. Philadelphia, 1812.

Pennsylvania Abolition Society. *The Present State and Condition of the Free People of Color of the City of Philadelphia*. Philadelphia, 1838.

Phelps, Amos A. *Lectures on Slavery and Its Remedy*. Boston, 1834.

Saunders, Prince. *Memoir Presented to the American Convention for Promoting the Abolition of Slavery*. Philadelphia, 1818.

Stewart, Maria W. "Lecture Delivered at the Franklin Hall," September 21, 1832, and "Religion and the Pure Principles of Morality," both in *Productions of Mrs. Maria W. Stewart*. Boston, 1835.

Tyson, J. R. *Discourse before the Young Man's Colonization Society of Philadelphia*. Philadelphia, 1834.

Walker, David. *Appeal in Four Articles: Together with a Preamble to the Colored Citizens of the World*. Boston, 1829.

Whipper, William. *An Address Delivered in Wesley Church . . . before the Colored Reading Society of Philadelphia*. Philadelphia, 1828.

Williams, Peter, Jr. *An Oration on the Abolition of the Slave Trade*. New York, 1808.

Young, Robert Alexander. *The Ethiopian Manifesto, Issued in Defence of the Blackman's Rights, in the Scale of Universal Freedom*. New York, 1829.

Secondary Sources

Books

Abzug, Robert. *Cosmos Crumbling: American Reform and the Religious Imagination*. New York: Oxford University Press, 1994.

Adams, Alice Dana. *The Neglected Period of Anti-Slavery in America, 1808–1832*. 1908. Reprint, Gloucester, Mass.: Peter Smith, 1964.

Aptheker, Herbert. *Abolitionism: A Revolutionary Movement*. Boston: Twayne, 1989.

——. *American Negro Slave Revolts*. New ed. New York: International Publishers, 1974.

——. *Anti-Racism in U.S. History: The First Two Hundred Years*. New York: Greenwood, 1992.

Barnes, Gilbert H. *The Antislavery Impulse, 1830–1844*. 1933. Reprint, Gloucester, Mass.: Peter Smith, 1973.

Bay, Mia. *The White Image in the Black Mind: African-American Ideas about White People, 1830–1925*. New York: Oxford University Press, 2000.

Benson, Lee. *The Concept of Jacksonian Democracy: New York as a Test Case*. Princeton: Princeton University Press, 1961.

Berlin, Ira. *Slaves without Masters: The Free Negro in the Antebellum South*. New York: Random House, 1974.

Birney, William. *James G. Birney and His Times: The Genesis of the Republican Party with Some Account of the Abolitionist Movement in the South before 1828*. 1890. Reprint, New York: Negro University Press, 1969.

Blue, Frederick. *The Free Soilers: Third Party Politics, 1848–1854*. Urbana: University of Illinois Press, 1973.

Bracey, John H., August Meier, and Elliott Rudwick, eds. *Blacks in the Abolitionist Movement*. Belmont, Calif.: Wadsworth, 1971.

Channing, Steven A. *Crisis of Fear: Secession in South Carolina*. New York: Norton, 1974.

Cheek, William F., and Aimee L. Cheek. *John Mercer Langston and the Fight for Black Freedom*. Champaign: University of Illinois Press, 1989.

Commager, Henry Steele. *Theodore Parker*. Boston: Beacon, 1947.

Cover, Robert M. *Justice Accused: Antislavery and the Judicial Process*. New Haven: Yale University Press, 1975.

Craven, Avery O. *The Coming of the Civil War*. 2d ed. Chicago: University of Chicago Press, 1957.

Cross, Whitney R. *The Burned-Over District: The Social and Intellectual History of Enthusiastic Religion in Western New York, 1800–1850*. Ithaca: Cornell University Press, 1950.

Davis, David Brion. *The Problem of Slavery in the Age of Revolution*. Ithaca: Cornell University Press, 1975.

———. *The Problem of Slavery in Western Culture*. Ithaca: Cornell University Press, 1966.

———. *The Slave Power Conspiracy and the Paranoid Style*. Baton Rouge: Louisiana State University Press, 1961.

Davis, Hugh. *Joshua Leavitt: Evangelical Abolitionist*. Baton Rouge: Louisiana State University Press, 1990.

D'Entremont, John. *Southern Emancipator, Moncure Conway: The American Years*. New York: Oxford University Press, 1987.

Dillon, Merton L. *The Abolitionists: The Growth of a Dissenting Minority*. New York: Harper and Row, 1974.

———. *Benjamin Lundy and the Struggle for Negro Freedom*. Urbana: University of Illinois Press, 1990.

Donald, David. *Lincoln Reconsidered: Essays on the Civil War Era*. 2d ed. 1956. Reprint, New York: Random House, 1961.

Duberman, Martin, ed. *Antislavery: The Crusade for Freedom in America*. New York: Norton, 1961.

———, ed. *The Antislavery Origins of the Civil War in the United States*. 1939. Reprint, Ann Arbor: University of Michigan Press, 1969.

Eaton, Clement. *The Freedom-of-Thought Struggle in the Old South*. New York: Harper and Row, 1964.

Egerton, Douglas R. *Gabriel's Rebellion: The Virginia Slave Conspiracies of 1800 and 1802*. Chapel Hill: University of North Carolina Press, 1993.

Ferguson, Robert A. *Law and Letters in American Culture*. Cambridge: Harvard University Press, 1984.

Fields, Barbara Jeanne. *Slavery and Freedom on the Middle Ground: Maryland during the Nineteenth Century*. New Haven: Yale University Press, 1985.

Filler, Louis. *The Crusade against Slavery, 1830–1860*. New York: Harper and Row, 1960.

Fladeland, Betty. *James Gillespie Birney: Slaveholder to Abolitionist*. Ithaca: Cornell University Press, 1955.

Fredrickson, George M. *The Arrogance of Race: Historical Perspectives on Slavery, Racism, and Social Inequality*. Middleton, Conn.: Wesleyan University Press, 1988.

——. *The Black Image in the White Mind: The Debate on Afro-American Character and Destiny, 1877–1964*. New York: Harper and Row, 1971.

Freehling, Alison Goodyear. *Drift toward Dissolution: The Virginia Slavery Debate of 1831–1832*. Baton Rouge: Louisiana State University Press, 1982.

Freehling, William W. *Prelude to the Civil War: The Nullification Controversy*. New York: Harper and Row, 1966.

——. *The Road to Disunion*. 2 vols. projected. New York: Oxford University Press, 1990.

Friedman, Lawrence J. *Gregarious Saints: Self and Community in American Abolitionism, 1830–1870*. New York: Cambridge University Press, 1982.

Gara, Larry. *The Liberty Line: The Legend of the Underground Railroad*. Lexington: University of Kentucky Press, 1961.

Garrison, Wendell Phillips, and Francis Jackson Garrison. *William Lloyd Garrison, 1805–1889: The Story of His Life Told by His Children*. 4 vols. New York: Century, 1885–89.

Genovese, Eugene D. *From Rebellion to Revolution: Afro-American Slave Revolts in the Making of the Modern World*. Baton Rouge: Louisiana State University Press, 1979.

——. *Roll, Jordan, Roll: The World the Slaves Made*. New York: Pantheon, 1974.

Gerteis, Louis S. *Morality and Utility in American Antislavery Reform*. Chapel Hill: University of North Carolina Press, 1987.

Goodman, Paul. *Of One Blood: Abolitionism and the Origins of Racial Equality*. Berkeley: University of California Press, 1998.

Hallowell, Anna Davis. *James and Lucretia Mott: Life and Letters*. Boston: Houghton Mifflin, 1885.

Harrold, Stanley. *Gamaliel Bailey and Antislavery Union*. Kent, Ohio: Kent State University Press, 1986.

Hart, Albert Bushnell. *Slavery and Abolition, 1831–1841*. 1906. Reprint, New York: New American Library, 1969.

Hinks, Peter. *To Awaken My Afflicted Brethren: David Walker and the Problem of Antebellum Slave Resistance*. University Park: Pennsylvania State University Press, 1997.

Hodges, Graham Russell. *Root and Branch: African Americans in New York and East Jersey, 1613–1863*. Chapel Hill: University of North Carolina Press, 1999.

Horton, James. *Free People of Color: Inside the African American Community*. Washington, D.C.: Smithsonian Institution Press, 1993.

Horton, James, and Lois Horton. *In Hope of Liberty: Culture, Community, and Protest among Northern Free Blacks, 1700–1860* (New York: Oxford University Press, 1997).

Howard, Victor B. *Conscience and Slavery: The Evangelistic Domestic Missions, 1837–1861*. Kent, Ohio: Kent State University Press, 1990.

Howe, Daniel Walker. *The Political Culture of the American Whigs*. Chicago: University of Chicago Press, 1979.

Hunt, Alfred N. *Haiti's Influence on Antebellum America: Slumbering Volcano in the Caribbean*. Baton Rouge: Louisiana State University Press, 1988.

Jacobs, Donald M., ed. *Courage and Conscience: Black and White Abolitionists in Boston*. Bloomington: Indiana University Press, 1993.

Jeffrey, Julie Roy. *The Great Silent Army of Abolitionism: Ordinary Women in the Antislavery Movement*. Chapel Hill: University of North Carolina Press, 1998.

Jones, Howard. *Mutiny on the "Amistad": The Saga of a Slave Revolt and Its Impact on American Abolition, Law, and Diplomacy*. New York: Oxford University Press, 1986.

Kraditor, Aileen S. *Means and Ends in American Abolitionism: Garrison and His Critics on Strategy and Tactics*. New York: Random House, 1967.

Kraut, Alan M., ed. *Crusaders and Compromisers: Essays in the Relationship of the Antislavery Struggle to the Antebellum Party System*. Westport, Conn.: Greenwood, 1983.

Litwack, Leon. *North of Slavery: The Negro in the Free States, 1790–1860*. Chicago: University of Chicago Press, 1960.

Litwack, Leon, and August Meier, eds. *Black Leaders of the Nineteenth Century*. Urbana: University of Illinois Press, 1988.

Mabee, Carlton. *Black Freedom: The Nonviolent Abolitionists from 1830 through the Civil War*. London: Macmillan, 1970.

Mcfeely, William S. *Frederick Douglass*. New York: Simon and Schuster, 1991.

McGowan, James A. *Station Master on the Underground Railroad: The Life and Letters of Thomas Garrett*. Moylan, Pa.: Whimsie Press, 1977.

McKivigan, John R. *The War against Proslavery Religion: Abolitionism and the Northern Churches, 1830–1865*. Ithaca: Cornell University Press, 1984.

McPherson, James M. *Ordeal by Fire: The Civil War and Reconstruction*. 2d ed. New York: McGraw-Hill, 1992.

———. *The Struggle for Equality: Abolitionists and the Negro in the Civil War and Reconstruction*. Princeton: Princeton University Press, 1964.

Melish, Joanne Pope. *Disowning Slavery: Gradual Emancipation and "Race" in New England, 1780–1860*. Ithaca: Cornell University Press, 1998.

Nash, Gary B., and Jean R. Soderlund. *Freedom by Degrees: Emancipation and Its Aftermath in Pennsylvania*. New York: Oxford University Press, 1991.

Newman, Richard, Patrick Rael, and Phillip Lapsansky, eds. *Pamphlets of Protest: An Anthology of Early African American Protest Literature, 1790–1860*. New York: Routledge, 2000.

Nye, Russell B. *Fettered Freedom: Civil Liberties and the Slavery Controversy, 1830–1860*. East Lansing: Michigan State University Press, 1963.

Oates, Stephen B. *The Fires of the Jubilee: Nat Turner's Fierce Rebellion*. New York: Harper and Row, 1975.

Pease, Jane H. *Bound with Them in Chains: A Biographical History of the Antislavery Movement*. Westport, Conn.: Greenwood, 1972.

———. *They Who Would Be Free: Blacks' Search for Freedom, 1830–1861*. New York: Athenaeum, 1974.

Perry, Lewis. *Radical Abolitionism: Anarchy and the Government of God in Antislavery Thought*. Ithaca: Cornell University Press, 1973.

Perry, Lewis, and Michael Fellman, eds. *Antislavery Reconsidered: New Perspectives on the Abolitionists*. Baton Rouge: University of Louisiana Press, 1979.

Phillips, Ulrich B. *The Course of the South to Secession*. New York: Appleton-Century, 1933.

Quarles, Benjamin. *Black Abolitionists*. New York: Oxford University Press, 1969.

Quist, John. *Restless Visionaries: The Social Roots of Antebellum Reform in Alabama and Michigan*. Baton Rouge: Louisiana State University Press, 1998.

Randall, James G. *The Civil War and Reconstruction*. New York: Heath, 1937.

Rael, Patrick. *Colored Americans: Forging Black Protest in the Antebellum North*. Chapel Hill: University of North Carolina Press, 2001.

Rhodes, Jane. *Mary Ann Shadd Cary: The Black Press and Protest in the Nineteenth Century*. Bloomington: Indiana University Press, 1998.

Richardson, Marilyn. *Maria W. Stewart: America's First Black Political Activist*. Bloomington: Indiana University Press, 1993.

Sewell, Richard H. *Ballots for Freedom: Antislavery Politics in the United States, 1837–1860*. New York: Oxford University Press, 1976.

Soderlund, Jean R. *Quakers and Slavery: A Divided Spirit*. Princeton: Princeton University Press, 1985.

Sorin, Gerald. *The New York Abolitionists: A Case Study of Political Radicalism*. Westport, Conn.: Greenwood, 1971.

Stanton, William R. *The Leopard's Spots: Scientific Attitudes toward Race in America, 1815–1859*. Chicago: University of Chicago Press, 1960.

Stewart, James Brewer. *Holy Warriors: The Abolitionists and American Slavery*, rev. ed. New York: Hill and Wang, 1996.

———. *Joshua R. Giddings and the Tactics of Radical Politics*. Cleveland: Case Western Reserve University Press, 1970.

———. *Wendell Phillips: Liberty's Hero*. Baton Rouge: Louisiana State University Press, 1986.

Stewart, James Brewer, with George Price. *"To Heal the Scourge of Prejudice": The Life and Writings of Hosea Easton*. Amherst: University of Massachusetts Press, 1998.

Still, William. *The Underground Railroad*. 1871. Reprint, Chicago: Johnson Publishing, 1970.

Tise, Larry E. *Proslavery: A History of the Defense of Slavery in America, 1701–1840*. Athens: University of Georgia Press, 1987.

Tyler, Alice Felt. *Freedom's Ferment: Phases of American Social History form the Colonial Period to the Outbreak of the Civil War*. New York: Harper and Row, 1944.

Volpe, Vernon L. *Forlorn Hope of Freedom: The Liberty Party in the Old Northwest, 1838–1848*. Kent, Ohio: Kent State University Press, 1990.

Waldstreicher, David. *In the Midst of Perpetual Fetes: The Making of American Nationalism*. Chapel Hill: University of North Carolina Press, 1997.

Walker, Peter. *Moral Choices: Memory, Desire, and Imagination in Nineteenth-Century American Abolitionism*. Baton Rouge: Louisiana State University Press, 1978.

Walters, Ronald G. *The Antislavery Appeal: American Abolitionism after 1830*. Baltimore: Johns Hopkins University Press, 1976.

White, Shane. *Somewhat More Independent: The End of Slavery in New York City, 1770–1810*. Athens: University of Georgia Press, 1991.

White, Shane, with Graham White. *Stylin': African American Expressive Culture from Its Beginnings to the Zoot Suit*. Ithaca: Cornell University Press, 1998.

Wood, Gordon S. *The Radicalism of the American Revolution*. New York: Knopf, 1992.

Wyatt-Brown, Bertram. *Lewis Tappan and the Evangelical War against Slavery*. Cleveland: Case Western Reserve University Press, 1969.

Yacovone, Donald. *Samuel Joseph May and the Dilemmas of the Liberal Persuasion, 1797–1871*. Philadelphia: Temple University Press, 1991.

———. *A Voice of Thunder: A Black Soldier's Civil War*. Urbana: University of Illinois Press, 1997.

Yellin, Jean Fagin. *Women and Sisters: The Antislavery Feminists in American Culture*. New Haven: Yale University Press, 1989.

Yellin, Jean Fagin, and John C. Van Horne, eds. *The Abolitionist Sisterhood: Women's Political Culture in Antebellum America*. Ithaca: Cornell University Press, 1995.

Zilversmit, Arthur. *The First Emancipation: The Abolition of Slavery in the North*. Chicago: University of Chicago Press, 1967.

Articles

Abzug, Robert H. "The Influence of Garrisonian Abolitionists' Fear of Slave Violence on the Antislavery Argument, 1829–1840." *Journal of Negro History* 55 (January 1970): 15–28.

Curry, Richard O., and Lawrence B. Goodheart. "'Knives in Their Heads': Passionate Self-Analysis and the Search for Identity in American Abolitionism." *Canadian Review of American Studies* 14 (Winter 1983): 401–14.

Dain, Bruce. "Haiti, Egypt, and Early Black Racial Discourse in the United States." *Slavery and Abolition* 14 (December 1993): 139–61.

Davis, David Brion. "Antislavery or Abolition?" *Reviews in American History* 1 (March 1973): 95–99.

Demos, John. "The Antislavery Movement and the Problem of Violent 'Means.'" *New England Quarterly* 37 (December 1964): 501–26.

Dillon, Merton L. "The Abolitionists: A Decade of Historiography, 1959–1969." *Journal of Southern History* 35 (November 1969): 500–522.

Fields, Barbara J. "Ideology and Race in American History." In J. Morgan Kousser and James M. McPherson, eds., *Region, Race, and Reconstruction*, 150–63. New Haven: Yale University Press, 1982.

———. "Slavery, Race and Ideology in the United States." *New Left Review* 181 (May–June 1990): 95–118.

Friedman, Lawrence J. "'Historical Topics Sometimes Run Dry': The State of Abolitionist Studies." *Historian* 43 (February 1981): 177–94.

Gerteis, Louis S. "Slavery and Hard Times: Morality and Utility in American Antislavery Reform." *Civil War History* 29 (December 1983): 316–31.

Hoganson, Kristan. "Garrisonian Abolitionists and the Rhetoric of Gender, 1850–1860." *American Quarterly* 45 (December 1993): 558–95.

Howe, Daniel Walker. "The Evangelical Movement and Political Culture in the North during the Second Party System." *Journal of American History* (March 1991): 1216–39.

Huston, James L. "The Experiential Basis of the Northern Antislavery Impulse." *Journal of Southern History* 56 (November 1990): 609–40.

Konefsky, Alfred. "Law and Culture in Antebellum Boston." *Stanford Law Review* (April 1988): 1119–59.

Littlefield, Daniel C. "Slaves and the Abolitionists." *Reviews in American History* 19 (1991): 485–91.

McCormick, Richard P. "The Jacksonian Strategy." *Journal of the Early Republic* (Spring 1990): 1–17.

Mathews, Donald G. "The Abolitionists on Slavery: The Critique behind the Social Movement." *Journal of Southern History* 33 (May 1967): 163–82.

McKivigan, John R. "Antislavery 'Comeouter' Sects: A Neglected Dimension of the Abolitionist Movement." *Civil War History* 26 (June 1980): 142–60.

Pease, Jane H., and William H. Pease. "Antislavery Ambivalence: Immediatism, Expediency, Race." *American Quarterly* 17 (Winter 1965): 682–95.

———. "Ends, Means, and Attitudes: Black-White Conflict in the Antislavery Movement." *Civil War History* 18 (June 1972): 117–28.

Price, Robert. "The Ohio Anti-Slavery Convention of 1836." *Ohio State Archaeological and Historical Quarterly* 45 (April 1936): 173–88.

Saillant, John. "Lemuel Haynes's Black Republicanism and the American Republican Tradition, 1775–1820." *Journal of the Early Republic* (Fall 1994): 293–324.

Stewart, James Brewer. "The Emergence of Racial Modernity and the Rise of the White North, 1790–1840." *Journal of the Early Republic* 18, no. 2 (Summer 1998): 181–217.

———. "Evangelicalism and the Radical Strain in Southern Antislavery Thought during the 1820s." *Journal of Southern History* 39 (August 1973): 379–96.

———. "'It Was a Proud Day': African Americans, Festivals, and Parades in the North, 1741–1834." *Journal of American History* (June 1994): 13–50.

———. "Peaceful Hopes and Violent Experiences: The Evolution of Reforming and Radical Abolitionism, 1831–1837." *Civil War History* 17 (December 1971): 293–309.

———. "Young Turks and Old Turkeys: Abolitionists, Historians, and Aging Processes." *Reviews in American History* 11 (June 1983): 226–32.

Yacovone, Donald. "The Transformation of the Black Temperance Movement, 1827–1854: An Interpretation." *Journal of the Early Republic* 8, no. 3 (Fall 1988): 282–97.

abolitionists, 35, 37; and PAS's petitions, 40, 41, 44–51, 53, 54, 56, 57–59, 132, 142; representatives of as slaveholders, 45–46, 71, 82–83; and District of Columbia, 49–53, 56, 114, 150; and Pennsylvania's Gradual Abolition Act of 1780, 71, 81; and African American activism, 89, 91; and slaveholders, 109; and mass mobilization, 133, 146, 147, 148–49; and women, 148–49

Connecticut, 18, 24, 34

Constitution, U.S.: amendments to, 6, 132, 136, 140, 141, 142–43, 144, 149, 150, 178, 183; and Massachusetts abolitionists, 6, 142, 144, 150; and District of Columbia, 21, 49, 50, 51, 52, 53, 141, 143; and PAS's petitions, 25, 41, 44, 45, 46, 142; and PAS's legal tactics, 26, 76–77, 78; and government's role, 27, 56; and slave trade, 32, 47–48, 141, 142, 143; and runaway slaves, 44, 65, 78, 79, 85, 140, 141, 142, 143; and African American activism, 89, 95, 103; and mass mobilization, 136, 140, 141–44, 149, 150, 222 (n. 44)

Constitutional Convention of 1787, 28, 41, 47, 56, 65

Corlis, John, 17

Cornish, James, 99

Cornish, Samuel, 13, 97–98

Courts of law. See Judiciary

Coxe, Tench, 21, 42, 47, 48

Crabbin, Alexander, 185

Crummel, Alexander, 19

Cuba, 68

Cummins, John, 185

Cushing, Caleb, 110, 112, 113

Danforth, John, 157

Davis, David Brion, 1, 8

Davis, Jefferson, 177

Debating clubs, 87, 100

De homine replegiando, 74

Delaware, 17, 34, 69

Democratic sensibility, 8, 9, 11, 15, 131, 175, 183

Despotism of Freedom, The (Child), 126

District of Columbia: and PAS's petitions, 5, 25, 40, 41, 49–56, 57; and PAS's legal tactics, 21; and U.S. Constitution, 21, 49, 50, 51, 52, 53, 141, 143; and state abolition societies, 52–53; congressional report on, 114; and mass mobilization, 132, 140, 141, 146, 148, 150; and traveling agents, 157

Douglass, Frederick, 7, 95, 105, 177, 178–79, 180, 191 (n. 1)

Dred Scott case, 61

Du Bois, W. E. B., 178

Duncan, J., 83

Dungy, Eliza, 182

Du Ponceau, Peter, 28, 78

Earle, Thomas, 30, 41, 51, 53–54, 116, 119–20

Easton, Hosea, 138, 160

Education. *See* African American education

Egalitarianism, 2–3, 6, 7, 9, 14, 38

Egerton, Douglas, 88

Elites: and abolitionist movement, 2, 178, 180; and Massachusetts abolitionists, 7, 35, 37, 109, 174–75; and Whiggism, 9; and reform movements, 32; opposition of, 33–34, 37–38; and Virginia abolitionists, 34, 35, 36, 37; and Garrison, 37, 132; black, 90–91; and mass mobilization, 137, 138, 144. *See also* Pennsylvania Abolition Society — and elites

Elizabeth (slave), 60

Emancipation: as private concern, 4, 27, 36; and gradual approach, 22, 24, 41, 45, 50; and government's role, 24, 25, 27, 36; and legislation, 29, 62, 119; in Massachusetts, 35, 36, 37; and PAS's petitions, 44, 45; and Dis-

trict of Columbia, 51, 53, 54; and
Revolutionary era, 52, 59, 67; and
African American activism, 89, 94,
95; and immediatism, 124
Emancipation Proclamation, 176, 183
Emancipator, 146, 162
Emerson, Ralph Waldo, 10
Emotional appeals: and Massachusetts
abolitionists, 2, 7; and PAS, 4, 7, 27,
65; and African American activism, 6,
13, 87, 90, 93, 96, 104, 106, 126, 179;
and religious revivals, 8; and Earle,
53–54; and NEASS, 104; and demo-
cratic sensibility, 175
Enlightenment, 4, 6, 90
Equiano, Olaudah, 105, 126
Essex County Anti-Slavery Society, 161
Essex County Gazette, 167
Essex Gazette, 164
Evangelicalism, 8, 9, 153
Everett, Edward, 2–3, 37, 110, 111,
112, 161–62, 166–68

Farmer, James, 141, 172–73
Federalism, 9, 10
Federally controlled territory: banning
of slavery in, 5, 49, 56, 132, 140, 143,
150. *See also* District of Columbia
Finney, Charles Grandison, 8, 153
First Great Awakening, 153
Fitzgerald, F. Scott, 1
Florida, 25, 40, 50, 64
Follen, Charles, 12, 138
Forten, James: and African American
literary tactics, 13, 90–91, 92, 94, 95–
96; and PAS, 83–84; and whites, 86;
and abolitionist narratives, 90; and
colonization movement, 99, 113; and
American Society for The Free Per-
sons of Color, 103; and Garrison,
114; and Phelps, 115; and Earle, 120;
and NEASS, 138; and emotional
appeals, 179
Fourth Amendment, 167–68
Fox, George, 16

France, 18, 27, 42, 45
Franklin, Benjamin, 21, 41, 42, 47
Free African Society, 88
Free blacks: and kidnapping cases, 5,
18, 21, 23, 26, 31, 42, 45, 46, 60, 62,
65, 66, 69, 74, 90, 126; and PAS, 5,
31, 69; and education, 18, 19; and
slave trade, 19; and legislation, 29; as
menace in Massachusetts, 36; and
white relations, 37; in Maryland, 64;
constitutional rights of, 77, 78, 80;
and African American activism, 87–
88; and colonization movement, 96,
97, 99, 100, 110, 112, 113, 114, 117–
18. *See also* African Americans
Freedom's Journal: and African American
activism, 11, 13, 19, 103; and PAS,
14; and District of Columbia, 52; and
Forten, 95; and colonization movement, 98, 99, 103–4; and Walker, 100
Free-market labor, 1, 193 (n. 7)
Free speech, and mass mobilization,
143, 144, 222 (n. 44)
Fugitive Slave Bill, 43
Fugitive Slave Law of 1793, 78–80, 81,
83
Fugitive slave laws: dropping of, 6; and
PAS's legal tactics, 29, 60, 62, 65, 66,
69, 78; and Maryland, 43–44, 67, 81;
and slaveholders, 44, 65, 185; and
U.S. Constitution, 65, 143. *See also*
Runaway slaves

Gabriel's Rebellion (1800s), 26, 35, 88
Gag rule: and petitions, 5, 57–58, 144,
148, 149; and Adams, 155
Gallatin, Albert, 21, 28, 42
Galloway, Benjamin, 185
Gardner, Charles C., 86, 138
Garnet, Henry Highland, 19
Garrison, William Lloyd: and *Liberator*,
1, 11; and immediatism, 1, 86, 104,
115, 116, 120, 124, 129; and aboli-
tionism's transformation, 1, 191
(n. 1); on Douglass, 7; anticoloniza-

Parrish, John, 17

Parrish, Joseph, 174

Parrott, Russell, 93, 94

PAS. *See* Pennsylvania Abolition Society

Paul, Nathaniel, 114

Paul, Thomas, 94

Payne, Charles, 175

Pemberton, James, 22, 41, 48

Pemberton brothers, 28

Penn, William, 61, 61–62

Pennock, Abraham, 53

Pennsylvania: elite abolitionist movement in, 2, 3; and Quakers, 17; reform movements in, 32; ending of slavery in, 38; and fugitive slave laws, 43–44; and free blacks' constitutional rights, 77, 78, 80, 95; and African American activism, 95; and colonization movement, 117; and women's activism, 135, 146, 148. *See also* Gradual Abolition Act of 1780

Pennsylvania Abolition Society (PAS): African Americans' role in, 2, 5, 6, 83, 88, 106, 117, 119; and judiciary, 2, 5, 21, 22, 23, 26, 33, 60, 61–65, 73, 74–77, 79, 80–83; women's role in, 2, 12; leadership of, 3, 4; and lawyers, 4, 5, 6, 21, 25, 28–29, 31, 60, 61, 62–68, 84, 85; and gradualist abolition movement, 4, 5, 22, 41, 49, 53; and emotional appeals, 4, 7, 27, 65; abolitionist strategy of, 4–6, 7, 16, 31, 33–34, 38, 39, 53, 58–59, 196 (n. 1); legal aid for African Americans, 5, 20, 29, 31, 60–64, 68, 84, 200 (n. 59); and Massachusetts abolitionists, 7–8, 35, 59, 108, 173–74; and immediatism, 7–8, 39, 120, 130; and individualism, 10; and *Freedom's Journal*, 14; formation of, 16, 20; official standing of, 22–23; and U.S. Constitution, 25, 26, 27, 142; utility men of, 30–31; opposition to, 32, 37–38; and radical abolition movement, 53, 54, 55, 58–

59, 84, 174; and colonization movement, 54, 96–97, 98, 108, 116, 118–19; and African American activism, 89, 106, 116–17, 119–20, 130; and NEASS, 107, 141; and Garrison, 114; and Lundy, 133, 152; and Chandler, 134

— and elites: domination of, 4, 11, 53, 174, 196 (n. 1); and legislation, 6; and republican world view, 16, 175; tactical influence of, 21–22, 23, 198 (n. 32); and government's role, 21–22, 31, 37; and emotional appeals, 27; and politics, 28, 38; and elite opposition, 33–34, 37–38; and petitions, 40, 41–44, 59, 142

— and government's role: and gradual attack on slavery, 4–5, 24–25, 27, 38, 40, 49–50, 53; and petitions, 5, 21, 25–26, 48–49; and antislavery trends, 20; and elites, 21–22, 31, 37; and public debate, 23; and legal tactics, 25, 26, 65; and slave rebellions, 26, 27; and pamphleteering, 26–27; and constitutionality of slavery, 27, 46; and opposition, 32, 33

— and legal tactics: and judiciary strategies, 2, 5, 60, 61–65, 74, 75, 76–77, 79, 80–83; and slavery, 4–5, 26, 38, 61, 65, 66, 75–81, 84; and legal aid to African Americans, 5, 20, 29, 31, 60–64, 68, 84, 200 (n. 59); and slaveholders, 5, 22, 26, 31, 61, 63–66, 69–81, 82, 124–25; and republican world view, 6, 31; and slave trade, 19, 35, 48, 65, 66, 68, 74–75, 119, 207 (n. 43); and black freedom suits, 22, 29, 62, 63–64, 66–71, 74, 76–81, 85, 204 (n. 9), 205 (n. 21); and Gradual Abolition Act of 1780, 22, 29, 64, 67, 72–74, 76, 78; and government's role, 25, 26, 65; and runaway slaves, 26, 31, 45, 60, 65, 69–70, 71, 74, 79–83, 85, 124–25; and indenture contracts, 31, 67, 69–71, 72, 75–76, 85;

opposition to, 32, 84–85; and petitions, 44; and African American activism, 66–67, 72, 83, 87; and writs, 74–75
— and legislation: and gradual abolitionism, 4; and antislavery memorials, 5; and republican world view, 6; and official incorporation, 22–23; and government's role, 25; and legal tactics, 26; and free blacks, 29; opposition to, 32; and state abolition societies, 33; and petitions, 39, 40, 41, 43, 44, 45, 49; and slave trade, 42, 48, 49; and black emigration, 43; and fugitive slave laws, 43–44
— and petitions: and sectional discord, 3, 32, 33, 55–58; and slaveholders, 3, 40, 45, 54, 56–57, 142; and slave trade, 5, 21, 25, 32, 38, 40, 42, 46–49, 51, 57; and government's role, 5, 21, 25–26, 48–49; and committee system, 20, 21; and constitutional rights, 25, 41, 44, 45, 46, 142; and legislation, 39, 40, 41, 43, 44, 45, 49; and politics, 39, 44, 49, 55, 57, 58; and deferential strategy, 39–41, 44, 49, 58–59, 132, 142; and U.S. Congress, 40, 41, 44–51, 53, 54, 56, 57–59, 132, 142; and District of Columbia, 40, 41, 49–56, 57; and elites, 40, 41–44, 59, 142; and lobbying efforts, 42–43, 44; and Gradual Abolition Act of 1780, 45; opposition to, 53, 56–57; and radical views, 53–54; mass mobilization compared to, 146
— and politics: and abolitionist strategy, 4, 6, 21, 31; and legal tactics, 26, 65, 84, 87; and elites, 28, 38; and state abolition societies, 33; and petitions, 39, 44, 49, 55, 57, 58; and legislation, 41; and runaway slaves, 130; and sectional discord, 174
Pennsylvania Anti-Slavery Society, 141
Pennsylvania Freeman, 95
Pennsylvanian, 117

Perfectionism, 14
Perry, Lewis, 10
Petitions: and gag rule, 5, 57–58, 144, 148, 149; and Massachusetts abolitionists, 7, 36, 121, 132, 146; and women, 12, 135, 139, 146–49, 150, 171, 172, 180; and African American activism, 13, 57, 88–89, 90, 91, 98; and NYMS, 18; and American Convention of Abolition Societies, 19, 41, 50, 51, 53; and Virginia abolitionists, 34; history of, 39; and District of Columbia, 52–53, 141; and U.S. Constitution, 56–58, 89, 143–44, 146; and mass mobilization, 59, 133, 136, 137, 140, 141, 143, 144, 146–49; of Maryland, 81; and traveling agents, 157; and local antislavery societies, 160; and state abolition societies, 161. *See also* Pennsylvania Abolition Society — and petitions
Phelps, Amos A.: and PAS's legal tactics, 84; and abolitionist narratives, 105; and colonization movement, 111, 113; and natural law, 115–16; and African Americans' rights, 121; and race issues, 123; and African American activists, 125, 138, 179; as traveling agent, 125, 154, 155, 156, 158, 159, 165, 169; and violence, 127; slavery as robbery, 129; and mass mobilization, 134, 135–37, 140, 143–44, 149, 150; and U.S. Constitution, 141, 142–43, 144; and women, 169, 173
Philadelphia Anti-Slavery Society, 174
Philadelphia Female Anti-Slavery Society, 148
Philadelphia Report, 99
Philadelphia Yearly Meeting, 16–17
Philanthropists, 4, 6, 21–22, 32, 96, 118, 138
Phillips, Wendell, 178
Pickering, Timothy, 28, 42
Pinckney, Charles C., 56

religious revivals, 8–9; and African American activism, 90; and colonization movement, 118; and democratic sensibility, 175

Rawle, William: and abolitionist strategy, 4, 26; and PAS, 28; and abolitionist law, 29–30; and petitions, 41, 43, 54, 55, 58; and District of Columbia, 49–50; and Miner, 51; and slave trade, 59; and fugitive slave laws, 65, 79; and colonization movement, 118; and slaveholders, 124; and NEASS, 174

Reconstruction period, 177

Reed, John, 78–79

Reed, William B., 28, 30

Reform movements: radical abolition movement, 1; and religious revivals, 9; and African Americans, 11, 19; and women, 11–12, 14, 135; and politics, 18; growth in, 31–32; and morality, 32, 199 (n. 39); and Chandler, 134; and mass mobilization, 138; and traveling agents, 154

Religion: and Revolutionary and early national periods, 2, 8–9; and women's reform movements, 11; and slave trade, 48; and African American activism, 87, 88, 94, 100, 102; and mass mobilization, 137; and traveling preachers, 153; and women's antislavery societies, 170, 171; and African American women, 182

Religious revivals, 1, 2, 8, 14

Remini, Robert, 10

Republican Party, 178

Respublica v. Blackmore (1797), 76–77, 80

Revolutionary era: and continuity of abolitionism, 1; and Quakers, 8, 16–18; and politics, 10; and African American activism, 13, 87, 89; and PAS, 16, 18, 23; and abolition societies, 16, 20, 178; and manumission, 20; and government's role, 23–

24; and legal profession, 28; ideals of, 40, 95, 141; and slave trade, 46–47; and emancipation, 52, 59, 67; and African American freedom suits, 62; and mass mobilization, 141; and newspapers, 163, 166; and reform movements, 183

Rhode Island, 18, 25–26, 37, 48

Richardson, Marilyn, 102

Roberts, Jonathan, 29, 30, 58, 118, 174

Roediger, David, 11

Rogers, Mary, 161

Rogers, Nathaniel P., 161

Romanticism, 6, 7, 125, 130

Ross, John, 76–77

Rousseau, Jean-Jacques, 20

Runaway slaves: and PAS's legal tactics, 26, 31, 45, 60, 65, 69–70, 71, 74, 79–83, 85, 124–25; and Maryland, 43, 60, 70, 72, 80, 81, 82; and PAS's petitions, 44; and U.S. Constitution, 44, 65, 78, 79, 85, 140, 141, 142, 143; and District of Columbia, 52; and Gradual Abolition Act of 1780, 72; and Massachusetts abolitionists, 126; and immediatism, 130; and mass mobilization, 132, 145. *See also* Fugitive slave laws

Rush, Benjamin, 21, 25, 32

Russwurm, John, 13, 97–98

Rusticus, 91, 92

Rutledge, John, 47

St. Domingo, 27

Salem Gazette, 164–65, 166

Saltonstall, Leverett, 131

Saunders, Prince, 98, 99

Saxton, Alexander, 11

Schwarz, Philip, 72, 88

Scituate Anti-Slavery Society, 121

Second Great Awakening, 8, 9, 153, 171

Sectional discord: and PAS's petitions, 3, 32, 33, 55–58; and slavery, 5, 35–36, 37; and abolitionist strategy, 20; and slaveholders, 28; and slave trade,

32, 42, 47, 48; and national political concerns, 35–36; and slave states' admission to Union, 50; and District of Columbia, 52, 56; and PAS's legal tactics, 75; and immediatism, 106; and colonization movement, 110; and mass mobilization, 133, 142, 150; and newspapers, 165, 167–68; and politics, 174; and women's activism, 181. *See also* National unity

Sedgewick, Theodore, 22, 28

Self-determination, 20

Self-help organizations, 87

Sergeant, John, 29, 30, 174

Series of Letters by a Man of Color, A (Forten), 95

Sevier family, 23

Sewall, Samuel, 139, 161

Sharpe, Grenville, 22, 25

Sherman, Isaac, 74

Shipley, Thomas: and black freedom suits, 31; and black emigration, 43; and District of Columbia, 51; and African American activism, 63, 97, 120; and Garrison, 84, 114, 120; as dissident within PAS, 84, 116, 119; and immediatism, 130; and runaway slaves, 143

Silas (slave), 74–75

Slaveholders: and PAS's petitions, 3, 40, 45, 54, 56–57, 142; and Quakers, 4, 17; and PAS's legal tactics, 5, 22, 26, 31, 61, 63–66, 69–81, 82, 124–25; and American Convention of Abolition Societies, 19; and state abolition societies, 19–20; and southern abolitionist groups, 20; and gradualist abolitionist laws, 24; as zealots, 27–28, 54; and manumission, 29; rights of, 30, 36, 45, 46, 50, 61, 66, 75, 84, 124, 125, 150; and Virginia abolitionists, 34; and fugitive slave laws, 44, 65, 185; and Gradual Abolition Act of 1780, 45, 61, 62, 67, 73–74, 76–77, 83, 208 (n. 69); and colonization

movement, 50, 96, 98, 99, 110, 113, 118; and District of Columbia, 52; petitions of, 81; and African American activism, 87, 90, 92, 102, 211 (n. 16); and U.S. Congress, 109; and Garrison, 114; and immediatism, 117, 129; and Shipley, 119; and AASS, 124; and violence, 125, 126; and mass mobilization, 133, 140, 141, 145; and women's activism, 139, 181

Slave rebellions, 26–27, 35, 50, 90, 102, 128–29

Slavery and Human Progress (Davis), 8

Slaves and slavery: and PAS's legal tactics, 4–5, 26, 38, 61, 65, 66, 75–81, 84; westward expansion of, 5, 25, 40, 41, 42, 55; legal protections of, 5, 26, 61, 64, 70; in federally controlled territory, 5, 49, 56, 132, 143, 150; outlawing of, 6; and slavery as sin, 9, 116, 166; and Revolutionary era, 20; and government's role, 23–24, 27, 36, 37, 38, 40, 167; and U.S. Constitution, 25, 26, 29, 167, 177; and legislation, 28–29, 33, 36, 167–68; in Massachusetts, 35; and PAS's petitions, 39, 42, 44–45, 46; and public debate, 50, 179; economic impact of, 56; slaves' lack of rights, 64, 125–26, 129; and African American activism, 87, 89, 92–95, 97, 98, 101–4; and immediatism, 104, 107, 129; and morality, 104; as state concern, 108; and Massachusetts abolitionists, 109, 125–27, 132, 220 (n. 81); and colonization movement, 110–12, 118; and natural law, 115–16; and violence, 128–29; and mass mobilization, 136–37, 150. *See also* Runaway slaves

Slave states' admission to Union: and PAS's petitions, 42, 49, 55, 57; and sectional discord, 50; and Massachusetts abolitionists, 109; and petitions, 146, 148

Slave trade: and PAS's petitions, 5, 21,

Underground Railroad, 69
United States Gazette, 99

Van Buren, Martin, 9–10
Vaux, Roberts, 28, 43–44, 54, 58, 119
Venet, Wendy, 183
Vesey, Denmark, 26, 50, 128
Violence: and PAS, 26, 27, 31, 70; and slaveholders, 125, 126; and Massachusetts abolitionists, 126–28; and traveling agents, 157; and NEASS, 166
Virginia: and Quakers, 17; abolitionists of, 18, 20, 34, 35, 36–37; and District of Columbia, 50, 53; and government's role, 56; legal developments in, 64; and PAS's legal tactics, 66, 68, 69, 70–71, 72, 73–74, 77–79, 80, 81, 82; and African American activism, 72, 88; and Turner, 128
Voting rights, 11, 119, 178

Walker, Amasa, 138
Walker, David: and print media, 12; and abolitionist strategy, 86–87; and African American literary tactics, 90, 93–94; and colonization movement, 97; and General Colored Association, 100, 101; and racial justice, 100–101; and slavery, 102; and Stewart, 102–3; and Garrison, 114, 129; and insurrection, 127
Waln, Nicholas, 21, 30, 48
Ward, Samuel Ringgold, 19
Washington (judge), 83
Washington, George, 29, 33, 42, 56, 90, 211 (n. 20)
Watkins, William, 105–6, 113, 114, 115
Watson, Harry, 9
Webb, Francis, 99
Webster, Daniel, 10, 30, 37, 109–10, 111, 167
Webster, Noah, 22
Weld, Theodore Dwight, 8, 153

Weston, Anne Warren, 148
Wheatley, Phyllis, 91
Whiggism, 9
Whipper, William, 89, 99
White, Shane, 24, 88
Whites: and African American activism, 3, 87, 88, 89, 90, 91, 92, 93–94, 97, 98, 105, 179–81, 213 (n. 50); democratic advances of, 11; and relations with free blacks, 37; and PAS, 38; and colonization movement, 96, 97, 98, 99, 100, 101, 114, 117–18; and integration, 97, 127, 156; and immediatism, 104; and radical abolition movement, 106; racial prejudices of, 113
Whitman, Stephen, 69–70
Whittier, John Greenleaf, 161
Wicks, Elizabeth, 182
Wilberforce, 22
Williams, Peter, 93
Wistar, Caspar, 28, 41
Wolcott, Oliver, 42
Women: and radical abolition movement, 2; and PAS, 2, 12; and abolitionism's transformation, 2, 179, 191 (n. 1); and morality, 6, 135, 139, 169; and Massachusetts abolitionists, 6, 174; and *Liberator*, 7, 171, 173, 227 (n. 67); rise of, in public sphere, 8, 135; and politics, 11, 14, 139, 148, 180–83; and reform movements, 11–12, 14, 135; abolition societies of, 12, 122, 132, 134, 135, 139, 146–47, 158, 161, 169, 170–71, 173; and petitions, 12, 135, 139, 146–49, 150, 171, 172, 180; and print media, 13; African American, 67–68, 102–3, 122, 170, 181–82; and African American/white coalitions, 122, 170; and Chandler, 134–35, 221 (n. 14); and mass mobilization, 134, 139, 146–49, 180; and grassroots organizations, 147, 155, 168–69, 172–73, 180, 226